Contents

Acknowledgements   v

Introduction: Global social work in a political context   1

Part One: The political context of contemporary social work   **4**
One   The political economy of social work   6
Two   Neoliberalism, social work and the state: retreat or restructuring?   21
Three   The privatisation of social work and social care   37

Part Two: Social work politics: past and present   **51**
Four   Social work's horrible histories: collusion and resistance   53
Five   Social work as a praxis for liberation: the case of Latin American   71
         reconceptualisation
Six   Refugees, migrants and social work   89
Seven   Social work, climate change and the Anthropocene   111

Part Three: Debating the politics of social work today   **133**
Eight   A new politics of social work?   135
Nine   The case for a social justice-based global social work definition   153

Conclusions: 'Making history'   169

References   181
Index   205

Acknowledgements

This book draws on our work with colleagues in a variety of radical social work networks across the global social work community. It would be impossible to thank them all individually, but we would like to acknowledge the support, friendship and comradeship of colleagues in the range of radical social work groups across the globe. These include the Social Work Action Network (SWAN) groups in Ireland, Greece, Canada and Britain. Similar groups in other global locations include the Boston Liberation Health Group, the New Approach Group in Hungary, the Progressive Welfare Network, Hong Kong, the Rebel Social Work Group in New Zealand/Aotearoa and the Arbeitskreis Kritische Soziale Arbeit (Critical and Radical Social Work Network) in Germany. We would also like to acknowledge the many inspiring representatives that we have met from the social work associations in Spain, Argentina and Brazil. In particular, we remember fondly the meeting we coordinated at the Global Social Work conference in Sweden to try and establish an international network together; the meeting was well attended and just about to start when the Brazilian colleagues arrived. Their presence was remarkable for two reasons: first, there were lots of them! Second, they all wanted to debate with us on the continuing relevance of Marxism to social work – not something we experience very often!

Our experience in social work has also been enhanced by the involvement of a range of service users and service-user organisations and colleagues in relevant campaigning organisations. Among the many organisations that we have worked with, we would like to thank Disabled People Against the Cuts, Recovery in the Bin, Black Triangle, Shaping Our Lives and Stand Up To Racism. In Britain, many social workers are active within both social work and their union. Helen Davies, Sharon Campion, Simon Cardy, Malcolm Jones, Bea Kay and Jimmie Main are active Unison members (and SWAN supporters) who regularly provide us with insights on working life on the social work front line.

As well as organisations, we would like to thank a number of colleagues who we have worked with in radical social work over the years: from the global community, the list includes Bessa Whitmore, Michael Reisch, Elaine Behring, Catherine MacDonald, Suzanne Dudziak, Jelka Zorn, Silvana Martinez, Fumihito Ito, Lúcia Garcia, Paul Michael Garrett, Dawn Belkin Martinez and Roberta Uchoa. Closer to home, we would like to thank Rich Moth, Linda Smith, Joe Greener, Rea Maglajlic, John Harris, Terry Murphy, Jeremy Weinstein, Natalie Farmer, Barrie Levine, Victoria Jupp-Kena, Lee Humber, Peter Beresford, Katherine MacKay, Des McDermott, Mark Baldwin, Chris Jones, Gurnam Singh, Maria-Inez Martinez, Alissa Ruane, Bob Williams-Finlay and the sadly missed Rona Woodward. Three people who deserve special mention for their inspiration and continuing commitment to radical social work theory and practice are Dora Teloni in Greece, Kerry Cuskelly in Ireland and Lam Chi Leung in Hong Kong – each represents everything that is good about radical social work and they have our utmost admiration for all they do!

We want to thank Policy Press for their continuing support of both the journal *Critical and Radical Social Work* (CRSW) and their commitment to publish radical social work texts. Thanks in particular to Julia Mortimer, Rebecca Tomlinson, Edwina Thorn, Catherine Grey and Isobel Bainton. We are grateful to Policy Press and CRSW for allowing us to use some material in Chapter Nine that originally appeared as an article by Vasilios, entitled 'Beyond the dichotomies of cultural and political relativism: arguing the case for a social justice-based "global social work" definition', *Critical and Radical Social Work*, 1(2): 183–200.

Finally, writing a book and taking part in various social movement activities takes time and can only be accomplished with the continuing support and co-participation of our partners. So we would like to record our thanks to Dorte Pape, Natalia Barrera Villota and Laura Penketh.

IF, VI, ML

Introduction: Global social work in a political context

As we approach the end of the second decade of the 21st century, the world is facing a growing number of, seemingly intractable, problems. Where does social work sit in relation to these problems and how should social work respond? Let us map out the terrain upon which these problems rest.

What Michael Roberts (2016) calls the 'long depression' shows no signs of ending. Financial instability and low economic growth continue to have an impact on global economic performance. In response to this crisis, large units of capital and states across the globe have been involved in a concerted attempt to reduce living standards, for the majority, as a means of restoring profitability across the system. This has been enshrined in policies of 'austerity', the claim that we can no longer afford what is thought of as the 'post-war welfare settlement' and that, as a result, 'there is no alternative' to savage cuts and welfare restructuring.

The attempt to transform the 'welfare state' (in all their variety across the globe) is important for social work. It has a significant impact on those who social work services work with (who find their services cut and stigmatised). For front-line practitioners, it means fewer resources to support service users, but it has also been matched by attempts to restructure and narrow the social work task. How do we understand these processes and, as social workers, how do we respond?

The 10-year depression and 'austerity politics' have also had the effect of eroding public confidence in 'mainstream' politicians and state actors. This has been particularly acute with regard to the crisis of social democracy, which increasingly looks like a universal phenomenon. The politicians of the centre, across the globe, act as if little has changed. For those of the social-democratic Left, this means that they have continued to promote the (failed) policies of the first decade of the century – promoting 'globalisation', trade liberalisation and the marketisation of public services. However, these politicians are uncomprehending of the rejection of their politics as 'populist movements' (of both the Left and Right) grow to challenge the political centre. Over the last few years, we have witnessed new social movements challenging the power of the powerful but we have also seen the growth of right-wing political networks that promote economic and political nationalism, xenophobia, and racism (with particular hostility towards migrants and refugees). These developments present huge challenges for social work and, once more, raise questions about how we respond.

As the 21st century unfolds, it is becoming clear that present economic arrangements pose a huge threat to our climate and the future of the planet and its ecological system. Is this of any relevance to social work? How can we develop a social work practice that is attuned to the planetary crisis we face?

These themes – economic crisis, welfare restructuring, climate change and refugee rights – represent some of the most pressing issues facing the social work profession globally today. The shifting political context of the 21st century is the backdrop against which present-day understandings of the role, tasks and possibilities of social work take place. This book is our attempt to navigate our way through this complex maze and try to understand the challenges it presents for social work.

The book has developed out of our experiences of working alongside a range of radical social work groups in a number of countries across the globe. Over the last 20 years, we have learnt a great deal about the limits and possibilities for a more engaged and radical practice by listening at the feet of practitioners involved in groups like the Social Work Action Network (in Britain, Ireland, Greece and Canada), the Boston Health Liberation Group, the New Approaches group in Hungary, the Progressive Welfare Network in Hong Kong and the various official social work organisations across much of Latin America. In all these groups, practitioners continue to engage in radical practice in difficult political contexts, but their practice continues to reaffirm that radical social work represents some of the best examples of good social work practice.

This book is an attempt to synthesise some of the best from the radical social work tradition globally. We want to look at how radical social work ideas can help explain the current global situation that social workers find themselves in and we want to look at and generalise from examples of good radical practice in the field.

The book is divided into three parts. Part One looks at the political context of contemporary social work. Here, we look at what might be termed the political economy of social work. Chapter One looks at the contemporary economic crisis and the alternatives to the 'perpetual austerity' that is being promoted by sections of our governing classes. Understanding the nature of these developments is important for all concerned with the future of social work and social care, for three reasons. First, the dominant policy response to the economic crisis has been to shift the costs of bailing out the global banking system in 2008 onto the poorest sections of the working class (pensioners, the disabled, the low paid and the unemployed). Of course, these are the sections who make up the majority of social work service users.

Second, while the roots of the current crisis lie in the failings of neoliberalism, the dominant political and ideological response to that crisis has been more of the same in the form of increased privatisation and public sector cuts, leading one writer to speak of 'the strange non-death of neoliberalism' (Crouch, 2011). It is also clear that for some governments, the crisis has provided them with a golden political opportunity to shrink the welfare state to levels not seen for decades, not least in Britain, where the percentage of spending on welfare is now at its lowest level since the 1930s. Third, the unprecedented assault on the lives and living standards of disabled people and people on benefits throws up major questions of how to respond, particularly for social workers and social work.

Chapters Two and Three explore the relationship between social work, neoliberalism and the state. This is a relationship that is rarely discussed in social work books – though the radical social work literature of the 1970s did look at the development of what Jones (1983) called 'state-directed social work'. Here, we focus on the relationship between the development of capitalism, the state, social work and the conditions of welfare transformation. The attempt to fundamentally transform welfare states has led to the growth of privatised, for-profit, service providers. These providers are funded and regulated by the state but, as private companies, they are not subject to the same democratic accountability as state-provided services and their priority is not meeting people's needs, but protecting their profit margins. This is the development of what we term 'state-directed social work' within the neoliberal welfare system.

The first three chapters, then, set the general political and economic context for contemporary debates about social work. In Part Two, we look at politics in social work 'past and present'. Chapter Four, perhaps controversially, discusses one aspect of social work that is rarely mentioned, its 'horrible histories'. Here, we look at a number of cases where social work has acted as the tool of the state to undertake brutal, oppressive and abusive acts. We view social work as an inherently political activity and that means looking at, and learning from, those episodes when social work acted in ways that, most of us would think, breached our various professional 'codes of ethics'.

Chapter Five, by way of a contrast, examines the Latin American 'reconceptualisation' movement. This movement is little known in social work circles across much of the 'West', yet it represents, we suggest, one of the most progressive and inspiring examples of engaged radical social work practice. If we want to reinvigorate radical social work for the 21st century, then it is important that we learn the lessons from this great movement of the 1960s across the Latin American continent.

Chapters Six and Seven take two of the most pressing social issues of the present, looking at the social work response to the refugee crisis (Chapter Six) and to the planetary crisis created by climate change (Chapter Seven). In both chapters, we look at the causes of the crises and locate them in the broader drives of contemporary capitalism, but we finish by looking at what social work can, has and could do to address the political crises created by these contemporary political and social problems. Throughout Part Two of the book, we have used boxed sections to highlight examples of good practice or to reflect back on continuities in social work's history that often get lost.

In Part Three, we look at some contemporary debates about the politics of social work today. In Chapter Eight, we engage in friendly debate with colleagues in what is sometimes called the 'critical social work' tradition. Our case is that the insights of the radical social work tradition offer a clearer set of ideas and theories that help us understand, explain and engage in the modern world. In Chapter Nine, we look at ongoing debates about the 'definition of social work', something, we suggest, that brings us back to our starting point: social work is an inherently political activity and the profession will be stronger when this is explicitly acknowledged.

Part One
The political context of contemporary social work

ONE

The political economy of social work

Introduction: 'the 1930s in slow motion'

Writing in the early 1990s, the veteran British-Palestinian Marxist Tony Cliff described the new decade as being like 'a film of the 1930s in slow motion'. As in the 1930s, Cliff argued, there was a global recession that had resulted in millions of people becoming unemployed. Also, as in the 1930s, accompanying that recession was the emergence of fascist movements such as Jean-Marie Le Pen's Front National in France. Cliff's conclusion, however, was far from fatalistic: 'The 1930s was a decade of extremes.... The fact that the film of the 1930s returns, but in slow motion, means there is much greater opportunity to stop the film and direct it in the way we want' (Cliff, 2000: 81). Like the Marxist literary critic Walter Benjamin some 60 years previously, Cliff was sounding a kind of 'fire alarm' to his contemporaries, 'a warning bell attempting to draw attention to the imminent dangers threatening them, to the new catastrophes looming on the horizon' (Löwy, 2005: 16). More than two decades on and some 10 years after the onset of a global recession that began in the US sub-prime housing market before morphing into an economic and political crisis in the Eurozone area, there is a sense that the film has sped up, both economically and politically.

Economically, the recovery from the crisis of 2008 has been very weak indeed. Commenting on separate reports from the Organisation for Economic Co-operation and Development (OECD) and from the United Nations Conference on Trade and Development (UNCTAD) issued in autumn 2016, an editorial in *The Guardian* newspaper described them as being 'thick with cloud and short on silver lining'. Despite promises from politicians and policymakers across the globe that, following the crash, things would change:

> nearly a decade later, what is most striking is how little has changed. In the US, the UK and the rest of the developed world, policymakers talk of the 'new mediocre', so tepid is economic performance. And in the developing world things look even worse. (*The Guardian*, 21 September 2016)

Echoing that theme in a speech in December 2016, the Governor of the Bank of England, Mark Carney, described the past 10 years as having been 'a lost decade' for the British economy; one would have to go back to the 1860s, Carney argued, to find a comparable period (Carney, 2016).

The effects of that 'long depression' (Roberts, 2016) have, of course, been experienced very differently by different sections of the global population. An Oxfam report published in early 2016 showed that 1% of the world's population now own more than the rest combined. Even more starkly, 62 people own as much as the poorest half of the world's population. 'An economy for the 1%' (Oxfam, 2016) showed that the wealth of the poorest half of the world's population – 3.6 billion people – has fallen by a trillion dollars since 2010. This 38% drop has occurred despite the global population increasing by around 400 million people during that period. Meanwhile, the wealth of the richest 62 has increased by more than half-a-trillion US dollars to US$1.76 trillion (Oxfam, 2016).

That inequality, coupled with the fact that the neoliberal promise that wealth would 'trickle down' has proved hollow for millions of people, has been one factor fuelling the political polarisation that has been a feature of the second decade of the 21st century. While rising racism and xenophobia have undoubtedly been contributory factors to a range of mid-decade political developments, including the 'Brexit' vote for Britain to leave the European Union (EU), the election of Donald Trump as President of the US and the rise of Far Right and neo-Nazi parties across Europe, most notably, Marine Le Pen's Front National in France. At least as important has been a sense of despair on the part of millions of people regarding their own future and that of their children and grandchildren. The polarisation, of course, has not all gone in one direction: the past few years have also seen the emergence of new social movements and political parties of the Left, for example, around presidential candidate Bernie Sanders in the US and Labour Party leader Jeremy Corbyn in Britain, as well as around Podemos in Spain and Syriza in Greece (though the extent to which the latter can still be described as a left-wing party is more questionable) (Watkins, 2016).

That economic instability both shapes and is shaped by wider political developments. Indeed, exploring the relationship between these two dimensions is at the heart of contemporary analyses of 'the new imperialism' (Harvey, 2004, 2005; Callinicos, 2009). At the time of writing, some of the more obvious features of the current situation include: war and counter-revolution in the Middle East; the biggest movement of refugees since the Second World War; and the emergence of a new Cold War, with 'hotspots' in areas like Ukraine.

Understanding the nature of these developments is important for all concerned with the future of social work and social care, for three reasons. First, while the response of national governments to the 'long depression' has varied to some degree from country to country and from continent to continent, the dominant policy response has been to shift the costs of bailing out the global banking system in 2008 onto the poorest sections of the working class (pensioners, the disabled, the low paid and the unemployed), in the now universally recognised term *'austerity'*. These are also the sections of the population who are most likely to come into contact with social work services.

Second, as we shall argue later, while the roots of the current crisis lie in the inability of the neoliberal project of the last three decades to overcome deep-rooted structural problems within the global capitalist economy, the dominant political and ideological response to that crisis has been more of the same in the form of increased privatisation and public sector cuts, leading one writer to speak of 'the strange non-death of neoliberalism' (Crouch, 2011). It is also clear that for some governments, the crisis has provided them with a golden political opportunity to shrink the welfare state to levels not seen for decades, not least in Britain, where the percentage of spending on welfare is now at its lowest level since the 1930s. Again, this poses a real existential threat to social work – a profession that is, in the Western world at least, a child of the welfare state – a threat that needs to be understood and challenged.

Third, the unprecedented assault on the lives and living standards of disabled people and people on benefits throws up major questions of how to respond, particularly for social workers and social work organisations in countries such as Greece and Spain, where the cuts have gone deepest. Should the main emphasis be on defending the post-war welfare state or do the new forms of social support that have been thrown up in the course of the crisis, such as the Solidarity Committees in Greece, prefigure more popular forms of social work that should be nurtured and developed? Moreover, how should social workers respond to the growth of new forms of racism such as Islamophobia and anti-Roma racism?

These are some of the key questions that we will seek to address in this book. The focus of this chapter, however, will be a narrower one. One factor that has facilitated the imposition of austerity policies across Europe – and, in the process, undermined potential resistance to these policies – has been the widespread acceptance of the neoliberal argument that 'there is no alternative' to austerity. Acceptance of that view, albeit reluctant, has led a majority of the population in many countries to tolerate as inevitable cuts to services, cuts to benefits and, more generally, levels of hardship (eg including the return of food banks on a mass scale) that would have been unthinkable prior to the crisis. It is a view that we unequivocally reject. Providing a basis for that rejection, however, requires us to do what social work texts rarely do and attempt to engage with some of the economic arguments that have been put forward to explain the crisis and to suggest how it might be resolved. Unless social work academics and practitioners seek to critically engage with these dominant analyses, there is a danger that they will also be persuaded to accept – and collude with – policies that are profoundly harmful to some of the most disadvantaged sections of society, including users of social work services, but that, in reality, are neither theoretically nor morally justifiable. The remainder of this chapter will therefore address what we will call *the political economy of social work*.

Explaining the crisis

In October 2013, a group of undergraduate students studying economics at the University of Manchester set up a Post-Crisis Economics Society (see: http://www.post-crasheconomics.com). The students' main demand was for a complete overhaul of the curriculum to include economic theories other than the neoclassical theories that made up the content of their teaching at Manchester (as at many other British universities). These theories, which have dominated mainstream economics for more than a century, assume that the capitalist system will always return to equilibrium – that goods will always find buyers – providing prices and wages are allowed to adjust without hindrance.

Not only, the students argued, had these theories failed to predict the great crash of 2008 (and had, in fact, even denied the very possibility of such a crash), but leading economics academics had played a key role in acting as cheerleaders for the policies and practices that had led to that crash. According to a spokesperson for the group, academic departments were 'ignoring the crisis' and by neglecting global developments and critics of the free market such as Keynes and Marx, the study of economics was 'in danger of losing its broader relevance'. Within a matter of months, similar groups had been formed in Cambridge and London, and by mid-2014, 41 groups had been set up in 19 different countries and had issued a common manifesto.

The post-crisis economics manifesto

Our critics have attempted to caricature our society as demanding "more Keynes and Marx". However, our argument is far broader: we are calling for an evidence based, pluralistic economics education.... The key point is that any reference to Marx is compartmentalised from the economic theory proper and his contribution is judged to be historical and now superseded. We argue that it would be far more valuable to use Marx's theories of crisis, exploitation, class struggle and the reserve army of unemployed as a lens through which to understand business cycles, income distribution and the labour market.... Teaching of Keynes in mainstream economics is not really Keynes.... Students at Manchester are not exposed to Keynes' theories first hand and are definitely not exposed to modern post-Keynesianism, which has developed and built on Keynes' framework substantially. Some would argue that poring over old texts is not the proper way to do a social science, and we agree to an extent. We only wish that particular thinkers' theories be taught insofar as they are relevant, and we think that these theories should be presented in their historical context where possible. It may be wise to teach thinkers from original texts if one wants to access their ideas rather than relying on watered-down impressions. (Post-Crash Economics Society, 2014)

The students were not alone in their critique of the neoclassical orthodoxy that had played such a major role in shaping the events of 2008. In a study of the financial crisis published in 2014, Martin Wolf, Chief Economics Commentator at the *Financial Times* and one of the UK's most respected economic spokespersons, acknowledged his own failure to predict the crash. This failing, he argued, was not because he was unaware of tensions developing within the global economy, but rather, he suggested, because:

I lacked the imagination to anticipate a meltdown of the Western financial system. I was guilty of working with a mental model of the economy that did not allow for the possibility of another Great Depression or even a 'Great Recession' in the world's most advanced economies. (Wolf, 2014: xvi)

Even more remarkable was the admission before a Congressional Committee by Alan Greenspan, chair of the US Federal Reserve for two decades and arguably therefore the most powerful player in the global economic establishment, that the slump had left him in 'a state of shocked disbelief':

He was questioned: 'In other words, you found that your view of the world, your ideology was not right, it was not working' (House Oversight Committee Chair, Henry Waxman). 'Absolutely, precisely, you know that's precisely the reason I was shocked, because I have been going for 40 years or more with very considerable evidence that it was working exceptionally well.' (Alan Greenspan, former chair of the Federal Reserve being questioned in the US Senate, cited in Roberts, 2012)

Despite this collapse of confidence and the inability of leading economists to explain the crisis, it is a remarkable fact that by 2016, eight years after the crisis began, the very same market fundamentalist policies that resulted in the 2008 slump continued to be vigorously promoted and enforced by bodies such as the European Central Bank and the International Monetary Fund, a fact that requires some explanation. In reality, it is the product of two factors, one theoretical and the other political.

The first reason for the continuing hegemony of neoliberal economic policies is quite simply that neither those in charge of national and global policy nor their academic advisers can envisage a theoretical alternative. When, for example, 60 leading US economists were asked in a 2012 survey 'If we are ever going to get out of this slump, what will it take?', the general view was 'don't know' (see https://thenextrecession.wordpress.com/2012/10/17/the-dilemma-of-the-mainstream/). Perhaps not surprisingly, then, despite the fact that austerity policies have manifestly failed in countries such as Greece (by 2015, Greek debt was higher and the economy smaller than when the policies were first implemented), not a single one of the other 27 EU members was prepared to support the Syriza government against the 'Troika' of the European Commission, the European Central Bank and the International Monetary Fund in its bid to end these policies in February 2015.

Second, the level of political resistance across Europe to the implementation of austerity measures has been uneven at best. In Southern countries, especially Greece and Spain, popular resistance has been at a relatively high level, whether through social movements, such as the Indignados movement and the Orange Tide social work organisation in Spain, or through the organised trade union movement in Greece, where 32 general strikes between 2010 and 2013 were an important contributory factor to the election of the left-wing Syriza party in January 2015. In Northern Europe, by contrast, resistance to austerity and to neoliberal policies has been more muted. This is not to say that there has been no resistance. Britain, for example, saw a 2-million strong strike in defence of retirement pensions on 30 November 2011. That struggle, however, like many others, ended abruptly in a shoddy climbdown by the official trade union leadership, a climbdown that British rank-and-file trade unionists lacked the confidence and the independent organisation to challenge.

It would be misleading, however, to suggest that there has been no questioning or criticism of the dominant orthodoxy. The depth of the crisis has prompted even some mainstream commentators and economists to revisit macroeconomic theories that look beyond the behaviours of individual 'rational consumers' and seek to make sense of the system as a whole, including the possibility that crises are an integral part of the workings of a capitalist economy. Martin Wolf, for example, has queried the neoclassical view that free-market economies always tend to equilibrium and that crises can only occur as a consequence of some external (or 'exogenous') shock:

> Depressions are indeed one of the states that a capitalist economy can fall into. An economic theory that does not incorporate that possibility is as relevant as a theory of biology that excludes the risk of extinctions, a theory of the body that excludes the risk of heart attacks, or a theory of bridge-building that excludes the risk of collapse. (Wolf, 2014: xvii)

Such criticisms of neoclassical economics tend to be informed by the theories of one or other of the two great economic thinkers referred to earlier: Keynes and Marx. It is to a consideration of these theories that we shall now turn.

Marx and Keynes: saving capitalism or ending capitalism?

The idea that crises are a feature of capitalist economies was one shared by the two giants of economic thought referred to by the Manchester students, namely, Marx and Keynes. While, however, Keynes believed – and earnestly desired – that such crises could be prevented or their effects ameliorated through government intervention, Marx, by contrast, argued that capitalism contained a long-term inbuilt tendency to crisis (Choonara, 2009; Fine and Saad-Filho, 2010). That tendency could be delayed by what he referred to as 'countervailing factors' (eg the exploitation of colonies) but would ultimately reassert itself. Given that Keynes was primarily concerned with saving capitalism while Marx devoted his life to its overthrow, it is perhaps not surprising that Keynes's ideas have tended to be more palatable not only to mainstream critics such as Wolf, but also to more radical critics of neoclassical economics, such as Joseph Stiglitz and Paul Krugman (Stiglitz, 2003, 2013; Krugman, 2008).

For Keynes, the principal cause of crisis is insufficient demand in the economy. The correct response to the onset of crisis, therefore, is for governments to replace that missing demand, either by increasing their own spending (eg through programmes of public works) or by cutting taxes so that consumers have more money to spend, which, in turn, will generate more demand, more jobs and so on. The fact that most governments responded to the crisis of 2008 by spending billions to bail out major banks and financial institutions led some to believe that what we were seeing was a return to the Keynesian policies of the post-war period. In reality, such government responses were prompted less by ideology than by the fact that the banks were simply (in a phrase much used at the time) 'too big to fail'. Indeed, as the experience of the merchant banker Lehman Brothers in 2008 showed, where one of these giants of finance capital did collapse, it deepened the crisis by pulling many others down with it and making things much worse (Harman, 2009).

US economist Nouriel Roubini's (2008) characterisation of the bailout, therefore, as 'socialism for the rich' was an accurate one, for the other side of the eye-watering sums given to the banks was austerity, privatisation and cuts in services for the mass of the population. In Chris Harman's (2009: 303) words: 'The new Keynesianism for capital was combined with a continuation of neoliberalism for those who worked for it'.

The mainstream view within economics continues to be that a combination of low interest rates and a dose of money printing ('quantitative easing') should be sufficient to get economies moving again. In reality, as Michael Roberts has argued, this has 'proved to be a chimera': 'Most of this extra credit or money has ended up in the stock and bond markets and in the cash reserves of the banks; very little has found its way to the so-called "real economy"' (Roberts, 2015).

The fact that neither zero interest rates nor quantitative easing have been sufficient to kick-start sluggish economies has led some Keynesian critics to argue that what is delaying the recovery is 'fiscal austerity' – spending cuts and deficit reduction – since its effect is to reduce demand in the economy. The solution, they argue, lies instead in a much greater fiscal stimulus – in other words, vastly increased government spending, with the deficit being addressed at some point in the future once the economy is healthy again. Leading British Keynesian theorist Simon Wrenn-Lewis, for example, has argued that the austerity policies of the UK Coalition government 'seriously blunted the recovery', taking at least 1% off growth in both 2010/11 and 2012. Arguing that both the Coalition government and the media have been profoundly mistaken in seeing deficit reduction as a priority, he argues that 'The key point is that deficit reduction should be left to a time when interest rates are high, so that they can be reduced to counteract the negative impact of austerity on demand' (Wrenn-Lewis, 2015).

Given the devastating effect that austerity policies are having on the lives of millions of people across the globe, the appeal of an argument which says that such policies are not only painful, but actually counterproductive, is not hard to see. In their opposition both to the politics of austerity and to rising inequality, adherents of both Marx and Keynes will often find themselves on the same side. Where they differ, however, concerns the extent to which policy reforms that remain within the framework of capitalism can overcome the deep-rooted problems facing the system.

First, Keynesianism is an 'underconsumptionist' theory in that it assumes that capitalism can escape crisis if the state intervenes to raise consumption the moment a recession seems likely to develop (Harman, 2009: 59). As the experience of the current crisis appears to show, however, no matter how much money governments throw at them, capitalists will only invest if they are guaranteed an acceptable rate of return on their profits. If not, then they will either simply save the money or alternatively 'invest' it in areas where they can make a quick return on their capital (such as the financial markets or even sub-prime mortgage markets, as they did prior to 2008) as opposed to investing it in the real economy. Such short-term investment, Michael Roberts (2016) argues, will not be sufficient to generate the kind of recovery or growth rates that were seen, for example, in the post-war period. The result is that even seven years after the beginning of the crisis, financial commentators in countries such as the UK were noting that the recovery, such as it was, was based not on investment or on increased exports, but rather on an upturn in consumer spending – hardly a sustainable basis.

Against the underconsumptionist arguments of the Keynesians, Roberts argues that what we are living through is a long-term crisis of profitability. Within the framework of capitalism, this will only be resolved either through the 'creative destruction' of large chunks of capital (eg through economic collapse or war) allowing the more profitable firms to expand, or by freeing up new funds for investment by forcing down the living standards of the mass of the people through cuts to wages, benefits and services (including the privatisation of public services). It is this latter approach that has underpinned the neoliberal project of the past 30 years and that also provides the rationale for current policies of austerity.

Jospeh Choonara makes a similar point:

> Four decades of neoliberal attacks, including almost a decade of austerity, have failed to reverse this decline of profitability. The Keynesian solutions that are offered by most reformist politicians are not capable of transforming this situation. Versions of Keynesianism have been attempted both in the past and in the current crisis – for instance by the Abe government in Japan – to no avail. In order to stimulate the economy, money has to either come from capitalists, further undermining profitability, or from workers, in which case the measures are hardly progressive. Or the money can be borrowed, which tends to lead to greater financial instability. (Choonara, 2016)

These arguments also apply to what some have characterised as the latest, and perhaps least anticipated, return of Keynesianism. In their apparent rejection of free-market globalisation and embrace of national investment and protectionist policies, the influence of Keynes has been detected in the policies of Donald Trump, elected US president in 2016. One of Keynes' biographers, for example, Robert Skidelsky (2016), has praised 'Trumpism's positive potential' and argued that he is proposing 'a modern form of Keynesian fiscal policy'. Even putting to one side the odious racist and nationalist themes that underpinned Trump's election campaign, given current levels of global economic integration in the 21st century, it is difficult to see how Trump could pursue such protectionist policies without damaging the world economy even more.

The alternative, these Marxist economists argue, is not to bail out the system in the way in which the Keynesians suggest, but rather to replace it with a very different kind of economic system driven not by profit, but by the overarching requirement of meeting human need. Until then, however, all that the current rulers of the world seem able to offer their peoples is what the former British Prime Minister Cameron at a Lord Mayor's State Banquet in London in 2013 described as 'permanent austerity' (Cameron, 2013). We will conclude this chapter by considering what such austerity has meant in two of the countries most affected by it: Greece and Britain.

The reality of austerity: Greece and Britain

It is difficult to compute the economic costs of the crisis of 2008. In Britain alone, for example, one 2011 estimate suggests that the costs to the Treasury of bailing out the banks was £123.93 billion, though, at several points, Treasury exposure (i.e. the amount guaranteed to be paid out) was 10 times that figure (Curtis, 2011). However, according to one leading economics academic and former Treasury adviser:

> The costs of the crisis are not simply the costs to the Treasury, important though these may be.... I have estimated taking into account the losses of output that would have occurred since 2008 without the financial crisis caused by the reckless lending of the banks, and projecting the losses forward until the end of 2012, that the total cost to the economy – all of us – is around 11 to 13% of GDP [gross domestic product]. (Desmond, cited in Curtis, 2011)

While the precise figures may be a matter of dispute, what is not in doubt is that in Britain and elsewhere, the costs of a crisis resulting from what Desmond calls the 'reckless lending of the banks' have been borne not by the banks or financial institutions (in Britain, unlike Iceland, no bankers have been jailed). Rather, they have been borne by the poorest sections of society, including low-paid workers, the unemployed, the young and the disabled. The narrative that has justified this assault on the welfare state and the living standards of the poor has gone under the name of 'austerity'.

'Austerity' is the short-hand term for the economic, ideological and political strategy that has dominated Europe for the best part of a decade since 2008. Its attraction for governments is that it appears to provide a clear and simple explanation for the current crisis (excessive government spending, especially on welfare) and a solution to that crisis (cutting wages, reducing public spending and raising taxes). In almost every case, that solution has also involved 'structural reform', meaning greater market flexibility, pension reductions, the privatisation of public enterprises and so on.

The Keynesian assessment of the success or otherwise of austerity policy has been discussed earlier and is neatly summarised by Martin Wolf:

> Austerity has failed. It has failed in the UK and it has failed in the Eurozone. Its failure was predictable and, by some at least, predicted. It turned a nascent recovery into stagnation. That imposes huge and unnecessary costs, not just in the short run, but in the long-term as well: the costs of investments unmade, of businesses not started and of hopes destroyed. (Wolf, 2013)

As a description of the devastating effect that austerity policies have had on the lives of millions across Europe, 'hopes destroyed' is perhaps something of an understatement.

Greece

Living in one of the weakest economies in the Eurozone, the Greek people have been made to pay a very high price for the bailout of Greek banks by the 'Troika' of the European Central Bank, the European Commission and the International Monetary Fund, not least because most of the money loaned goes straight back into the coffers of banks in Germany and other major European countries to repay earlier loans. Just what the bailout has meant for public health services was spelled out in a paper in the medical journal *The Lancet* in 2014 (Kentikelenis et al, 2014).

A key condition of the Troika bailout was that health expenditure in Greece be capped at 6% – lower than that of any other pre-2004 EU member country. Seeking to surpass even that target, in 2012, the government made huge cuts in hospital operating costs and pharmaceutical spending. As the former Minister of Health Andreas Loverdos admitted, 'the Greek public administration … uses butcher's knives [to achieve the cuts]'.

Predictably, the results have been devastating. One of the most affected areas has been prevention and treatment programmes for illicit drug users, at a time of rising levels of addiction. In 2009/10, the first year of the austerity programme, a third of all street work programmes were closed while the number of syringes and condoms distributed fell by 10% and 24%, respectively. Not surprisingly, there has been a huge increase in the number of new HIV infections – from 15 in 2009 to 484 in 2012 – and preliminary data also suggest a doubling of tuberculosis among this population (all figures from Kentikelenis et al, 2014).

Reductions to local budgets have led to cuts in public health practices such as mosquito-spraying, resulting in the re-emergence of locally transmitted malaria for the first time in 40 years. In addition, cuts to hospital budgets of 26% have resulted in greatly increased workloads for staff and longer waiting times. Cuts to pharmaceutical expenditure have meant that some drugs are now unobtainable because pharmacies have built up unsustainable debts and can no longer afford to stock them. A study cited by Kentikelenis and his colleagues found that in one province (Achaia), 70% of respondents said that they had insufficient income to purchase the drugs prescribed by their doctors. Pharmaceutical companies have reduced supplies because of unpaid bills and low profits.

Despite a rhetoric of 'maintaining universal access and improving the quality of care delivery', in reality, the introduction of charges (or the increase in existing charges) for out-patient visits and for prescriptions have created barriers to access. In addition, the difficulties of securing health care if you are not employed mean that an estimated 800,000 people now have no access to health care and depend on the voluntary clinics that have sprung up across Greece.

Mental health services have also been seriously affected. According to health economist David Stuckler, who has studied the impact of austerity policies on suicide rates across the globe, in terms of 'economic' suicides, 'Greece has gone from one extreme to the other. It used to have one of Europe's lowest suicide rates; it has seen a more than 60% rise' (Henley 2013). In general, each suicide corresponds to around 10 suicide attempts and – it varies from country to country – between 100 and 1,000 new cases of depression. In Greece, says Stuckler, 'that's reflected in surveys that show a doubling in cases of depression; in psychiatry services saying they're overwhelmed; in charity helplines reporting huge increases in calls' (Henley, 2013).

Ioakimidis and Teloni have explored the impact of these austerity policies on social services in what, they argue, was the only EU country where comprehensive social assistance, a safety net of last resort, did not exist. Even before the crisis, they suggest, 'Greek workers in the welfare sector and social workers were over-worked and underpaid' (Ioakimidis and Teloni, 2013). Nevertheless, in the years before 2009, EU funding allowed for the development of 'Home Care', with hundreds of projects at the local and regional levels, employing around 4,000 staff and supporting more than 100,000 service users (albeit at the cost of marginalising state-provided welfare). The underpinning philosophy of Home Care was to promote independence for service users, who included elderly and disabled people, by providing care and support directly in their own homes. As Ioakimidis and Teloni (2013: 40) note: 'In a country where adult care never really existed, it is not a surprise that the project immediately became very popular'. The crisis, however, put an end to all that. Home Care depended on EU funding and when that dried up, the then Conservative government discontinued the scheme. It was reintroduced by the socialist (PASOK) government in 2010 but in an extremely reduced form, based on means testing with strict eligibility criteria. The result, according to Ioakimidis and Teloni (2013: 42), was that by 2013:

> [T]he number of Home Care projects has been significantly reduced, continuation of the scheme remains uncertain, and employees have not been paid for several months.... More importantly, more than half of the service users are now considered ineligible, leaving some of the most vulnerable groups without any support whatsoever. The project only targets pensioners, excludes disabled people and older people without pension support. Most of these people struggle to survive, receiving food from charity soup kitchens.

In January 2015, the left-wing Syriza party was elected to government with a commitment to ending austerity and renegotiating the bailout with the European banking institutions. However, after six months of what one leading player described as 'mental water-boarding' by the Troika of the European Bank, the European Commission and the International Monetary Fund, and despite massive popular support (reflected, above all, in a huge vote against the latest bailout terms in a popular referendum), the Syriza government caved in to the Troika's demands in July 2015 and implemented the required cuts and privatisations (Ovenden, 2015). One illustration of what the climbdown meant in practice was provided in October 2016, when Greek pensioners, protesting against the latest cut to their already meagre pensions, were tear-gassed in front of the Greek Parliament by riot police acting on the authority of the Syriza government.

Britain

If Greece entered the crisis with the least developed welfare state in Europe, then Britain, by contrast, would be seen by many as having one of the longest-established welfare states in the Western world and one of the most developed in respect of universal provision. It is a perception that requires some qualification. First, while for most of the post-war period, health-care provision in the UK in the form of the National Health Service (NHS) has been genuinely universal (in the sense that that treatment is free at the point of need), this has never been true of social care and social work, which have always been based on a mixture of means testing and discretion (Beresford, 2016). Second, the period since the early 1990s has seen the erosion of universal provision through the increasing marketisation and privatisation of the health service, particularly in England, by both Conservative and New Labour governments. Thus, by 2014, between a quarter and a half of all community services in England were run by Richard Branson's Virgin Care (see: www.virgincare.co.uk; see also White, 2016).

The imposition of austerity policies, especially since the election of Conservative–Liberal Democrat Coalition government in 2010, has further eroded that welfare state in three main ways. First, in place of what was once called 'social security', unprecedented cuts across all areas of benefits (especially disability benefits), the introduction of sanctions regimes that have contributed to up to 1 million people being forced to use food banks, and a spare room or 'bedroom' tax affecting around 600,000 people will increase the number of children living in poverty by 200,000, undermine families and force tens of thousands of people to uproot and move to other areas of the country or face eviction (*The Independent*, 2016). All of this has been underpinned by a brutal ideological offensive against people on benefits that has contributed to a significant increase in levels of disability hate crime, increased rates of depression and anxiety, and an increase in the rate of suicide among those on benefit.

Second, in social care, a combination of cuts of around 30% to local authority budgets since 2010, increasingly restrictive eligibility criteria for services and inadequate personal budgets have left millions without the support they need and increasingly dependent on the family, in particular, women family members.

Third, the Health and Social Care Act 2012 in England and Wales will remove the duty on the Secretary of State for Health to provide a comprehensive health service, while the requirement in the Act that up to 49% of services can be tendered out to 'any qualified provider' will rapidly lead to the privatisation of the NHS in England and Wales.

'Austerity' in the sixth richest country in the world

The young couple trudge into the church hall looking gaunt, meek and beaten. They have walked for three miles in heavy rain, their thin clothing so drenched it sticks to their skin as they huddle by a radiator for warmth. Across the room, a 34-year-old mother weeps into her hands as her shopping trolley is filled with food which will stop her two children going to bed that night with hunger pains. Over by the racks of second-hand jackets, shirts and jumpers for sale for 20p each, sit two jobless men without a penny in their pockets, pondering how the three-day emergency rations they've just been handed can last a week-and-a half.

Behind them a smartly dressed married couple who've never been on benefits before suffer the indignity of explaining how they have lost their jobs and home and cannot feed their three kids. (Excerpt from a 2013 report on food charities in the UK, cited in O'Hara, 2014)

Conclusions

The present global political and economic situation – what the writer Tariq Ali has dubbed the 'new world disorder' – presents the social work profession with great challenges. The ways in which social workers across the globe are responding to these challenges will be the subject of later chapters. Before then, however, it is necessary to continue the task that we have begun in this chapter of mapping the ways in which social work has been transformed during the neoliberal era and the implications of that transformation for whatever emancipatory potential it retains. That will involve looking, first, at the changing relationship between social work and the state and then, in Chapter Three, at the impact of privatisation on social work and social care.

TWO

Neoliberalism, social work and the state: retreat or restructuring?

Introduction

In this chapter, we will explore the relationship between social work, neoliberalism and the state. Such a focus is unusual in a social work text. Theoretical discussion of the state seldom figures in contemporary social work literature. There are a number of possible reasons for this. One may be the assumption that what is sometimes referred to as the 'retreat of the state' from welfare over the past three decades, as well as the development of globalisation, has rendered nation states less important than was previously the case. Another reason may be the influence within the critical social work literature of Foucauldian or post-structuralist perspectives, which see power as omnipresent, 'saturating' all relationships, with the state simply one source of power among many others. Probably the main reason for the neglect of the state within the mainstream literature, however, is the continuing influence of a view of social work as essentially a non-political project, an ethical or professional response to human need in particular societies in which the state provides, at most, a context in which this activity takes place.

All of these views will be challenged in the course of this chapter. Before then, however, it is necessary to make some preliminary observations. First, it is not the case that all currents within social work have ignored the state–social work relationship. The Marxist-influenced radical social work literature of the 1970s, while acknowledging the gains provided by post-war welfare states, nevertheless questioned the then dominant social-democratic view of such states as essentially benign, highlighting instead the repressive features of the welfare state and seeking to address in theory and in practice the challenges and contradictions of working 'in and against the state' (Bailey and Brake, 1975; LEWRG, 1979; Simpkin, 1983). Similarly, the movement for the 'reconceptualisation' of social work in Latin America from the 1960s onwards challenged the 'non-political' view of social work and state promoted by the dominant US-linked clinical perspectives:

> The result was a qualitative leap, as the profession began to define not only new frameworks and purposes but also positioned social workers side by side with the masses, whether they were called the 'exploited', the 'marginalised' or the 'excluded'. (Rangel, 2005: 13)

Second, interest in the role of the state has re-emerged over the past decade in the wake of the return of capitalist crisis. As Bob Jessop (2016: 210) has observed in his magisterial study of the state, the fact that, in 2008, the global banking system was only saved from a financial catastrophe of its own making through massive intervention by supposedly irrelevant national states proved, if proof were needed, that 'the national state generally remains the addressee of last resort in appeals to resolve economic, political and social problems'. Since then, as he notes, 'The North Atlantic and Eurozone financial and economic crises, the state's role in crisis management, and serious fiscal and sovereign debt crises have revived interest in the limits of state power and in the challenges of global governance' (Jessop, 2016: 5).

Third, when imperialism is back with a vengeance on the global agenda and the world seems a more dangerous place than it has been for more than half a century, it is a strange time to talk of the 'retreat of the state'. On the contrary, in recent years, states across the globe have been demonstrating their seemingly unlimited capacity for brutal repression and mass destruction all the way from Guantanamo Bay to the Ukraine – above all, in wars throughout the Middle East that have led to the biggest movement of refugees since the Second World War (a movement that has, in turn, been repeatedly blocked by the actions of local states and European Union [EU] state institutions).

Nor, in fact, are such displays of state power inconsistent with the operations of neoliberalism. *Guardian* journalist Jack Shenker's observations concerning the relationship between neoliberalism and the state in Mubarak's Egypt in his superb study of the Arab revolutions and counter-revolutions have much wider application:

> One of neoliberalism's great strengths is to appear as if it is the irresistible outcome of decentralised, common sense management decisions, the origins of which are so diffuse that they are impossible to identify accurately or resist. In reality the opposite is often true. (Shenker, 2016: 62)

As he goes on to argue:

> Neoliberalism is a political project, and its implementation always involves a mass transfer of resources from the poor to the rich.... Without the state intervening to open up new markets and repress dissent among the citizenry, liberalization policies could never have been pushed through. (Shenker, 2016: 68–9)

As in Egypt, states, whether in the UK, Greece, South Africa or elsewhere, have played a key role in the reshaping of welfare to make it more amenable to the wider project of neoliberal capitalism. The nature of that reshaping, and, in particular, what has been involved in the transition from the welfare state to the neoliberal welfare state, will be addressed in the first part of this chapter. The next part of the chapter will look more specifically at the ways in which social work, both within the state and in the third sector, has been transformed in recent decades and the role that the state has played in this process. It is worth noting that very few of the major changes that have taken place in recent decades, such as the shift towards care management approaches in the 1990s in Britain, Japan and elsewhere, came from within the profession; for the most part, they were imposed by governments in the face of strong opposition from social work professionals. One factor undermining resistance to such top-down changes was an unwillingness by professional organisations to address the politics behind such 'reforms'.

Finally, and more positively, some of the most promising developments in global social work practice in recent years have emerged from within social movements as a response to the imposition of neoliberal or austerity policies, or in the face of the crises of war or environmental catastrophe. Elsewhere, we have described these as forms of 'popular social work', which contain a potential within them to go well beyond traditional social work responses to crises (see, eg, Lavalette and Ioakimidis, 2011a; Jones and Lavalette, 2013). These are exciting and significant developments. They do, however, raise the question of how we should view them and their relationship to state-provided social work services – as supplement, as alternative or as prefigurative examples of how social work could be in a differently organised society?

Theorising neoliberalism

As the late Chris Harman (2007) argued, there has always been an ambiguity at the heart of the term 'neoliberalism':

> Did it refer to a way of running the capitalist system that could be changed with a change in government policy, or did it refer to something intrinsic to the present phase of capitalism that only challenging the system as a whole could overcome?

If the former, then the problem was not capitalism per se, but rather a particular ideology or set of policies that should be replaced by an alternative set of policies. As an example of this view, Harman cited the French sociologist Pierre Bourdieu: 'The main issue is neoliberalism and the retreat of the state. In France neoliberal philosophy has become embedded in all the social practices and policies of the state' (Bourdieu, cited in Harman, 2007). This, Bourdieu continued, 'was the effect of a shared belief ... which has created a climate favourable to the withdrawal of the state and submission to the values of the economy' (Bourdieu, cited in Harman, 2007).

To a greater or lesser extent, Bourdieu's view was shared by most of the leading figures in the anti-capitalist or global justice movement that emerged out of the protests against the World Trade Organization in Seattle in 1999. Issues such as globalisation, rising inequality or privatisation – some of the key components of neoliberalism – were seen by them as being 'the problem', rather than the logic of capitalism as a global system. As Harman noted, the logic of their position was to argue for a change of policy or direction at the top of society, often involving a return to the policies of the post-war years when levels of inequality were much lower and the welfare state was more extensive.

Such a view is open to two objections. First, it risks viewing 'welfare states' in the post-war period of 'the long boom' as essentially different from other state forms, neutral if not always benevolent, rather than being a response to a particular (and highly exceptional) phase of capitalist development. Even the award-winning British director Ken Loach's excellent documentary about the 1945–51 Labour government, *The Spirit of '45*, tends to present a largely uncritical portrayal of a government that, alongside its considerable achievements, sent in troops on 18 different occasions to break strikes, left the former bosses in charge of the newly nationalised industries and reimposed dental and prescription charges in 1951 (Miliband, 2009). As Marxist critics of the Attlee government such as John Saville and Ralph Miliband argued, whatever its achievements, even that government operated very clearly within the framework of capitalism and had no hesitation in putting the needs of capital before those of the working class.

A second objection to the arguments of those whose response to neoliberalism is to argue for a return to the policies of the post-war period is that these policies were the product of a very particular – and highly unusual – period of capitalism's development. As Michael Kidron (1968) argued in *Western capitalism since the War*, in the context of the Cold War, that boom was sustained by exceptionally high levels of arms spending that could not be maintained without undermining economic growth, both East and West. The neoliberal policies adopted by governments from the 1970s onwards were, above all, a response to the crisis of profitability exposed by the breakdown of the global economy in 1973. As Harman (2009: 240) argues, that response involved:

> Imposing 'flexible labour markets' so as to get longer working hours and more intensive production (in Marx's terms absolute and relative surplus value) and to try to cut back on welfare expenditure. This was the rationale behind 'neoliberal' policies with counter reforms of welfare and the use of marketization and privatization measures to get workers competing with each other.

Or, as John Harris (2014: 8) has argued, 'neoliberalism's priority is the creation of conditions attractive to capitalist profitability in the global market'.

As the earlier quote from Bourdieu shows, it is common to describe the changes that have taken place in global welfare since the late 1980s in terms of 'the retreat of the state'. At one level, this is an accurate description of a process that has involved the state either contracting out welfare services to private providers or non-governmental organisations (NGOs), or simply withdrawing from areas of provision and leaving individuals, families and communities to get by as best they can. In another sense, however, the concept of 'retreat' is not helpful since it suggests that the state has become less important or is playing a less active role in welfare. In fact, as Harman (2007) argued:

> The reality is that capital uses the state as much today as it did in the heyday of 'Keynesianism' – indeed, even more so, insofar as it is faced with more crises needing intervention. Neoliberalism as an ideology does not guide practice when it comes to this matter. The difference with the post-war decades is that capital is anxious to cut back on many of the positive reforms it granted in a more profitable era, and states respond accordingly.

None of this means that modern states can do without welfare. The three-part rationale for the British post-war welfare state developed by the Marxist historian John Saville in the mid-1950s still provides a useful framework for making sense of welfare regimes today. That welfare state, Saville argued, was best understood as a product of the interaction of three quite different factors:

> The struggle of the working class against their exploitation; the requirements of industrial capital (a convenient abstraction) for a more efficient environment in which to operate and in particular the need for a highly productive labour force; and recognition of the property owners of the price that had to be paid for their political security. (Saville, 1957: 5–6)

All three of these factors continue to apply more than half a century later. So, for example, as we have argued elsewhere, the huge expansion of social work education in China by the ruling Communist Party in the 1990s and 2000s, with its strong emphasis on social work's role in promoting social stability, is best understood as a response to concerns within the Chinese ruling class over growing political and industrial unrest, particularly following the brutal crushing of the student protests in Tiananmen Square in 1989 (Ferguson, 2012).

Generally, in terms of welfare, what we are seeing is the state increasingly abandoning its role as 'provider' of welfare services but asserting its role as regulator and director of services. The state's role remains paramount but the direct provision of services is increasingly outsourced to a range of private and voluntary sector organisations, with 'welfare gaps' picked up by the informal sector (often service user families). In other words, we are witnessing a significant shift in the mixed economy of welfare and this is impacting upon social work services. In the past, several social work academics described social work services provided by the state as 'state social work' (eg Jones, 1983). As the state moves away from the direct provision of services, what we are seeing is the growth of 'state-directed social work', tightly regulated and controlled by state agencies but provided by a range of service provider organisations, including 'for-profits'.

The impact of the neoliberal turn on the organisation and provision of welfare services can usefully be periodised in two phases. In the first phase (the 1980s to approximately 2008), McDonald (2006: 37) suggests that the primary commonalities across states 'revolve around the linkage between employment policy and engagement with associated labour market programmes, the promotion of individual responsibility and increasingly conditional access to social support'.

Among other things, that involved: a shift from welfare to workfare, with work seen as the route out of poverty; more individualised forms of social support, including 'cash for care' and personalisation schemes; and increased conditionality. An example of the latter from Latin America is what the *Economist* magazine has called 'the world's favourite new anti-poverty device': conditional cash transfer programmes (CCTs). First tried out in Brazil as the *Bolsa Família*, CCTs, as their name suggests, supply monetary benefits as long as recipients can demonstrate that they have met certain conditions, such as children's school attendance. They have proved popular with governments not only in Latin America, but also across much of the Global South. According to Lavinas, in 1997, only three Latin American countries had launched such programmes; a decade later, the World Bank reported that 'virtually every country' in the region had one, and others outside it were adopting them 'at a prodigious rate' (Lavinas, 2013). By 2008, 30 countries had them, from India, Turkey and Nigeria, to Cambodia, the Philippines and Burkina Faso; even New York City had put one in place (Lavinas, 2013). As with the neoliberal policies implemented by the Mubarak government in Egypt, the 'encouragement' by international financial bodies (in this case, the World Bank) for governments to adopt such schemes has been a crucial factor in their widespread use. Yet, while they have undoubtedly relieved the poverty experienced by some of the most marginalised in society, they suffer from a number of serious limitations, not least the fact that, as Lavinas (2013) argues:

> [T]hey remain *ad hoc* instruments, unconstrained by legal and institutionalized principles of rights. The distinction is crucial: instead of being one dimension of a wider, universal system of social protection, such programmes enforce a principle of selectivity, targeting the poor as a residual category while insisting they assume individualized responsibility for their fates – thus working to diminish social solidarity and cohesion. The schemes are also designed to extend commodification, on the one hand disbursing monetary rewards to the poor in exchange for their participation as consumers, while on the other offering governments an alibi for scaling back provision of public goods. They thus pave the way for a retrenchment of welfare rather than its expansion.

The second phase of neoliberal restructuring of welfare has been the period since the onset of global economic crisis in 2008 until the present time. As we saw in Chapter One, global institutions and national states have made use of that crisis to promote an ideology and politics of 'austerity' and to fundamentally reconfigure the relationship between the state and its citizens. Jessop suggests that austerity can be studied in three ways. First, there are *conjunctural austerity policies*, usually presented as short-term responses to periods of economic difficulty, with the implication that once these difficulties have been overcome, then 'business as usual' can be resumed. This was how austerity policies were initially presented from 2010 onwards across Britain and much of the Eurozone. Gradually, however, that discourse has been replaced by a second one of *enduring* or *permanent* austerity. Such a politics, as Jessop (2015: 233) notes, 'Is intended to bring about a more lasting reorganisation of the balance of forces in favour of capital rather than to make policy adjustments to safeguard existing economic and political arrangements'. Thus, for example, the decision by the then British Chancellor of the Exchequer George Osborne in 2016 to reduce welfare spending as a proportion of gross domestic product (GDP) to levels not seen since the 1930s at the same time as reducing top rates of tax clearly reflects an ideological commitment to a smaller state rather than an economic requirement to balance the books.

Finally, there is what Jessop calls the *austerity polity*, which, he argues 'results from a continual and fundamental reorganization between the economic and the political in capitalist formations' (Jessop, 2015: 233). The experience of Greece in recent years at the hands of the Troika of the European Commission, the European Central Bank and the International Monetary Fund shows the extent to which parliamentary democracy can be dispensed with if it conflicts with or impedes the operations of wider neoliberal concerns. Former Greek Finance Minister Yannis Varoufakis, for example, has expressed his astonishment on hearing his German counterpart Wolfgang Schauble respond to the election of a Syriza government committed to challenging austerity by saying 'Elections cannot be allowed to change an economic programme of a member state!' (Varoufakis, 2016).

Neoliberalism, the state and social work

What, then, has this reshaping of the economic and political polity meant for social work? Reference was made at the beginning of this chapter to the view that social work is a 'non-political' profession, an ethical response to human need. In reality, throughout its history, professional social work has been shaped by forces outside its own ranks, not least the state, arguably to a greater extent than almost any other profession. As John Harris (2008: 663) has argued in a review of five different 'moments' in the historical development of social work in Britain:

> Rather than thinking about social work as a professional project that has
> orchestrated its own genesis and development, it is positioned at these

different moments as an element in their respective welfare regimes, concerned with managing and regulating the sphere of the 'social'.

A number of internal and external factors, including a weak professional identity, a contested knowledge base and a lack of strong professional organisation, have meant that in the face of a ruling-class desire to regulate and control the behaviour of those sections of society perceived as deviant or dangerous, the organisation and content of the social work role has been shaped by the state to an even greater extent than professions such as medicine or teaching. As Jordan (1984: 114) has noted:

> Social work has played various roles in contrasting systems of social provision, and has served a number of political ends. Its great virtue – that it is almost infinitely adaptable to circumstances – also makes it open to exploitation for any kind of policy objectives.

The state: friend or foe?

A proposed new law in Scotland would provide every child with a 'Named Person' to whom the child (or his or her family) could turn if he or she was experiencing difficulties. The Named Person would most likely be a health visitor, a school guidance teacher or sometimes the head teacher at the child's school. The new Act has been developed in consultation with organisations representing children in care and is seen by some of them as a way of offering additional protection and support to children. The Act has been fiercely opposed, however, by left-wing journalists, social work professionals and some children's organisations (as well as by some right-wing Christian groups) on the basis that it represents a massive extension of state power, the main effect of which will be to undermine families.

One result has been the 'horrible' histories of social work, which will be explored in Chapter Four. In our own times, states have intervened actively to reshape social work in the interests of neoliberal capitalism. As Harris (2014: 8) has argued, that reshaping has been based on three main propositions, which, he argues, have been played out in social work across the world:

- Markets are efficient and effective and should be introduced in as many and as wide a range of contexts as possible;
- Individuals should be responsible for themselves and run their own lives;
- Services in the public or voluntary sectors should be modeled on management knowledge and techniques drawn from the private business sector.

Here, some examples of what that reshaping has meant in specific countries will be considered.

China

Reference was made earlier to the expansion of social work education in China since the early 1990s. Several factors contributed to that expansion (Sigley, 2016) but the most important was arguably the government's need to promote 'social stability' in the wake of two key developments. The first of these, referred to earlier, was the crushing of the mass student movement in Tiananmen Square in 1989, and the second was the growing social divisions resulting from the social and political effects of the marketisation of the economy that began soon after that massacre. As in the West, it is helpful to identify two phases of neoliberal development. The period following the decision by the Chinese Communist Party in 1992 to inaugurate a 'socialist market economy' led to the wholesale privatisation of state-owned enterprises. The consequences of that shift were devastating for ordinary workers and peasants. According to the activist network China Labour Net:

> More than 60 million workers in the state and collective sectors were sacked, a scale never seen in history.... At the same time, the flourishing private sector led 120 million poor rural residents to leave the land and roam the country as migrant workers in search of employment. The overwhelming number of them ended up working in private enterprises with wages so low that workers are barely able to sustain themselves, and with little social security. (Yu and Ruixe, 2010: 27–28)

Even these poorly paid jobs and that limited social security, however, disappeared with the onset of the global economic crisis of 2008. According to the writer Hsiao-Hung Pai (2012: 11):

> Despite state proclamations of a 'rising' China, the reality is that China has been struck hard by the global recession and is as bitterly divided as the rest of the world. The 'iron rice bowl' no longer exists. More than 600,000 small and medium-sized firms closed in China in 2008, throwing millions out of work. The deepening slump has encouraged a reverse migration, back to the countryside.

Unsurprisingly, social upheaval on this scale has given rise to massive social problems – drugs, family breakdown, mental illness, homelessness and so on. No less important, it has also led to huge social unrest, including record numbers of workers taking strike action in recent years. The government's response has been to promote a 'harmonious society policy' within which social work has been accorded a central role. In an interesting review of the recent development of social work in China, Sigley (2016: 108) notes that:

> [F]rom its inception the harmonious society campaign has emphasized 'social management' and recognized that NGOs and NPOs [Non-Governmental Organisations and Non-Profit Organisations] have a significant role to play in promoting social stability. The profession of social work, for example, was given an elevated position within the 'Harmonious Society' document, which described the development of a large cohort of professional social workers as 'an urgent task for socialist construction and the development of a harmonious society'.

As Sigley also notes, however, there is a potential tension between the long-standing practice and preference of party bureaucrats at both national and local levels to 'fix' social problems by political and administrative means, on the one hand, and the promotion of a profession that, even in its most conservative forms, encourages self-help and self-determination on the part of marginalised individuals and communities, on the other. Given the interest in more radical forms of social work in Hong Kong, Taiwan and mainland China expressed, for example, in well-attended conferences of the Progressive Social Welfare Association based in Hong Kong and the production of a manifesto for progressive social work (PSWN, 2011), it will be interesting to see how that tension plays out over the next few years.

South Africa

Social work in South Africa has its roots in apartheid ideology, born out of what was called the 'poor white problem' of the depression of the 1930s (Sewpaul, 2012). Thus, from its earliest beginnings until the first democratic elections in 1994, public sector social work functioned within apartheid structures and policies. (The 'architect of apartheid', Hendrick Verwoerd, was himself a social work academic.) As Sewpaul (2012) notes: 'Those working in non-governmental and faith-based organisations did not evade the horrendous arm of apartheid laws. A host of legislative and policy directives demanded that services be provided separately (and unequally) for the different race groups'.

The overthrow of apartheid provided the opportunity for the development of both a different kind of society and a different kind of welfare. After the democratic transition in 1994, South Africa declared itself to be a developmental state (Edigheji, 2006) and social welfare and social work moved towards the 'developmental approach' (Patel, 2005). The basis for this was the 'White Paper for social welfare' (RSA, 1997), which contains the principles, policies and programmes for developmental social welfare in South Africa. Therefore, both state departments and non-governmental welfare organisations (dependent on state subsidies for survival in most cases) shifted their focus towards the developmental approach, guided by various statutory imperatives such as the 'Financing policy', the 'Integrated service delivery model' and the 'White Paper for social welfare'. Social development also became the emphasis in social work education and curricula at all the various tertiary training institutions.

Progressive as this may sound, in fact, as Marjorie Mayo noted in a discussion of community development approaches in Bailey and Brake's (1975) seminal collection *Radical social work*, the concept of 'development' is inherently ambiguous:

> [D]evelopment, progress, community and participation are all problematic terms – development and progress of what kind, for whose benefit in what type of community, composed graphically or in class terms, participating in what and with what degree of real power and influence? (Mayo, 1975: 130)

Answering these questions requires that we locate development approaches in their wider political and economic context. In post-apartheid South Africa from 1996 onwards, that context was explicitly one of neoliberalism:

> The adoption of the neo-liberal Growth, Employment and Redistribution (GEAR) strategy in 1996 ... was a major shift from the Reconstruction and Development Programme, the major policy of the African National Congress at the time of the national democratic transition, aimed at ushering in liberation and a 'better life for all'.... The GEAR structural adjustment programme normalised corporate capitalist power in post-apartheid South Africa.... The popular developmental approach is thus framed within the context of GEAR and its neo-liberal ideologies. Such emphasis on the free-market, privatisation, personal responsibility, self-reliance and even development itself competes with a more politicised, radical and structural social work and does not augur well for social work with its professional commitment to social justice. (Ferguson and Smith, 2012: 978)

Thus, in a context of widespread poverty and income inequality that, according to economist Thomas Piketty (2014), is even higher than it was under apartheid, state-driven developmental social work increasingly means poor communities being expected to pull themselves up by their own bootstraps. In contrast to China, however, there is a long tradition in South Africa of powerful social movements, movements that played a key role in the overthrow of apartheid, as well as a highly organised working class. Radical forms of community work were often a feature of these movements. They, alongside new movements formed in the wake of the massacre of miners by the state at Marikana (under the command of a chief of police who was also a former social worker!) and around the issue of tuition fees, potentially provide a basis for more radical forms of social work practice and education than currently prevail (Alexander et al, 2012; Sewpaul, 2013; Motlalepule and Smith, 2017).

Britain

Britain was one of the first countries to engage in the neoliberal reshaping of social work and, arguably, it is there that the process has gone further than anywhere else. From the outset, it is a reshaping that has been driven from the top and one in which the state has played – and continues to play – a central role. The three key elements were put in place by the NHS and Community Care Act 1990 (Harris, 2003). These were, first, the deliberate creation of a market in social work and social care by re-designating local authorities as purchasers, not providers, of care, responsible for commissioning and purchasing services from private and voluntary sector organisations. Second, the social work role shifted from one in which social workers engaged directly with clients or service users through the use of a range of different methods (primarily casework, group work and community work) to one of assessment and care management in which social workers assessed clients' needs and then organised 'packages of care' to be provided by other agencies. Third, users of social work services were reframed not as clients, but as 'customers', who would shop around to find the most appropriate services for their needs from a social care market.

These processes, identified by Harris as *marketisation, managerialisation* and *consumerisation*, have transformed social work in the UK (as well as generating considerable resistance, to be considered later) (Harris, 2014). The British experience has been thoroughly documented elsewhere by different writers, so we will confine ourselves here to a few more general comments (Harris, 2003; Ferguson, 2008).

First, a dominant theme over the past decade has been the *individualisation* of services, primarily through the policy of individual budgets known as personalisation (or, in Scotland, self-directed support). While its origins lie in the disabled people's movement, the policy has largely been driven from the top but cleverly constructed around a discourse of 'choice and control' that has played to both worker and service user dissatisfactions with the bureaucratic, top-down and controlling nature of many state-provided welfare services in areas such a mental health and learning disability. At best, the experience of personalisation has been mixed (Beresford, 2014; Needham and Glasby, 2014; Pearson and Ridley, 2014). While some service users receiving the more generous direct payments have been positive about the policy, in many areas, personalisation has primarily been used as a means of reducing spending and undermining social forms of provision such as day centres, which, for all their limitations, have provided an important means of social support for people who are socially isolated. Here, as elsewhere, a consistent complaint from social workers is that despite a dominant rhetoric which suggests that personalisation will allow social workers to return to more relationship-based work, the opposite is frequently the case. In many cases, the emphasis on budgets and cost reductions, based on ever-tighter eligibility criteria, has led to an increase, not a reduction, in bureaucracy (Ryan, 2016).

A second key theme has been the reshaping of the social work role. Since the Thatcher years, the attitude of successive governments to the social work profession has been highly ambivalent. On the one hand, as different writers have noted, social work has often been excluded from key government initiatives, such as the Sure Start project under New Labour (Jordan and Jordan, 2000) or the Coalition government's 2011 Troubled Families programme. It has also been marginalised in such areas as mental health (Bamford, 2015). At the same time, the experience of the past decade suggests that the state continues to see the social work profession as having a role to play in managing individuals, families and communities perceived as problematic. Thus, considerable funding was invested by the then New Labour government in a social work reform process following the highly publicised death of a small child, Peter Connelly, in 2008 at the hands of his carers. More recently, the Conservative government has promoted a major reform of social work education in England, the aims of which are to align the value base of social work much more closely with neoliberal individualism, to dilute the social science knowledge base of the profession, to produce social workers who are much readier to blame clients for their own problems and to prepare sections of the profession for privatisation (SWAN, 2014). In the words of the minister who launched the reform programme:

> In too many cases, social work training involves idealistic students being told that the individuals with whom they will work have been disempowered by society. They will be encouraged to see these individuals as victims of social injustice whose fate is overwhelmingly decreed by the economic forces and inherent inequalities which scar our society. (Gove, 2013)

Instead, Gove has argued, social problems such as poverty, drug misuse and homelessness should be seen as the result of individuals making 'wrong choices', with the role of social workers being to encourage them to make 'better choices'. It is, in other words, a wholly victim-blaming approach that downplays or ignores the extent to which people's lives are shaped by wider structural forces.

Greece

The final example from Greece is a rather different one. As discussed in Chapter One, Greece is the European country that has become the testing ground not only for the politics of austerity promoted by the 'Troika' of the European Commission, the European Central Bank and the International Monetary Fund, but also for strategies of resistance to that austerity. One form of resistance from below has been the creation of a nationwide network of solidarity committees, usually involving health and social work professionals working on a voluntary basis to address the care needs of those who have been abandoned by the statutory services. As the following boxed article indicates, these committees are important not only as a humanitarian response to unmet need (including support for refugees), but also as potential examples of 'prefigurative welfare', both more inclusive and more openly political (eg in challenging racism) than services provided (or not provided) by the state. At the same time, they raise important questions for radical social workers about the role of the state in welfare. Can such committees ever be a substitute for state-provided services? Given their limited resources, is there not a great danger of burnout on the part of those involved? Should the main energies of those on the Left not be directed towards defending the welfare state? It is perhaps not surprising that the Syriza government is enthusiastic about the committees given that it is that government that is now implementing the austerity policies demanded by the EU. Nevertheless, the committees are an inspiring example of what a radical social work response might involve.

Greece's solidarity movement: 'It's a whole new model and it's working'

'A long time ago, when I was a student,' said Olga Kesidou, sunk low in the single, somewhat clapped-out sofa of the waiting room at the Peristeri Solidarity Clinic, 'I'd see myself volunteering. You know, in Africa somewhere, treating sick people in a poor developing country. I never once imagined I'd be doing it in a suburb of Athens.'

Few in Greece, even five years ago, would have imagined their recession- and austerity-ravaged country as it is now: 1.3 million people – 26% of the workforce – without a job (and most of them without benefits); wages down by 38% on 2009, pensions by 45%, GDP by a quarter; 18% of the country's population unable to meet their food needs; 32% below the poverty line. And just under 3.1 million people, 33% of the population, without national health insurance.

So, along with a dozen other medics including a GP, a brace of pharmacists, a paediatrician, a psychologist, an orthopaedic surgeon, a gynaecologist, a cardiologist and a dentist or two, Kesidou, an ear, nose and throat specialist, spends a day a week at this busy but cheerful clinic half an hour's drive from central Athens, treating patients who otherwise would not get to see a doctor. Others in the group accept uninsured patients in their private surgeries.

'We couldn't just stand by and watch so many people, whole families, being excluded from public healthcare,' Kesidou said. 'In Greece now, if you're out of work for a year you lose your social security. That's an awful lot of people without access to what should be a basic right. If we didn't react we couldn't look at ourselves in the mirror. It's solidarity.'

The Peristeri health centre is one of 40 that have sprung up around Greece since the end of mass anti-austerity protests in 2011. Using donated drugs – state medicine reimbursements have been slashed by half, so even patients with insurance are now paying 70% more for their drugs – and medical equipment (Peristeri's ultrasound scanner came from a German aid group, its children's vaccines from France), the 16 clinics in the Greater Athens area alone treat more than 30,000 patients a month.

The clinics in turn are part of a far larger and avowedly political movement of well over 400 citizen-run groups – food solidarity centres, social kitchens, cooperatives, 'without middlemen' distribution networks for fresh produce, legal aid hubs, education classes – that has emerged in response to the near-collapse of Greece's welfare state, and has more than doubled in size in the past three years.

'Because in the end, you know,' said Christos Giovanopoulos in the scruffy, poster-strewn seventh-floor central Athens offices of Solidarity for All, which provides logistical and administrative support to the movement, 'politics comes down to individual people's stories. Does this family have enough to eat? Has this child got the right book he needs for school? Are this couple about to be evicted?'

As well as helping people in difficulty, Giovanopoulos said, Greece's solidarity movement was fostering 'almost a different sense of what politics should be – a politics from the bottom up, that starts with real people's needs. It's a practical critique of the empty, top-down, representational politics our traditional parties practise. It's kind of a whole new model, actually. And it's working.'

It also looks set to play a more formalised role in Greece's future under what polls predict will be a Syriza-led government from next week. When they were first elected in 2012 the radical left party's 72 MPs voted to give 20% of their monthly salary to a solidarity fund that would help finance Solidarity for All. (Many help further; several have transferred their entitlement to free telephone calls to a local project.) The party says the movement can serve as an example and a platform for the social change it wants to bring about. (Henley, 2015)

Conclusion

This chapter highlights the limitations of a narrative of 'state withdrawal' as a means of understanding 'what is going on' in respect of social work and social care. In fact, the neoliberal state, far from having withdrawn from the field of social welfare and social work, is playing a more central role than ever in shaping both the content of the social work role and the tasks of social workers (as well as the behaviour of poor people, up to and including 'psycho-compulsion', the provision of cognitive-behaviour therapy for those seen as not being sufficiently motivated to seek work [Freidli and Stearn, 2015]). From Latin America to China, governments are actively reshaping the social work profession to address the challenges of 'permanent austerity', unprecedented levels of inequality and shrinking public services. Challenging that reshaping must start from the clear recognition that social work is a political activity and that these developments require a political response. Any other perspective will leave us disarmed in the face of an existential threat to the profession.

As we progress through the rest of the book we will discuss the way in which social workers across the globe are responding to this reshaping. Before then, however, it is necessary to address another central plank of the neoliberal reshaping of welfare in which states have also played a key role, namely, privatisation, and to explore the implications of this for global social work and those who rely on it.

THREE

The privatisation of social work and social care

Introduction

The privatisation of what were previously state-controlled services has been a key plank of the neoliberal project since its beginnings in the 1970s. One of the first acts of the military junta that overthrew the democratically elected government of Salvador Allende in Chile in 1973 was to institute the wholesale privatisation of the Chilean economy under the supervision of the 'Chicago Boys', economists from Chicago University committed to market fundamentalism. Since then, privatisation has been a key element of neoliberal economic 'reform' everywhere, from the Structural Adjustment Programmes (SAPs) imposed on countries in the Global South from the 1990s onwards by the International Monetary Fund (IMF) and World Bank, to the more recent crippling austerity packages imposed on the people of Greece by the Troika of the European Commission, European Central Bank and IMF.

Social work and social care have not been immune from this process. While the privatisation of professional social work is at an earlier stage in most countries, it is clearly in the sights of governments keen to open up the profession to market forces and, in the process, create a more compliant workforce, less informed by social science theories or committed to the value of social justice (Murphy, 2016).

The first part of this chapter will explore the rationales – ideological, political and economic – for privatisation. Privatisation, like neoliberalism, is often viewed, first and foremost, as ideology and there is no question that the rhetoric of 'private good, public bad' has been enormously influential, taking on the mantle of a kind of common sense among global elites. Yet, an overemphasis on the ideological roots of privatisation can lead to an underestimation of the political and economic forces that underpin it, forces that will be explored in some detail later.

In the second part of the chapter, we will examine the ways in which the global social work and social care landscape has been changed as a result of the many privatisations and outsourcing over the last three decades of what were previously state-controlled services.

Finally, we will critically examine the claims of the neoliberal advocates of privatisation. Has it really led to increased choice and control, as they claimed it would? What has it meant for those who use social work and social care services and for those who work in them? What has its impact been on the quality of those services?

Why privatisation?

The notion that something can exist and not be a source of profit is an affront to capitalist sensibilities. David Harvey's comments about the relationship between capital and nature can also be applied to the way in which social care services are viewed within neoliberal capitalism:

> Nature is necessarily viewed by capital ... as nothing more than a vast store of potential use values – of processes and things – that can be used directly or indirectly in the production and realization of commodity values.... While some aspects of nature are hard to enclose (such as the air we breathe and the oceans we fish in), a variety of surrogate ways can be devised usually with the help of the state to monetize and make tradeable all aspects of the commons of the natural world. (Harvey, 2014: 250)

As we shall see later, the creation of 'quasi-markets' in health and social care in Britain and other countries in the 1990s was precisely such as 'surrogate' way of making profit from people's poverty and ill-health.

Nevertheless, throughout much of the world for several decades after the Second World War, large parts of the economy, as well as health-care provision and social security, were in the hands of the state. Why were ruling classes prepared to tolerate the public ownership of key industries and health provision then but unwilling to countenance such ownership today? One early answer to that question came from the pen of Marxist historian John Saville, reference to whose arguments was made in Chapter Two.

Saville was clear that the welfare state was a gain for working-class people and that pressure from below was an important factor in leading to its creation. However, it would be a mistake, he argued, to see the welfare state purely as a response to working-class demands. No less crucial for its creation was what he referred to as 'the needs of capital'. One of these needs is for a healthy workforce. The Boer War more than half a century earlier had highlighted to the British ruling class the dangers of an undernourished proletariat, with nine out of 10 applicants for military service being rejected as unfit. Successful military and economic competition demanded the maintenance of a healthy workforce, something that the market, left to its own devices, clearly could not provide (for further discussion, see Ferguson et al, 2002).

By extension, the same argument applied to the creation of nationalised industries in the post-war period. Growing economic and military competition between the leading capitalist powers in the first decades of the 20th century required that the state become increasingly involved both directly and indirectly in the economy. At its most extreme, this involved the total subordination of the economy to the state in the 1930s, as in Hitler's Germany and Stalin's Russia. However, the phenomenon of greater or lesser state involvement in the management of the economy was a fairly universal phenomenon during the 1930s, through the Second World War and into the post-war period – and was something that capitalists were prepared to tolerate. Discussing the widespread nationalisations that took place in Britain and other countries during the 1940s and 1950s, Harman (2009: 116) writes:

> For the state the purpose of nationalized industry was to enable domestic accumulation to match that undertaken by foreign rivals so as to be able to survive successfully in economic and/or military competition…. The state might plan production within the enterprises it owned but its planning was subordinated to external competition, just as the planning within any privately owned firm was.

Harman, like Saville more than half a century earlier, therefore challenged the view that either nationalisation or the provision of free health care in itself equalled socialism (eg as the leading Labour Party theoretician Antony Crosland [1956/2006] had argued in his book *The future of socialism*). As Saville (1957) put it:

> As for the claim that the Welfare state is an early form of a socialist society, it must be emphasised that both in Western Europe and the United States social security schemes are placed firmly within the framework of a free enterprise economy and no one suggests that what is a natural development within a mature capitalist economy should be given new names.

Both Saville's and Harman's comments provide a useful corrective to those, both then and now, who see state ownership in itself as necessarily progressive or even socialist. Their arguments also challenge the widely held view that welfare states, in their different forms, are somehow 'non-capitalist' islands within a capitalist sea, a view most famously expressed in Gosta Esping-Andersen's (1989) celebrated distinction between 'commodified' and 'decommodified' sections of the economy, and, more recently, in David Harvey's (2004) argument that the privatisation of state-owned industries (include welfare provision) is an example of 'accumulation by dispossession', the plundering of the state sector to benefit the private sector. Both sets of arguments assume that, in some way, state-controlled industries represent some kind of challenge to private capitalism despite the fact that workers in these industries enjoyed no more control over production than those in private industry and very often the same bosses remained in place following nationalisation, a process now reversed in the former Soviet Union and Eastern Europe, where the former Communist Party bureaucrats are now often owners of privatised firms.

The reality of nationalisation was very different. As Cliff and Gluckstein (1998: 220) observe in their discussion of the post-1945 Labour government under Prime Minister Clement Attlee:

[M]odern capitalism required a well-developed infrastructure, including transport and power supplies, in order to function efficiently. Now this 'social overhead' capital tended to be costly, requiring long-term investment, and its benefits accrued to industry as a whole rather than the individual entrepreneur. For these reasons the infrastructure in most countries was developed and controlled by governments. In 1945 British capital was ready to break with tradition. It was unwilling to tie up large sums in rebuilding necessary but largely unprofitable areas of industry after the ravages of war. So the bulk of Attlee's nationalization programme did not worry capital in the least.

If the emphasis on privatisation is more than simply an ideological throwback, what, then, is its rationale and how should we respond? The answer, as we suggested in Chapter One, is that it was a key plank of the ruling-class response to the end of the long post-war boom in the early 1970s and the crisis of profitability that it exposed. It sought to address that crisis in several ways (Harman, 2009).

First, it was a pragmatic response to what the US economist James O'Connor (1991 [1973]) had previously described as 'the fiscal crisis of the state'. While global capitalism was expanding during the years of the long post-war boom, increased state expenditure, both on infrastructure (such as roads, airports, etc) and on health and social security, was tolerated or even encouraged. With falling profit rates and the return of global economic crisis in the early 1970s, however, that state expenditure began to be presented as a 'drain' on growth and pressure grew to cut state spending. In Britain, for example, the first round of cuts to welfare took place not under a Conservative government, but under the 1974–79 Labour government, at the behest of the IMF.

Second, the shift to privatisation was aimed at increasing competition between firms and also the exploitation of workers. There was a widespread perception in the 1970s that the managements of nationalised industries were complacent while their workers were lazy and underworked. As Harman (2007) notes:

> The logic of this view was that breaking up state owned monopolies and opening them to the market would force their managers to be much harder on the workers, and would intimidate the workers into accepting worse conditions. Certainly the approach of privatisation often encouraged managers to force through methods to push up productivity. And once privatised, it was easy for companies to 'contract out' a range of activities, so breaking the links that tie weak groups of workers to potentially more powerful ones.

Ben Fine (1999: 42) similarly argues that 'privatisation has been an important way in which the relations between capital and labour have been reorganised' and is connected to so-called 'labour market flexibility'.

Third, privatisation plays an important ideological role in appearing to depoliticise welfare and other forms of what were previously state provision by shifting responsibility away from the state to private firms. As Harman (2007) observes, it may do this though outright privatisation or through the kind of surrogate measures referred to earlier by Harvey:

> At the same time, privatisation is not absolutely necessary to create the illusion of the automatism of the market. The breaking up of state run institutions into competing units (NHS [National Health Service] trusts, foundation hospitals, city academies, 'self-governing' colleges, 'agencies') can try to achieve the same goal; so can 'market testing' within particular entities. So too can deregulation aimed to produce competition between different nationally based, and often still state owned, companies. This is what the European Union is trying to do to a whole range of industries such as electricity and postal services. The end result of privatisation in a country like Britain can be that whole sections of 'privatised' services such as electricity, water and rail can be run by foreign state owned companies.

As an illustration of what that 'illusion of automatism' means in practice, a series of industrial disputes in Glasgow in 2016 involved low-paid workers employed in Arms-Length External Organisations (ALEOs), delivering what were previously council-provided services but nominally independent of the council. In reality, such organisations are both funded by and controlled by the locally elected council (an example of state-directed social services). Their apparent independence, however, meant that elected councillors were able to claim that there was nothing that they could do to resolve the dispute (Kiernan, 2016).

In respect of Harman's second point, in a development that highlights the hollowness of privatisation rhetoric, the contract to deliver railway services in the West of Scotland in 2015 was awarded by the left-leaning Scottish National Party government to Abellio – a nationalised Dutch railway service (BBC, 2014)!

Privatisation, social care and social work

How, then, has the global social work and social care landscape changed as a result of the privatisation and outsourcing agenda of the last three decades? As noted earlier, Chile under the Pinochet dictatorship was the initial test bed for neoliberal policies. Since then, however, many Latin American countries and large parts of Africa have been the recipients of IMF 'help' in the form of SAPs, which, as Patrick Bond et al (2006: 50) have noted, have typically 'meant the loss of state welfare programmes and in turn the need for civil society to pick up the pieces'. In his book *The Egyptians*, Jack Shenker (2016: 50) gives a graphic description of what such SAPs meant in the context of Hosni Mubarak's Egypt:

Through a series of laws passed through the 1990s and early 2000s, Egypt's public sector was divided into dozens of 'holding companies' which could then dispose of their assets on the open market. No longer were state institutions to be thought of as economic development projects, the success of which would be judged by whether or not they met the political and social goals of the state. Now they were merely an epic estate agent's inventory. Huge corporate tax exemptions were established.... New labour laws established fixed-term hiring as a norm and allowed employers to renew the temporary contracts of their staff indefinitely without offering them any longer-term employment rights; workers also faced new limits of their right to strike. Egypt's rulers were so enthused by structural adjustment that they went further and faster in implementing it than even the IMF had expected.... [B]y the end of Mubarak's reign no fewer than 336 public entities had been privatized.

As Shenker notes, it is a scenario that would be familiar to the peoples of dozens of countries in the Global South, from Jamaica to Jordan, who have been on the receiving end of IMF-driven SAPs over the past two decades. Since the Great Crash of 2008, however, citizens of European countries have experienced very similar programmes. Social work and social care were not the first areas to come under the privatisers' spotlight – other areas were far more lucrative – but from the early 1990s onwards, a sea-change took place in the shape and ownership of what one writer has called the 'public services industry' (Gosling, 2011). Here, the experience of three countries will be considered: the UK, Sweden and South Africa.

The UK

In contrast to the provision of health care, which, until recently, was funded through general taxation, free at the point of need and organised through a centralised NHS, social care services in the UK have always been much more fragmented, locally provided and often dependent on the payment of a charge (Beresford, 2016). Nevertheless, until the early 1990s, the state, in the form of local councils or the NHS, continued to be the main provider of social care services (albeit with the family also playing a central role). The picture has changed massively since then. The introduction of a 'quasi-market' in social care has meant that whereas in 1993, 95% of home care was provided directly by local councils, by 2012, that figure had fallen to 11%. Similarly, in 1979, 64% of residential care and nursing homes were provided either by local councils or by the NHS; by 2012, that figure had fallen to just 6% (Moriarty et al, 2014). Small wonder, then, that the privatisation of residential social care has been described by one commentator as 'arguably the most extensive outsourcing of a public service yet undertaken in the UK' (Gosling, 2011: 8).

The privatisation has taken two main forms: first, the outsourcing of local authority services to private or third sector providers; and, second, the promotion of individual budgets (personalisation or self-directed support). Both of these policy developments were accompanied with the familiar rhetoric of 'choice and control' for people using services. The reality has often been very different.

First, the introduction of competition to win contracts has led to a 'race to the bottom' in respect of the wages and conditions of staff in both private and third sector organisations, with worrying implications for the quality of service provided (Cunningham, 2008). Within the UK home care sector, more than 300,000 care workers are on zero-hours contracts, with very few employment rights, and frequently restricted to 15-minute visits to the vulnerable people in their care (White, 2016: 139) – hardly a basis for good-quality care.

Second, the introduction of the market into social care has changed the ethos and dynamic of the sector, with growing involvement by providers whose primary concern is profit rather than the needs of their service users. While the typical business is still a small family-owned firm operating in a converted house, big business and organised money are increasingly represented through chains of purpose-built homes so that the five largest chains accounted for nearly 20% of beds in 2015 (Burns et al, 2016). The British journalist Polly Toynbee cited an advertisement from Gravity International, an investment company specialising in 'sourcing and providing alternative investment products' with bases in Malaga, Dubai and Chester, offering an 18% return on investing in buildings that could be run as children's homes (Toynbee, 2014).

Third, as the global crisis of 2008 graphically illustrated, capitalism in its globalised form continues to be a system based on boom and slump. During periods such as the current 'long depression', market failures are commonplace, and the social care market is not exempt from such failures. The collapse in 2011 of Southern Cross, the biggest provider of residential care for older people in the UK, with 37,000 residents in 750 care homes, demonstrated all too clearly the dangers of leaving the provision of care for vulnerable people to market forces (Ferguson and Lavalette, 2014).

Even outside such periods of crisis, however, the claim that the market provides a better quality of care than publicly provided services does not stand up to scrutiny. A Care Quality Commission (CQC) report into learning disability services in England in 2012, for example, found that almost half of all locations inspected were non-compliant with the two outcomes of the care and welfare of people who use services and of safeguarding people who use services from abuse. However, NHS locations were nearly twice as likely to be compliant with both of the outcomes compared to independent providers, while residents tended to stay for much longer in independent that is, private, homes than in NHS facilities (CQC, 2012). A more recent report by the CQC found that 41% of community-based adult social care services, hospice services and residential social care services inspected since October 2014 were rated as inadequate or requiring improvement (CQC, 2015).

Despite these failures, however, the commitment of all the main political parties (with the partial exception of the Scottish National Party government in Scotland) to increasing the role of the market in social care and social work shows no sign of abating. The focus of the UK government in recent years has moved onto the privatisation of both children's services and social work education. Furthermore, the integration of health and social care services, which is a policy priority in all parts of the UK, is likely to speed up the process, especially as the Health and Social Care Act 2012 in England removes all barriers to the privatisation of the NHS.

Sweden

There is, apparently, a joke on the Swedish Left that everybody would like the Swedish model of welfare – and the Swedes would like it more than anyone else! The joke highlights the extent to which the post-war welfare state in Sweden, traditionally viewed as the epitome of genuinely universal welfare, has been eroded and transformed in recent years in ways that would be very recognisable to social workers in the UK and elsewhere. Jessica Jonsson (2015: 358) has summarised these broader changes in the following way:

> The success of neoliberal ideology in Sweden has succeeded in gradually forcing the welfare state to retreat from its traditional and legitimate responsibilities for providing welfare and improving the living conditions of less privileged groups based on the traditional principles of the welfare state – that is, equal opportunities, social solidarity and social security for everybody. Following the neoliberal changes in the 1980s and the financial crises of the early 1990s, comprehensive neoliberal reforms have been continued both by Social Democratic (1998–2006) and right-wing governments (1990–1998, 2006–2014). Deregulations and re-regulations of the welfare state have led to new forms of 'governance' ... by introducing managerialism, privatisation and cuts in welfare provisions. Such changes have resulted in increasing socioeconomic inequalities, discrimination and social problems in Sweden.

The results are depressingly familiar. Thus, according to figures from the Organisation for Economic Co-operation and Development (OECD, 2015): relative poverty and income inequality have increased more in Sweden than in any other country studied by the OECD; the poverty rate in 2010 was more than twice as high as a decade previously; and children and young people, especially those from immigrant backgrounds, are increasingly marginalised (one factor contributing to the riots that erupted in Husby, a suburb of Stockholm, in 2013).

As in the UK, the state's retreat from welfare has meant a growing role for both the private sector and non-governmental organisations (NGOs). According to Shanks et al (2015):

> The Swedish personal social services have ... revealed evident signs of marketisation; the private sector has become an important provider of social care. For example, a majority of the residential care units for children and youth are today run by private companies in a care market.

Jonsson similarly identifies the transformation of care for older people, with a greatly increased role for the private sector, contributing, she argues, to a series of care scandals not dissimilar to those that have occurred in the UK. In an example of the 'hybridisation' identified by Moriarty and her colleagues, Swedish NGOs, she argues, are both acting as a bridge towards full-scale privatisation and also legitimising the idea of a market in social care, based not on universal rights, but on charity or on what you can afford to pay (Jonsson, 2015: 364–5).

As elsewhere, however, neoliberalism in Sweden is breeding resistance. Jonsson points to the emergence of new organisations of Swedish social workers like *Nu bryter vi tysnaden* ('Now We Break the Silence'). In language reminiscent of the UK-based Social Work Action Network manifesto, such initiatives, she notes:

> Criticise the development of an increasing burden on social services and the reduction of social work to administrative actions, where social workers spend too much time on documentation and evaluation and which have destructive consequences both for the working conditions of social workers and for those people in need of social services. (Jonsson, 2015: 370–1)

Against this, she argues:

> Social work as 'a profession for social change' and the improvement of the living conditions of less privileged groups has an important role to play in an alliance for change in resisting the neoliberal reorganisation and retreat of the welfare state in order to fight against inequalities and injustices. Social workers should actively participate in public debates about, and actions against, the retreat of the welfare state from its responsibilities for people. (Jonsson, 2015: 370–1)

South Africa

As noted earlier, the countries of the Global South were the test beds for many of the SAPs imposed by the IMF and World Bank during the 1980s and 1990s. Against a background of wholesale privatisation of these countries' public utilities, many hoped and expected that the road taken by post-apartheid South Africa would be a different one. After all, the magnificent victory in 1994 of the people of South Africa over the barbaric apartheid regime had been inspired by a Freedom Charter that, among other things, promised free education, free universal health care and an end to hunger. It is undoubtedly the case that major changes have taken place since then, both in terms of the extension of basic rights, such as the right to strike and to form political parties, and also economically, with millions more now benefitting from access to electricity, improved housing and social grants. Yet, with the abandonment by the African National Congress (ANC) government in 1996 of the redistributive Reconstruction and Development Programme put by COSATU, the main trade union federation, and its replacement by the Growth, Employment and Redistribution (GEAR) strategy, the country was firmly set on a neoliberal path (Ministry of Finance, 2006). Sewpaul (2013) has identified the main elements of GEAR as being:

- trade liberalisation;
- cutbacks in state expenditure on social spending;
- the privatisation of state assets;
- increased consumerism and the commodification of every facet of human life;
- the profit motive above human well-being and dignity; and
- efficiency, with the aim to do more for less.

One consequence of this policy was that by 2009, South Africa had overtaken Brazil as the most unequal country in the world. In relation to welfare, the dominant discourse in South Africa is the familiar one of the promotion of self-reliance, the importance of individuals, families and communities looking after themselves, and responsibility shifting from the state to the community, albeit wrapped up in the African concept of *Ubuntu* and a theoretical framework of social development. What is again striking, however, is the extent to which the core elements of neoliberal social work – marketisation, managerialism and consumerism – appear once more in a discourse that would be immediately familiar to social workers from Britain to Japan. Discussing the key policy document for financing welfare published in 2009, for example, Sewpaul (2013: 21) notes that it is 'Replete with managerial and market discourses. It speaks of business plans, contracts, affordability, efficiency, outputs, performance audits, outsourcing, venture financing, and service purchasing, thus effectively reconstructing the people we work with as *customers*'.

The complaint of one South African social worker cited by Sewpaul is strongly reminiscent of the voices of the experienced British social workers interviewed by Chris Jones (2001) in his influential paper 'Voices from the front line: state social workers and New Labour':

> Government is looking at social work in a very commercialised way. And if you look at the theory and principles of social work – warmth, empathy, genuineness and the people-centred approach – I think we are becoming now forced to move away from this, we are actually forced to rationalise. We tend to focus now more on survival than actually servicing our clients.... Eventually your role will have to

change completely ... you might as well have become an accountant. (Cited in Sewpaul, 2013: 22)

Privatisation, social work and social care: the balance sheet

The outsourcing of public utilities was justified by the free marketeers on the grounds of both efficiency and ethical superiority. Not only could the market deliver services more efficiently than the state, it was claimed, but in offering citizens (or customers, as they were now known) greater choice and control, it increased their freedom and 'empowered' them. Thirty years into the neoliberal era, such claims ring very hollow indeed.

In respect of efficiency, as Alan White (2016: 13) observes in his study of the 'shadow state' – the companies that now run much of Britain, such as Serco and G4S – the question has never really been answered: 'New Labour rarely if ever carried out detailed comparisons of outsourced provision with that performed in-house, nor were assessments of savings made: that lack of assessment has carried on to this day'. In fact, as White's study shows, these big companies were often far more effective at winning contracts than delivering them. Like George Monbiot's earlier (2000) study *Captive state: The corporate takeover of Britain*, White provides clear evidence that the record of these large companies in running public services, including social work and social care services, has been appalling. Two examples will illustrate the point.

In 2008, the Labour government in the UK asked ATOS, a French multinational company that specialises in information technology (IT) services, to reassess some 2.5 million disabled people on benefits for eligibility for benefits using a newly developed Work Capability Assessment (WCA). The strongest indication of how poorly ATOS carried out this test is shown by the fact that in 2014, when claimants were being assessed at the rate of 11,000 per week, some 35% of challenged decisions were being overturned on appeal at a cost of £70 million in 2013/14 to conduct the appeals. More important, however, has been the human cost. A study carried out by University of Liverpool academics in 2015 found that after taking into account the socio-economic background of different parts of the country, as well as long-term trends in mental health, a total of 590 additional suicides could be related to these assessments between 2010 and 2013. There were also an additional 279,000 extra cases of mental ill health and 725,000 more prescriptions for antidepressants (Barr, 2015).

Nor have other attempts by government to force people back into employment via outsourcing been any more successful. Action for Employment (A4E), founded in 1991 and with an annual turnover of more than £200 million, has been the largest provider of the government's welfare-to-work programme. The company was awarded a contract for the Pathways to Work scheme in 2008, with a target to get 30% of participants into employment. In February 2012, the Public Accounts Committee heard that the success rate was 9%, which, as a number of commentators pointed out, was actually worse than doing nothing (White,

2016: 60). Committee Chair Margaret Hodge questioned why A4E had been awarded new contracts to deliver the Work Programme despite this 'abysmal' performance. The decision to award the company new contracts is even more astonishing given that the company was also being investigated for fraud at this time, leading to the company's founder Emma Harrison (also Prime Minister David Cameron's 'families tsar') being forced to step down in 2012.

Even more concerning than poor performance, however, particularly in the field of elderly care, where the continuity of care is crucial to well-being, is market failure. Reference was earlier made to the catastrophic collapse in 2011 of Southern Cross, the biggest provider of residential care for older people in the UK. However, while much of the attention has focused on the viability of the big providers, many small care homes have been going under. Thus, between 2003 and 2010, almost 1,400 private care homes closed, often with less than four weeks' notice. According to a study by sector analysts LaingBuisson, the care home sector in the UK is closing more beds than it is opening for the first time since 2005, with a net loss of 3,000 across the UK last year. Homes most at risk are those dependent on residents paid for by local councils at rates far below those paid by self-funding residents: proprietors say that rates are actually below break-even point (LaingBuisson, 2015).

Outsourced services can also be criticised on the grounds of their lack of accountability and transparency. The two issues are closely linked. White discusses the experience of Tory-run Barnet Council in North London, which, in 2011, put around £600 million of services out to tender. A *Guardian* report gave a glimpse of what this 'radical experiment in privatisation' meant for local residents:

> For those who live and work in Barnet, their local affairs are now handled remotely by people hundreds of miles away, who know nothing about them or the area. Payroll for what remains of council staff is done in Belfast, while for schools it's Carlisle. Pension queries go to Darlington. Benefits end up in Blackburn.... Got a complaint? Then you have to speak to someone you'll never see – that is, if you can speak to them at all. (Chakraborrty, 2014)

The privatisation was challenged by a vigorous campaign involving the local authority, trade unions and residents' groups. The full implications for accountability of transferring services from elected councils to private companies is evident in the following account of where supporters of the campaign challenged the council at a meeting of the new Board set up to implement the plan. The campaigners were asked to leave the meeting because 'confidential' issues were about to be discussed. When they asked what these issues were, they were told that they were 'too confidential' to be disclosed:

> A row kicked off and the chair of the board walked out of the meeting.... [He was] caught on camera saying, when asked why he

wasn't listening to the families that were present, 'This is a board meeting of a company. It is not a local authority meeting and therefore that right does not extend'. At which point one audience member said: 'That is exactly our problem with our services being outsourced'. (White, 2016: 145)

The story illustrates that for all their limitations, with state-controlled services, there is a degree of accountability and transparency. There are forums where elected representatives can be challenged, it is more difficult for them to hide behind 'commercial confidentiality' and, at the end of the day, elected representatives can be removed if they have failed to deliver on their manifestos. No such right of recall exists in relation to private companies, whether based locally or, as is increasingly the case with large providers of health and social care, in overseas tax havens.

Conclusion

A common thread connects the different elements of the critique of privatisation offered in this chapter: the poorer quality of services; the competition that results in a 'race to the bottom' in health and social care services; the market failures; and the lack of accountability and transparency. It is so obvious that it should hardly require saying but here it is anyway: the primary, overriding purpose of private companies, whether it is in the manufacture of military equipment, pizzas or toilet rolls, is to make a profit, with all other considerations secondary. It is scarcely surprising, then, that when private companies move into the field of social care, their first concern is not with meeting people's needs. The point was made forcefully more than half a century ago by the architect of the NHS in Britain:

> The danger of abuse in the health service is not in the way that ordinary people use the service. Abuse is always at the point where private commercialism impinges on the service – where an attempt is made to marry the incompatible principles of private profit with public service.
>
> The solution is to decrease the dependence on private enterprise.
>
> A free health service is a triumphant example of the superiority of the principles of collective action and public initiative against the commercial principle of profit and greed. (Bevan, 1952)

That is why, for all the deficiencies of state-provided welfare services, the struggle to keep such services public, while simultaneously pushing for greater democratisation, a stronger user voice and less reliance on biomedical models of health in areas such as mental health and learning disability, continues to be a priority whenever and wherever such services are threatened with privatisation.

Part Two
Social work politics: past and present

FOUR

Social work's horrible histories: collusion and resistance

Introduction

Reisch and Andrews (2002: 3) describe social work as a profession suffering from historical amnesia and assert that 'in an increasingly ahistorical culture, we are ignorant of those elements of our past that challenged the status quo'. Reisch and Andrews's concern is to recover examples of the profession's radical histories in the US. This is necessary work, and in Chapter Five, we explore the 'reconceptualisation movement' that was active in Latin America in the 1960s as an episode of radical social work that has been 'hidden' from our history.

In this chapter, however, we want to look at a different aspect of social work history. Our view is that the ahistorical culture in social work that Reisch and Andrews describe has also had the effect of suppressing discussion of what we term social work's 'horrible histories'. Mainstream social work histories often portray a benign profession that has gradually evolved and developed to support people in times of need, an inherently benevolent profession that constantly struggles for recognition (for a critique of this view, see Harris, 2008). At the heart of such approaches lies the belief that social problems have little to do with the way our societies are organised. Therefore, exploring social or political histories of social work does not give us enough information about the 'here and now' of the profession's mechanics. In fact, such curiosity may even harm the profession through unearthing awkward and unpopular aspects of the profession's past activities.

In contrast, in this chapter and Chapter Five, we argue that social work, as a contested profession, has a history that is complex and divided: within the profession, there are examples of social work that are inspiring as well as those that are, frankly, shameful. It is our contention that we need to learn from, and celebrate, those periods when social work rose to great heights and embraced the struggle for a more equal and just world, when social work was prepared to 'speak truth to power', and when the profession clearly aligned itself with the interests of the marginalised and excluded. Equally, we suggest that we must also be aware of and reflect upon those periods when social workers were involved in practices that reinforced oppression and exploitation in the interests of the powerful. These dark episodes emphasise what a social work in the interests of the powerful can mean for both social workers and those who use our services. They also show that social work's unwillingness to deal with the historical injustices affecting both the profession and the people we work with potentially damages the profession.

We start by outlining an example from Greece, where decades of political tension and the suppression of civil rights culminated in a seven-year military Junta (1967–74). Much of the resistance against the dictatorship came from young people, mostly school pupils and university students. When the military found it difficult to control 'unruly young people' and many teachers seemed to be too politicised to deal with the issue, the Greek Association of Social Workers (GASW) seemed willing to run to the state's assistance. The GASW initiated a public relations campaign and communicated to the dictator:

> Social workers have not been utilised in schools yet. They can play a great role in this context. Not only providing early diagnosis of possible difficulties – something that even teachers can do – but identifying the family, social and physiological and biological reasons of such slowness. (GASW, 1968: 2)

The dictatorship's minister of welfare, in response, circulated a memo titled 'Arrangements for social workers and their professional utilization', suggesting that:

> The Greek government during the general ongoing labour reform will look after all the remaining social work demands.... On the other hand, we really appreciate social workers' contribution in the constructive implementation of our social programs.... The ministry of social services will take all the appropriate measures for the advantageous and coherent organization of social workers in commission. (Ioakimidis, 2011: 515)

The GASW celebrated such collaboration, reassuring Colonel Papadopoulos, head of the military junta, that: 'The whole 660 currently qualified social workers are able to face and resolve issues of social adjustment' (GASW, 1968). In the same year (1970), the GASW stressed to the government that social workers: 'are better scientifically equipped than teachers in preventing the social tribulations [in schools]' (Ioakimidis, 2011: 515).

Many contemporary social workers would find such cordial communication between a vicious dictatorship and social workers' official representative body difficult to comprehend. The idea that social workers could collaborate with the military in order to suppress pro-democracy activism would sound mystifying and definitely would not fit with the presumed 'benign role' and the Kantian ethics promoted by mainstream social work discourses.

Some may want to focus on the 'poor morality' of the social work practitioners involved in the events just described and dismiss them as isolated and rare events. However, the disturbing social work histories we discuss in this chapter cannot be dismissed as mere historical quirks and neither can we distance ourselves from them by blaming the individual social workers involved while absolving the profession of any responsibility. Instead, we suggest that in order to understand these events, we have to take into consideration all those broad – and often contradictory – parameters that shape society and influence the actions of people, institutions and organised groups. Such a process can be difficult and painful but it is also necessary to help us answer crucial questions about the contradictory nature of the profession itself.

It is necessary to explore some of the darkest chapters of social work history through the political prism of the particular historical periods within which they occurred. For analytical purposes, we have categorised these histories in two broad and interrelated sections. In the first section, we explore the role of social work in the process of the top-down construction of the ideal-type family as envisaged and constructed by the ruling elites. The second section moves beyond the confines of the family and explores the involvement of social work in broader 'experiments' of social engineering with catastrophic consequences for whole communities.

Children of nation, children of empire

Preoccupation with the nature, values and evolution of the institution of the family has been central to the history of social work. In capitalist societies, such a preoccupation has historically reflected the desire of the state to ensure the perpetuation of working-class families as a disciplined unit of production and consumption. Welfare services have been instrumental in this process.

The 'care and control' dichotomy of welfare states, discussed in previous chapters, finds no more complete and powerful expression than in the context of family services, for although in the most advanced capitalist states, the welfare system has been able to provide varying levels of care, the element of harsh social control of the poorest in society has always been present. In the West, these cases can be linked, most notably, with the rise of eugenic theories and their pseudo-scientific preoccupation with the creation of the 'superior race'. In the Global South, brutal and often genocidal 'family policies' were primarily linked to colonialism and the politics of assimilation.

Nazi Germany

The most notorious example of social work complicity is related to the practice of social, youth and community workers in Nazi Germany. Walter Lorenz (2004: 33) suggests that in the 1920s and 1930s, 'as social service staff came more directly under state control the position of value neutrality demonstrated its blindness to political misuse most catastrophically in Hitler's Germany'. Social policy in this context had a double purpose: on the one hand, it aimed at physically and socially segregating and exterminating those families and individuals 'unworthy' of being citizens of the Reich (see next section); on the other hand, it focused on educating the family and ensuring that all members had a clear understanding of the distinct role required by the state.

The expected roles for men in this context primarily included the functions of being a breadwinner, a good citizen and a good soldier. Women's role, on the other hand, was almost exclusively determined by their mission as mothers. The Nazi state expected women to give up on their careers, have several children, take care of the family and help create, physically and culturally, the perfect 'Aryan'. This was summarised by Goebbels' suggestion that 'The role of women is to be beautiful and to bring children into the world' (Haste, 2001: 74).

State policies ensuring the successful realisation of those aims were implemented through a system of rewards based on generous loans and moral commendations. Social workers and social pedagogues were directly involved in the process of monitoring the development of families and indoctrinating children. Young women were expected to stay healthy, exercise and devote their lives to the infamous concept of 'The 3 K's – Kinder, Küche, Kirche (Children, Cooking, Church)'.

The formal and informal education of children primarily focused on how to become good and obedient citizens. In its most sinister dimension, the education system indoctrinated children in the pseudo-science of eugenics, while encouraging them to join the Nazi Youth Organisations and prepare for the inevitability of war:

> There were to be two basic educational ideas in [Hitler's] ideal state. First, there must be burnt into the heart and brains of youth the sense of race. Second, German youth must be made ready for war, educated for victory or death. The ultimate purpose of education was to fashion citizens conscious of the glory of country and filled with fanatical devotion to the national cause. (Zentner and Friedemann, 1991: 79)

Part of the education of the German youth, often facilitated by social workers and social pedagogues, included field visits to centres for the detention of people with disabilities. These visits were used as 'freak shows', where German youth could witness the 'realities' of racial hierarchy first hand. While Nazi authorities focused on the 'reconstruction' of the Aryan family, social services also focused on the removal of 'defective' children from the community. Johnson and Moorhead (2011) explain that this policy was developed for two reasons: first, as a result of the social eugenic policy of the day; and, second, to send a message to the community that the Nazi government was in control of the public and private lives of German citizens. Social workers were actively involved in these programmes and worked closely with authorities in identifying 'unworthy' children and facilitating their extermination (Kunstreich, 2003). Johnson and Moorhead (2011) suggest that:

As early as 1934, genetic health courts were created for the sole purpose of enforcing Nazi health laws and decrees. Documents from this era reveal that public health officials, doctors, teachers, and social workers were also required to report children who were deemed to have a disability or emotional problem.

According to Giles (1992, cited in Johnson and Moorhead, 2011), social workers and nurses had the responsibility to submit official documentation with regards to individuals that they considered unfit.

Spain under Franco

Although the politics of creating the ideal family was central to the mission of social work in most European countries, it was in the countries that experienced military rule that such a mission took on the character of an ideological 'crusade'. In fact, in many European countries, the idea of developing the social work profession was itself conceived and nurtured by military regimes. In Spain, the brief progressive example during the civil war (1936–39) offered women and children a glimpse of an alternative society based on the principles of solidarity, social justice and gender equality. These were the very principles that Franco's military regime, which emerged victorious after the civil war, attempted to obliterate. As early as 1937, Franco's regime recognised the importance of social services on the terrain of ideas. In winning 'hearts and minds', family policies and child protection were essential.

Spanish social services under Franco were initially modelled on the services in Nazi Germany. They required the unpaid labour of women, curtailed women's political rights, were constructed on the basis of absolute discipline and obedience, and adopted grotesque notions of racial purity. Following the Nazi blueprint meant that women in Franco's Spain had lost control and ownership of their bodies. Women were seen exclusively as mothers, whose prime mission was to conceive, deliver and care for 'the children of the nation'. Maintaining the purity of the race was of the utmost importance.

In Spain, unlike in Nazi Germany, the concept and celebration of 'race' was not obsessed with physical appearance, but primarily focused on the construction of a well-defined cultural, social and political national entity. In this case, the enemy was not so much the Jew or the disabled, but communism and modernity. This was epitomised in Castro Villacanas' (1948) description of national purity:

> We want our friends, our servants and our fiancées to be Spanish. We want our children to be Spanish. In our holy Spain we want only our traditions. If you want to call this nationalism, this is fine with me. We do not want progress, the romantic, liberal, capitalist, bourgeois, Jewish, Protestant, atheistic and Masonic Yankee progress.

In fact, the Catholic Church played a key role in developing social services that would be fully compliant with these principles. The anti-clericalism of the Second Republic was replaced by anti-communism as the most important mission of the Spanish Catholic Church. This new crusade for Spanish Catholicism targeted the 'hydra of social and political revolution that had flourished with the Republic' (González Duro, 2008). Nearly all social work schools in Spain at the time were under the direct control of the Church. The curriculum and admissions process ensured that the chances of 'political contamination' among social work students and practitioners were minimal. National Catholicism, unconditionally subordinated to the fascist regime, was directly in charge of social services and social work education.

For the first decades of the dictatorship, social workers – whose desired profile was that of 'exemplary Catholic ladies' – were assigned paternalistic and assistance-oriented roles in relation to the relief and moral control of the poor (Sanz Cintora, 2001, cited in Martinez, 2017).

Martinez (2017: 74) suggests that:

> The mission statement of the second school of social work in Spain, founded in Madrid at the beginning of the dictatorship, can serve to illustrate the ideological backlash in the field of social work brought about by the newly established political regime. According to this school's mission statement, social work [*asistencia social*] was 'a feminine area of study which aims [were] either a preparation of women for a service to society or an improvement of their education in order to become good and Christian mothers.

Apart from focusing on 'winning hearts and minds' and shaping the nationally pure 'New Spaniard', welfare services under Franco were actively involved in one of the darkest chapters in the modern history of Spain. Although the suppression that faced left-wing and republican families after the end of the civil war has been well documented, only recently have stories about the abduction and trafficking of babies begun to be openly discussed and investigated. The Spanish 'Pact of Forgetting' ('*el pacto del olvido*'), introduced in 1975 after the death of Franco, which banned research and investigations into the regime's atrocities, was not enough to prevent the hundreds of families whose children had mysteriously disappeared from hospitals and welfare institutions from demanding justice. Over a period of more than 30 years after the civil war, social services were implicated in an illegal mechanism set up by state and Church officials aimed at kidnapping children – mostly from left-wing and poor families – and offering them for illegal adoption to 'nationally minded' families (BBC, 2011b). At the epicentre of these revelations was the Catholic Church, which, over a period of half a century, had served as the closest ally of Francoism. The Catholic Church had constructed and controlled a nexus of welfare institutions ideologically obedient to Francoism, and social work education and practice itself emerged as a historical product of this period. Gómez and Buendia (2009: 2) suggest that such was the control of the Catholic Church over social work education that in the immediate post-civil war period, the main curriculum was divided into three main sections, all directly promoting religious moralism aligned with Franco's political agenda:

> The curriculum consisted of three courses and each of these was structured on religious training. The first course, generically called 'Religious Education', revolved around the four disciplines: General Psychology, General Sociology, Social Service Methodologies, and the Practices of Social Services. The second course, also called Religious Education, was less generic and concerned with the Social Doctrine of the Church. It emphasised the subjects: Differential and Genetic Psychology, Social Structure, Individualized and Group Social Services, and the Practices of Social Services. The third and final course, again called Religious Education, established a moral code which was way beyond the professional code of ethics of today.

The ideological legacy of this period is recognised by Vázquez (1970: 40), who suggests that:

> The initiative to professionalize social work began in the Catholic sector. Consequently, during many years, the content of the programs of study, the development of the schools of social service, and above all, the orientation given to professional activities have a marked confessional quality. To do justice to its origins, those who study Spanish social services cannot ignore the confessional quality of its genesis.

The notion of social work as a political reaction to social movements was not always directed towards families and children. In Spain during the Franco period, activists were routinely described as mentally ill and incarcerated in mental institutions. A recent comprehensive study into the pathologisation of political activism reveals how the whole concept of Francoist psychiatry was constructed on the notion of intellectual degeneration caused by communist ideas (González Duro, 2008); tellingly, the study was entitled 'The reds were not crazy'.

Greece

Similar questions have also been raised in Greece. Nearly 60 years after the end of the civil war, and although the sinister practice of 'child-gathering' (ie the removal of children from left-wing families) is acknowledged and documented, its extent and impact on thousands of children and families is still considered a taboo question. Research in Greek social work suggests that the profession was so immersed in the politics of 'child-gathering' that nearly *all* social work practitioners in the 1950s had, in one way or another, been involved in the notorious 'child colonies' (Ioakimidis, 2011).

Children from regions controlled by the Greek Left were moved to these institutions, which resembled 19th-century workhouses. They were separated from their families and were subjected to systematic brainwashing and torture. Mando Dalianis, in her unique longitudinal study that includes interviews with affected children over a period of 30 years, provided evidence of the horrific nature of those institutions (Mazower and Dalianis, 2000). As she explains, in the colonies, the children's experience was of a harsh set of activities aimed primarily at tackling communism, both on the battlefield and in the local communities, and only secondarily to respond to some immediate humanitarian needs:

> Conditions in these villages in many ways resembled prison life and there was the same rigid sense of a division between 'inside' and 'outside' worlds separated usually by walls or guarded barbed-wire fences. They were run on quasi-military lines, often by former officers, who employed corporal punishment and made the children wear uniforms. Letters were censored, just like in prison, and the atmosphere was generally unfriendly. As in prison, there were no clocks or calendars, and the day was regulated by the ringing of a bell. The children were marched everywhere, even on occasional visits to the world outside, to the cinema or local park. Most teachers were indifferent or cruel to their charges, though there were some exceptions. (Mazower and Dalianis, 2000: 99)

It is important to highlight that, in these contexts, social work was conceived, developed and presented as a respected 'science of charity' in opposition to the principles of solidarity inspired by socialist movements. In fact, both in Spain (behind Republican lines during the civil war) and in Greece (during the years of National Resistance), societies had already experienced short but thriving periods of developing alternative social structures and institutions. These social alternatives were based on gender equality, collectivism, direct democracy and solidarity. In both cases, women had experienced a brief period of relative emancipation and active political involvement before being forced to return to the home and family, what was often portrayed as their 'natural kingdom'. In this sense, social work provided an ideological response to the grass-roots politics of social solidarity, one steeped in ideas of nationalism and women's oppression. These ideas were often pioneered by women of the local aristocracy. As Vervenioti (2002: 115) argues:

> 20 upper class women, the so-called commissioned Ladies of the Queen's Fund, pulled the strings of women. They, as biological and ideological reproducers, as 'cultural carriers' of the Greek nation, superseded the government in matters of internal and external affairs very effectively in the 'save the children' enterprise.... While Greek

women had the legal status of minor, the right-wing women were crucial in establishing the specific form and agenda of the official Greek government.

The detachment of social work education from the university sector until 1994 ensured that training was the sole responsibility of charities linked to the 'Ladies of the Queen' and Church institutions. Until the middle of the 1960s, the vast majority of social work trainees had to attend at least one placement linked to children who required 'protection from communism and nationalist education'. The GASW, desperate to obtain a degree of professional recognition on a par with senior civil servants, was complicit with these practices throughout this period. During the 1967–74 military dictatorship, the GASW attempted to promote itself as the junta's major ally that could effectively ensure social control in school settings with rebellious pupils.

Colonial social work and indigenous children: Canada, Australia and Denmark

Whereas the dark histories of European social work were primarily concerned with the construction of the nationally minded, obedient and racially superior family, in countries of the capitalist periphery, the profession was exported as a potent colonial tool. The First International Conference of Social Work took place in Paris in 1928. The fact that it was attended by 2,500 delegates from 42 countries suggests that by the third decade of the 20th century, there was more than sufficient interest among welfare workers to 'internationalise' the profession. In a period overwhelmingly defined by the internal and external contradictions of colonialism, social work was not only influenced by colonial politics, but seemed to be the direct product of an era when 'the number of rulers officially calling themselves, or regarded by western diplomats as deserving the title of, "emperors" was at its maximum' (Hobsbawm, 1987: 56). As the character of colonisation in the 19th century and beginning of the 20th century shifted from a primarily 'mercantile' form to a more complex system of production and the unification of markets, the prominence of capital expansion meant that the old methods of military colonisation could be successfully replaced by means of market unification and cultural assimilation.

In the context of the partition of the world's wealth and territory among a handful of states, these calculations had a twofold objective: on the one hand, colonial powers were 'united' in their concern to firmly secure their grip over native populations through the suppression of their self-determination; on the other hand, they were locked into a vicious antagonism for global domination against each other. The latter escalated into two world wars and numerous regional conflicts. The former required a variety of 'soft' methods (assimilation, the suppression of local cultures, the reconfiguration of social institutions, bureaucratisation and the modernisation of local economies) and 'hard' methods (violent subordination, segregation, disenfranchisement and the politics of fear). The development of social work was invariably seen as a 'soft' approach to perpetuating colonial rule through social control and the reconfiguration of sociocultural institutions.

Although the emergence of the 'indigenisation' debate in recent years has generated some interesting arguments challenging the colonial nature of social work, not much attention has been paid to the ways in which social work played a key role in the oppressive politics of assimilation. In these contexts, social services actively attempted to suppress indigenous cultures and to forcibly extend settler values to native communities. Once again, the institution of the nuclear family was deemed to be the 'gold standard'. Individualistic approaches to child protection were also used as a quantifiable measure of assimilation success. Inevitably, these approaches failed spectacularly and led thousands of aboriginal families into misery and suffering. It would not be an exaggeration to claim that these policies were never meant to succeed anyway. By definition, the process of assimilation pre-designed conditions that would lead to the alienation, marginalisation and stigmatisation of native populations in order to justify more draconian state interventions. The infamous Canada Scoops, for example, a methodical process of child removal from aboriginal families, offers a sobering example of drastic assimilation under the guise of social care. According to The Aboriginal Justice Implementation Commission, within a period of nearly 20 years (from the early 1960s until the late 1980s) the child welfare system:

> removed Aboriginal children from their families, communities and cultures, and placed them in mainstream society. Child welfare workers removed Aboriginal children from their families and communities because they felt the best homes for the children were not Aboriginal homes. The ideal home would instil the values and lifestyles with which the child welfare workers themselves were familiar: white, middle-class homes in white, middle-class neighbourhoods. Aboriginal communities and Aboriginal parents and families were deemed to be 'unfit.' As a result, between 1971 and 1981 alone, over 3,400 Aboriginal children were shipped away to adoptive parents in other societies, and sometimes in other countries. (The Aboriginal Justice Implementation Commission, 1999)

Likewise, in Australia, the Aboriginal Protection Act 1869 gave the colonial administration such extensive powers over the lives of indigenous children that communities experiencing assimilation through the child protection system have become known as 'stolen generations'. The oppressive role of Australian social workers has been evidenced in the recent *Report of the National Inquiry into the Separation of Aboriginal and Torres Strait Islander Children from Their Families* (NISATSIC, 1997), which acknowledges the fact that social workers routinely used unsubstantiated allegations of neglect in order to remove children from Aboriginal families. The report states that:

The children were still being removed in bulk, but it wasn't because they were part white. They had social workers that'd go around from house to house and look in the cupboards and things like that and they'd say the children were neglected (Molly Dyer evidence 219, speaking of the practice of the Victorian Aborigines Welfare Board in the 1950s). (NISATSIC, 1997: 28)

A lesser-known case of social work complicity with the brutality of colonial assimilation occurred in Greenland in the early 1950s. It involved welfare practitioners from Danish charity organisations who worked closely with the government of Denmark in attempting to 'modernise' Greenland through the creation of a new and re-educated generation exposed to the advancements of the Danish lifestyle. As part of this social engineering project, officially described as an 'experiment', several children were forcibly removed from their communities in Greenland and given to middle-class foster-families in Denmark. The Danish press were quick to celebrate the success of the 'experiment': 'The way of life here in Denmark is so different from what these children of nature are accustomed to but their ability to adapt is remarkable. Disagreements – caused by their reaction to civilisation – happen very rarely' (BBC, 2015b).

Scotland's lost children

In 2014, the Scottish newspaper the *Daily Record* reported on the horrific experience of the children of one family at the hands of the Scottish care system in the 1950s. George, Jimmy and Tommy Clark were taken from their family home in Greenock and put into local authority care after their parents were ruled incapable of looking after them. 'Boarded out' to a family in a remote part of Scotland, the brothers – then aged four, six and nine – say that for the next four years, they slept in a filthy chicken coop and were forced to steal dog food to survive.

According to the report, the brothers were now challenging the system to ensure that Scotland's so-called lost children were reunited with their siblings. For George Clark:

People were shocked by the film, 12 Years A Slave. But Scotland has its own shameful history of slavery too. Over 100,000 kids were shipped from children's homes to Australia, New Zealand and Canada until the late 1960s to work on farms and factories. There were also children like us, used as slaves and cheap labour, boarded out by local authorities across Scotland (www.dailyrecord.co.uk/news/scottish-news/secret-slaves-scotland-revealed-3300900).

The horrific experience of many of these children has been documented by the Golden Bridge Project (see: https://www.iriss.org.uk/resources/multimedia-learning-materials/golden-bridge) and also in the movie *Oranges and Sunshine*.

Britain's 'children of empire'

From the middle of the 19th century, British authorities and a number of well-known charities involved in broad social work activity were involved in the forced migration of children from Britain to various countries then part of the British Empire – especially Canada, Australia, New Zealand, South Africa and Zimbabwe (then Rhodesia). Initially, the motivation was a combination of 'child-saving' philosophies where, especially for a number of leading Christian charities (such as Barnardo's, Quarriers and the Catholic Emigration Association), the migration was portrayed as an 'opportunity' for pauper children to avoid the physical and moral hazards of the newly sprawling towns and cities of industrial Britain. For local government bodies (such as the Poor Law Unions), migration was favoured because the cost of transporting dependent children was far less than the potential cost of looking after them in workhouse institutions.

In the second half of the 19th century, large numbers of children were shipped to Canada in a process often dubbed 'philanthropic abduction'. The children were almost always under the age of 11, though some were much younger:

> The child migrants were mostly aged between four and fourteen and were usually rounded up and accompanied by a Poor Law guardian or a representative of the organisation sending them. Sometimes there was no representative and the word 'care' didn't come in to it. (Bean and Melville, 1989: 2)

In 1880, 540 children were forced to migrate to Canada; by 1880, the number had risen to 2,104 per year (Kershaw and Sacks, 2008). 'At the peak of [this] … phase of child migration – 1870 to 1925 – at least 25 large philanthropic organisations were sending children to Canada' (Bean and Melville, 1989: 38). Canada remained an important destination until the practice ended in the late 1930s. An estimated 100,000 children had been shipped to Canada from Britain between 1869 and the late 1930s (Government of Canada, 2016).

The conditions that the children endured were often harrowing. The children were moved from the bustling streets of towns and cities in Britain and placed in isolated, rural farms in Canada, where they had to adapt to a vastly different climate and way of life. Most had families but migration brought separation from their family and support networks. They were forced to work long hours in gruelling labour, often in cruel and abusive conditions. This was state-sanctioned child abuse on a grand scale.

By the beginning of the 20th century (in the aftermath of the Boer War), the argument in favour of child migration had changed. Now Barnardo's described their child migrants as 'Bricks for Empire-Building' (Kershaw and Sacks, 2008: 9). By populating the Empire with 'good British stock', the Empire could ward off future rebellions and insurgencies (like those then recently witnessed in South Africa in the war against the Boer farmers). One of the first to adopt this new philosophy of migration was Thomas Sedwick, 'a social worker', who took 50 young boys to New Zealand in 1910. As they left Britain, he wrote to the King: 'The first party of town lads for colonial farms beg to convey to Your majesty the expression of our most dutiful and humble devotion to your Throne and person on our departure for the Dominion of New Zealand' (cited in Bean and Melville, 1989: 79).

In the 20th century, the process of child migration was linked to eugenic philosophies. As the Archbishop of Perth (cited in Humphries, 2011:12):

> At a time when empty cradles are contributing woefully to empty spaces, it is necessary to look for external sources of supply. And if we do not supply from our own stock we are leaving ourselves all the more exposed to the menace of the teeming millions of our neighbouring Asiatic races.

The children shipped to Australia were checked to ensure that they had good eyesight, no flat feet and were of general 'healthy disposition':

> Child migration to Australia ... especially of those of solid Anglo-Saxon stock – was encouraged. Physical stamina was important, and children were prepared for living in the outback by sleeping outside in tents and learning to swim. They also underwent a series of medical tests.... They didn't take anyone wearing glasses or who was colour blind. (Kershaw and Sacks, 2008: 10)

In the late 1930s, the Fairbridge Society set up training schools and colleges in Southern Rhodesia – though their first migrants did not arrive until after the Second World War. Their stated aim was to 'Fill the empty spaces of Empire with selected children of sound stock from the over-crowded towns and cities of the United Kingdom' (cited in Bean and Melville, 1989: 98). In Southern Rhodesia, the intention was to select children who could eventually join the local white elite. To fill their allocated role in the social structure, the children went through significant selection. They undertook IQ tests, health checks and a background assessment of their social standing. The background checks were undertaken by trained social workers – members of the British Federation of Social Workers (Bean and Melville, 1989: 99).

After the Second World War, Australia became the most important destination for the migrant 'children of empire'. An estimated 10,000 children were shipped from Britain to Australia between 1945 and 1970 (BBC, 2006). As Chenery (2011) notes:

> When bleak postwar Britain answered Australia's call for 'good white British stock' to build its population, it saw an opportunity to empty overflowing institutions of the innocent victims of poverty, illegitimacy

and broken homes. In the child trafficking that became known as the child migration schemes it cost £5 a week to keep a child in care in Britain but just 10 shillings in Australia. Institutions that took children would be paid a subsidy for each one of them. All the reputable agencies – Barnardo's, the Salvation Army, the Fairbridge Society, National Children's Home, the Catholic and Anglican churches – colluded in sending children to the other side of the world for 'a better life'. They were thought a particularly attractive category of migrant, according to a 1945 prime ministerial brief to state premiers, 'on account of their easier assimilation, adaptability, long working life ahead and easier housing'.

The children were told that their parents were dead – or their mothers unfit – but that they were destined for better lives, with warm beds, full stomachs and a proper education. The reality was very different. As Bean and Melville (1989: 111) note 'The history of child migration to Australia is in many ways a history of cruelty, lies and deceit'. For many, it was also a gateway to hell as they ended up in institutions where physical and sexual abuse was standard. Those unlucky enough to be dispatched to institutions run by the Christian Brothers in Bindoon, Tardun and Clontarf, for example, were subjected to regular, routine abuse (Bean and Melville, 1989; Humphries, 2011). The story of the migrant children, sent across, first, the Empire and then the Commonwealth, by leading children's charities, with the knowledge and collusion of local authority children's departments, stands as one of the most shameful episodes in social work's history in Britain.

Margaret Humphreys and the Child Migrants Trust

In 1986, a woman from Adelaide, Australia, wrote to Margaret Humphreys (at the time, a social worker in Nottingham, England) claiming that, at the age of four, she had been sent to Australia, unaccompanied, on a boat from England. She claimed that this voyage was undertaken with the full knowledge of the UK authorities.

Humphreys was at first incredulous. However, after undertaking some research, she found the story to be true. In fact, Margaret Humphreys soon discovered that as many as 150,000 children had been deported from children's homes in Britain and shipped off to a 'new life' in distant parts of the Empire. The practice continued up until the late 1960s.

Many of the children were told that their parents had died, even though, for most, this was not true. Many of the parents were told that their children had been adopted in Britain – again, an outrageous lie. Siblings were separated and for numerous children, it led to a life of horrendous physical and sexual abuse in institutions in Western Australia and elsewhere.

Margaret Humphreys campaigned relentlessly for the rights of the forced migrant children and their families. In 1987, she set up the Child Migrants Trust – which continues to have a base in Australia and Britain.

Despite her 'discovery' of the children of empire in 1986, the children and families did not receive an official apology until 2010. It was only in 2017, over 30 years after the initial 'discovery', that the British government set an official inquiry into the child migrant trade.

Social work and social Darwinism

As we discussed in the previous section, the political and professional position of social work as an agent of the state has implicated the profession in the development and implementation of oppressive family policies underpinned by theories of 'the nation', moralism and cultural assimilation. However, it is the profession's involvement in the politics of racial segregation and exclusion that has generated the most appalling and shocking social work histories. An inconvenient reality is the profession's love affair with eugenics and social Darwinism. Jones (1983: 46) has persuasively demonstrated that ideological proximity when saying that:

> Drawing on social Darwinism, the COS [Charity Organisations Society] insisted that one's location in the social and economic world was in large measure a reflection of character, those at the bottom of the pile being the most deficient and disorganised.

Eugenics was so influential in social work at the beginning of the 20th century that a passing review of archived casework notes in the UK would almost certainly indicate several references to this pseudoscience. Ideological dependence on the state aside, these deterministic theories offered social work the illusion of scientific status and posture that was lacking in comparison to other professions.

Despite British social work's flirtation with Sir Francis Galton's grotesque ideas, it was in Nazi Germany where eugenics theories were put into practice in a systematic way and on an industrial scale. In Germany, the adoption of social Darwinism was neither merely symbolic nor peripheral to state policies. In fact, these ideas shaped the core of the Hitler's vision. The creation and reproduction of the Aryan race could not be achieved without the parallel segregation and eventual extermination of the inferior races. Annihilation of those 'unworthy' of life was seen as the absolute and final solution. Within a period of 10 years (1934–44), millions of people with physical or intellectual disabilities, Slavic minorities and Roma communities, and gay men and women were subjected to mass detention, hard labour, sterilisation and extermination. The catastrophic culmination of these policies was the Holocaust, which resulted in the killing of over 6 million Jews.

Social workers were heavily involved not only in advancing the ideas of social Darwinism, but also in actively utilising them. They were involved in the process of diagnosing racial inferiority and facilitating the detention of those deemed 'unworthy'. Lorenz (2006: 35) explains that:

> The system relied on all welfare personnel filing case reports in which they listed the family histories of epilepsy or alcoholism [and] assessed the chances of rehabilitation of offenders or of children with learning difficulties. Sticking to their professional task with the air of value neutrality and scientific detachment they did not feel responsible for the consequences of their assessments.

Hope in the face of horror

Irena Sendlerowa was a social worker in Poland during the Second World War. She organised a small group of colleagues to smuggle Jewish babies and children out of the Warsaw ghetto between 1942 and 1943 and place them with Polish families. Irena's team smuggled the children out by hiding them in ambulances, taking them through the sewers or wheeling them out hidden in suitcases or boxes. The workers noted the names of the children on cigarette papers and sealed them in glass bottles, which were then buried. After the war, the bottles were dug up and attempts were made to reunite the children with their families – though most of them had perished in concentration camps (Connolly, 2007).

A similarly notorious example of social work's active and systematic collaboration with a regime promoting policies of racial segregation and social engineering is that of South Africa. Racist policies defining colonial rule in South Africa were typified and fully operationalised in the period of apartheid (1948–91). This was a complex, brutal and multilayered system of segregation designed to physically, politically, socially and culturally exclude non-white populations. Racial segregation also aimed at maximising labour exploitation through the consolidation of colonial rule. Non-white populations, deemed as inferior, were classified in different administrative categories according to the colour of their skin, were deprived of civic and political rights, and were allowed access only to substandard and segregated education, health and social services.

Mainstream white South African social work, which had largely accepted segregationist ideologies well before 1948, readily adopted and functioned within the context of racial separation culminating with the creation of apartheid. Legislation demanded that social workers, particularly in the public sector, provide services only to those designated as the same race as themselves while social work education was also defined by a differential university education based on race (Sewpaul, 2013). Smith's (2014: 313) analysis encapsulates the evolution of such historical and indefensible complicity in South African social work when suggesting that:

> The origins of social work in South Africa are found within the forces of racist capitalism, social conflict and unequal power relations – shaped by the hegemonic ideologies of the various eras during the 20th century and even earlier colonial and imperialist origins. Through hegemonic discourses, social work generally supported the maintenance of the racist status quo and the capitalist mode of production, with individualist and liberal ideologies of freedom of choice and personal responsibility.

Oppressive social work practices influenced by the principles of social engineering have not, however, been restricted to countries with undemocratic or military regimes. The disturbing case of social workers' involvement in US sterilisation projects is another example. The eugenics movement in the US officially began in the late 19th century, reached its zenith in the 1920s and 1930s, fell out of favour during the Second World War, and then made a comeback in the 1950s (Anastas, 2011). As in the cases we reviewed earlier, the principles of US eugenics projects were inextricably linked to the effort to devise mechanisms of social control through the promotion of an *ideal-type* representing their own values and characteristics. Social problems such as poverty, crime and unemployment were seen as largely 'hereditary' within the inferior classes and therefore treated through practices aimed at preventing these classes from 'reproducing'. Despite the impression that the forced sterilisation of the poor in the US was a thing of the distant past, recent research suggests that in some states (most notably, in North Carolina), this practice lasted until well into the 1970s. In North Carolina, where sterilisation projects were widespread and, unlike other states, not confined to institutional settings only, more than 7,600 poor, vulnerable and minority citizens were permanently affected by this practice (Boggs, 2014). Evidence suggests that many sterilisations were recommended by social workers, who would base their 'diagnosis' solely on observations of home environments or poor school performance (Boggs, 2014):

> The US National Association of Social Workers recently conceded that 'As early social workers researched and developed programs to provide solutions to alleviate American social ills, and encouraged greater investment in the social safety net, long held beliefs about the capacity of poor, mentally ill and other social "outsiders" colored a variety of government policies and the medical establishment'. (Anastas, 2011)

Conclusion

In this chapter, we have attempted to present some of the most disturbing historical cases of social work complicity. What we suggest is that at key political junctures, many professional social work organisations (eg the GASW in Greece during the military junta or the National Association of Social Workers in the US during the McCarthy period) were more concerned to protect the interests and survival of the profession at the expense of any overarching commitment to social justice. Often masked under a narrative of eclectic positivism, the ideology of professionalism meant that there was a systematic depoliticisation of social work, which turned it into a work task for processing the poor, the disadvantaged, the political and the oppositional in the interests of the powerful.

In most of the cases we reviewed, social work as a profession was tightly controlled by the state. In the cases where social work associations sided with the oppressor and social work education was regulated by the state (or Church), there was very little room for individual social workers to create a viable movement for resistance. However, some did resist. Reducing horrible social work histories to textbook footnotes or justifying them as mere episodes of compromised judgement and poor morality blurs the crucial contribution of numerous, known or unsung, social workers who bravely fought for social justice. The contributions of African-American social worker Thyra Edwards, who travelled to Barcelona and joined the anti-fascist international brigades during the Spanish Civil War, or the story of Polish-Jewish practitioner Irena Sendlerowa, who saved nearly 2,500 children from the Warsaw ghetto between 1940 and 1943, would be incomplete if we did not consider the fact that many – if not most – of their contemporary colleagues sided with the fascist and Nazi forces at the time.

FIVE

Social work as a praxis for liberation: the case of Latin American reconceptualisation

Introduction

In contrast to the horrible histories discussed in Chapter Four, in this chapter, we explore the Latin American *reconceptualisation movement*, a radical social work movement that was extraordinary in terms of both its intellectual contribution and its generation of transformative praxis. It is our contention that the reconceptualisation movement has been one of the most comprehensive, influential and far-reaching examples of emancipatory social work globally, yet it remains little known in social work circles across much of the world. The movement was an integral part of the 'radical triangle' (along with 'Liberation Theology' and 'Popular Education') that emerged in Latin America in the 1960s and 1970s and redefined the role and scope of the applied social and pedagogical professions. Although it is not easy to discuss in isolation any one component of the 'radical triangle', in this chapter, we will try to focus on the powerful influence of the reconceptualisation movement on the social work profession in Latin America and internationally.

Apart from its groundbreaking theory and practice, the reconceptualisation movement stands out from other radical social work movements for another reason too. Never have social work activists been targeted by state violence more aggressively and systematically than those involved in the Latin American reconceptualisation in the 1970s. Although records from international social work organisations suggest that the victimisation of social work activists has not been an uncommon phenomenon (IFSW, cited in SWAN-Greece, 2011a), the degree of suppression that Latin American social workers suffered in that period has been unparalleled in the history of the profession. The Argentinian Association of Social Workers, for example, suggest that in the first months following the 1976 military coup, 24 practitioners were murdered, while the records of the Association indicate that there are still 59 *desaparecidos* (missing) practitioners (Ministerio de Educación, 1984). Equally, data from the Chilean Association of Social Workers confirm the violent persecution, disappearance or assassination of 17 social workers following the coup in that country in 1973 (Colegio de Asistentes Sociales de Chile, 2008). Although the precise figures of murdered and violently persecuted social workers in this period are unknown due to the ruthlessness and arbitrariness of the military regimes, it would be safe to calculate the numbers of persecuted social workers into the hundreds.

One of them was Argentine Professor Luis M. Früm, who published his article in 1971 on 'Ideology in social work', which eloquently presented the contradictory ideological function of the profession:

> Assuming that ideology guides our work, can we talk of 'reconceptualised' Social Services without reconceptualising the ideology that sustains it?... In this sense, the process of selecting a specific methodology is one that addresses the specific needs in real life; it could be referring to either a system which desires to be preserved or the specific need of a social class to transform reality. (Früm, 1971: 23)

Früm's observations in his article captured the most central task of the reconceptualisation movement: 'making sense of the ideological function of social work as a precondition for creating an alternative profession and eventually a just world' (Früm, 1971). Five years after the publication of this text, Früm was dismissed from his position as Chair of Social Work Methodology at his university, targeted by the military regime's infamous 'Dispensability of civil servants' laws. A few months after his dismissal, he went missing. His body was eventually found in a morgue in the area of Villa Mercedes, 'face down, blindfolded and hands tied with chains and a wire. Dressed in his pyjamas and shot in the neck' (*El Diario Dela Republica*, 2014).

Früm was probably the best known social worker murdered in this period. The most notable pioneers of the other two parts of the 'radical triangle' were also targeted during this purge. Catholic Priest Camilo Torres was executed in 1966 by the Colombian army and the critical pedagogue Paulo Freire lived in exile from 1964 until 1980, in both cases, as a direct consequence of their intellectual and political contributions.

The ferocity of the suppression and targeting of social workers and activists involved in the 'reconceptualisation' movement was, in a sense, a testimony to its wide popular influence (which transcended borders across the whole of Latin America). Between 1965 and 1975, the movement evolved from a rather marginal 'anti-paradigm' to the most dominant and influential social work approach in Chile, Argentina, Brazil, Uruguay, Colombia, Mexico and Puerto Rico. Its political legacy is still powerful across Latin America and visible in global social work.

It is not easy to present a linear history of reconceptualisation, for its development was dynamic, evolving through a series of interrelated responses to the contradictions of the 'modernisation' of social services across the region. Although, during roughly the same period, social work in much of the developing world had experienced the tense process of reforms coordinated by the United Nations (UN) and United States Agency for International Development (USAID), only in Latin America did social workers create a movement, structured and militant enough to earn the description of an 'anti-paradigm', a 'rupture' with mainstream social work (Barreix, 2003). The main reason behind the Latin American social work 'exception' can be found in the unique constellation of social, cultural and economic elements that gave rise to broader radical and popular movements.

Justice for Luis María Früm

In April 2015, Argentina's Federal Court found 11 former military officers guilty of crimes against humanity. Their historical crimes, committed during Videla's dictatorship, were mostly related to thousands of arbitrary and violent disappearances of pro-democracy activists. Among the defendants were the murderers of academic and radical social work pioneer Luis María Früm. The Argentinian Association of Social Workers welcomed the sentencing of Früm's murderers, describing it as 'Justice delivered after 38 years of pain'.

Luis María Früm, qualified as a social worker at the Institute of the Ministry of Social Assistance. Early in his career as a social worker and academic, he challenged the 'technocratic' basis of mainstream social work in Latin America, which, under the veil of political neutrality, assisted the perpetuation of neo-colonial macroeconomic policies. Früm became instrumental in the reconceptualisation movement in Argentina. This movement sought to create a social work paradigm that promotes the 'liberation of the oppressed communities and social classes'. He was recognised as one of the reconceptualisation movement's organic thinkers and his monographs on the ideology of social work were widely read among progressive academics across Latin America. He became a Professor and Director of the School of Social Work at the National University of San Luis. He used his professorial role as a means for developing genuinely participatory and democratic pedagogies in social work academia. He was also a founding member of the Conceptual, Referential and Operational Scheme (ECRO) group, the editorial collective behind the radical social work movement's most influential publications.

He continued his progressive academic and activist work even after the military Junta led by Colonel Videla suspended the constitution and suppressed democracy in Argentina. Luis María Früm was immediately targeted by the military and his activities were closely monitored by the intelligence service. In March 1976, he was dismissed from his academic position under the 'Dispensability of Civil Servants Act', a law designed to silence progressive civil servants. On 19 June 1976, a group of military officers showed up at Luis María Früm's family home in Villa Mercedes. When he opened the door, he was arbitrarily arrested and removed from his home by force. Several days later, he was found dead in a lake, 40km away from his home. He was shot in the neck and his body was blindfolded and handcuffed, still wearing his pyjamas.

Over 40 years since his murder, Luis María Früm's work and life are still celebrated and remembered by social workers across Latin America as an inspiring example of a social worker fighting for social justice even in the most dangerous and oppressive circumstances.

Hundreds of social workers were murdered or 'disappeared' in Latin America in the 1960s
and 1970s due to their activist and politically progressive work.

'The food of the minority is the hunger of the majority' (Galeano, 2009)

Until the late 1950s, social work in Latin America was a rather marginal, Church-related, activity. Although it claimed to be a 'profession', in reality, it was difficult to differentiate it from traditional philanthropy. In most countries of the region, the lack of social policies and unwillingness to create organised social services meant that social work only existed nominally as an organised profession. Social work in the socio-economic context of 'Hacientismo', the Latin American variation of landed social relations, was a world apart from the organised profession in the industrialised 'West'.

'Hacientismo' had its roots in the colonial socio-economic relations evolved during the Spanish Empire. The colonisation of the subcontinent by the Spanish Empire, already complete by the late 16th century, had effectively divided Latin America into four administrative regions: New Grenada (corresponding to modern-day Colombia, Ecuador, Panama and Venezuela), New Spain (Mexico, Central America and Spanish West Indies) and Río de la Plata (Argentina, Bolivia, Paraguay and Uruguay). Colonial Brazil was controlled by the Kingdom of Portugal.

Unsurprisingly, the colonial powers concentrated their efforts on the aggressive exploitation of natural resources. This was achieved through the creation of a system of which the main pillars were land appropriation and racial segregation. Large plantations were created, mostly in the central and northern zones of the cone, while in the southern areas the focus was on mining and the extraction of minerals. Slavery was of central importance to the colonial system. Unlike North America, in the southern cone, the colonial powers did not intend to physically exterminate the indigenous populations. Instead, the main priority was to incorporate them into the colonial production system as a labour force. Nevertheless, much of the indigenous population could not survive the European diseases brought to Latin America by settlers. In order to deal with labour shortages, the Spanish Empire resorted to extensive slave trading, forcibly transferring millions of Africans to Latin America and the Caribbean. The mix of African, indigenous and European populations resulted in very diverse cultural and racial communities. In order to retain their power, the new rulers created a complicated system of racial hierarchy, with varied levels of privilege according to race (*Sistema de Castas*). The *Mestizos*, people of mixed race and the majority group, although having fewer rights than the European-born ruling classes, enjoyed a bit more privilege than the indigenous or Afro-Latin American communities. The 'divide and rule' principle introduced in colonial times survived well into the 20th century, and its legacies are still evident in most Latin American countries.

Within this context of oppression, peasants (from the 17th century) started organising and articulated demands for agrarian reform. Unlike the northern part of the American continent, in Latin America, peasant rebellions moved beyond racial lines and often succeeded in creating effective grass-roots alliances. The rebellious spirit of the Latin American peasantry shaped the 'national liberation' movements of the 19th century that eventually defeated the Spanish Empire and divided the region into nation-states. Despite the defeat of colonial rule and the high hopes of the oppressed classes, the newly born states maintained the perpetuation of vast inequalities. Land and wealth remained in the hands of the privileged few while the majority of the population – and, in particular, the communities of indigenous and African origin – suffered from chronic marginalisation. Moreover, the emergence of the US as an imperial power established new forms of 'colonisation', favouring the use of economic means, interference in domestic affairs and the establishment of puppet regimes rather than direct military interventions.

In the 1950s, major advances in transportation and industrialisation in much of the formerly 'colonised world' had effectively created a new international division of power: 'a massive shift of industries producing for the world market from the first generation of industrial economies which had previously monopolized them to other parts of the world' (Hobsbawm, 1994: 362). Such shifts provided the foundations of what would later be called 'economic globalisation'. Despite the tectonic socio-political changes it caused, unlike the case of 19th-century Europe, the old 'latifundia' did not disintegrate. Instead, old oligarchies were incorporated into the new system, which combined the accumulation of land, colonial hierarchies and the process of rapid industrialisation. The result was that the poorest communities experienced the 'worst of both worlds': old ruling classes retained feudalistic social relations and repelled demands for agrarian reform, while in the newly created cities, inequality crushed the hopes of the working classes. Galleano (2009: 5) described this system of multiple oppressions in his iconic book *Open veins of Latin America*, which immediately became an indispensable 'primer' among radical social work students and practitioners:

> The division of labor among nations is that some specialize in winning and others in losing. Our part of the world, known today as Latina America, was precocious: it has specialized in losing ever since those remote times when Renaissance Europeans ventured across the ocean and buried their teeth in the throats of Indian civilizations.... It continues to exist at the service of others' needs, as a source and reserve of oil and iron, of copper and meat, of fruit and coffee, the raw materials and foods destined for rich countries which profit more from consuming them than Latin America does from producing them.

In 1961, US President John Kennedy introduced his short-lived 'Alliance for Progress', a set of ambitious economic reforms and financial stimuli, supposedly aimed at creating growth and accelerating industrialisation in Latin America. Economic domination aside, a major objective of this agenda was to prevent the emergence of revolutionary movements like Fidel Castro's in Cuba, which had captured the imagination of the oppressed communities. The developmentalist reforms introduced by the 'Alliance for Progress' were destined to fail as apart from the flawed economics that characterised them, they were also deeply neo-colonial in nature. Based on old clichés, developmentalism identified the poorest communities not as victims of the system, but as the main reasons of stagnation. Overpopulation and the demographic 'time bomb' were highlighted as a hindrance to development, and it was inevitably the poorest who were presented as the main culprits for all the misfortunes of Latin America. Galleano (2009: 8) explains how 'Various US missions have sterilized thousands of women in Amazonia, although this is the least populated habitable zone on our planet'.

Unsurprisingly, these neo-colonial experiments, instead of fostering economic growth, contributed towards the growth of militant anti-imperialist movements. The developmentalist approach had underestimated the fact that Latin American societies had long lost faith in reforms and policies 'imported' by colonial powers. 'Modernisation' had not brought about the desired social change and the most oppressed communities directed their discontent into organised political action. The historically strong tradition of rebellion in the region gained momentum and eventually gave rise to well-organised movements seeking to 'emancipate' Latin American. These movements varied from well-organised guerrilla movements (such as the FARC in Colombia) to successful electoral alliances (such as the rise of Salvador Allende to President of Chile in 1970). What really characterised Latin America's 'age of rebellion' was its organic nature, which transcended cultural, geographical and often class boundaries. One has to remember that, almost simultaneously, peasants pushed for (and in the case of Guatemala's '10 years of Spring', achieved) meaningful land reform, indigenous communities joined communist parties *en masse* (Hobsbawm, 1994) and popular guerrilla movements were created and often led by members of the white metropolitan intelligentsia (as in the case of the Cuban Revolution, as well as FARC and M19 in Colombia). In many respects, the formidable force of Latin America's popular radicalisation had defied all known scripts, and unlike in other regions, social workers, educators and even priests swiftly swapped loyalties and found themselves in the forefront of these movements.

Social work reconceptualisation: a child of its time

Like all transformative movements, reconceptualisation did not develop in isolation; it was the product of the broader political commotion that gave rise to radical politics across Latin America. The modernisation policies of the 1950s and 1960s required a broad range of well-trained personnel. Social workers, who had had a peripheral semi-professional role in the rudimentary social services of the region until then, became the 'chosen' profession assigned with the mission to operationalise the principles of community development on the ground. 'Developmentalist' approaches created a critical mass, organised and coherent enough to be described as a profession. For the first time in its history, social work was provided with space, status and resources comprehensive enough to lift the profession from the hitherto anaemic vocation of 'social assistance'. The (re)birth of the social work profession in the 1960s was largely based on Anglo-American positivism and it swiftly incorporated in its methodology technocratic tool kits promising immediate solutions to the chronic problems associated with the region's 'underdevelopment'. Social workers were employed in UN–US coordinated community projects, most of which emphasised community development, informal education and family planning. It needs to be noted that in the early years of this professional transformation, there was a great degree of optimism about the profession and what could be achieved.

Such transformation was also reflected in the rapid expansion of social work education. During this period, many social work programmes were organised across the region, benefiting from the support of the UN. Moreover, the provision of social work education moved to universities instead of the private and religious tertiary institutions that had monopolised the training of social workers until that point. The new generation of students and practitioners, educated within the context of technocratic reformism, were able to break free from the constraints of conservative philanthropy and engage with a wider range of courses and themes, such as political economy, community development, demographics and so on.

Ironically, the call for de-professionalisation, central to the radical arguments of the reconceptualisation movement, would never have developed without the pre-existing process of successful professionalisation introduced in the 1950s and early 1960s. The rapid expansion of social work education in the 1950's and 1960's meant that the class base of the profession shifted away from the traditional philanthropy of the middle class. Eventually more working class students entered the social work profession altering irrevocably the image of social work as a church-based, middle class, gendered vocation.

However, by the early 1960s, the initial optimism was gradually replaced by scepticism and disillusionment. Social work methodologies taught at the universities proved to be ineffective and irrelevant to the Latin American context as, in most cases, they were direct translations of US textbooks. Practitioners who were involved in the social assistance projects in both rural and urban areas witnessed first-hand the failures of a system supposedly designed to create growth and development.

While analysing the social work reconceptualisation movement, it is important to highlight the close proximity of and dialectical relationships between the three different professions (theology, education and social work). The radicalisation of all three activities evolved simultaneously and was a direct response to the shared realities of practitioners in the community intervention projects in impoverished regions. Teachers were sent into these community and welfare centres in order to contribute towards the eradication of illiteracy. Social workers were utilised in community development/family planning tasks, and priests engaged with the spiritual and material support of the poorest communities. The three professions coexisted in these centres and shared concerns, ideas and actions. Their criticisms mostly focused on the issue of the inequalities generated through the developmentalist approach. Crucially, they also recognised the ways in which reformism restrained the articulation of alternative and transformative models. Liberation theologian Gustavo Gutierrez (1971: 26) suggested that 'Developmentalism came to be synonymous with reformism and modernisation, that is to say synonymous with poor measures really ineffective in the long run and counterproductive to achieve real transformation'.

Increasingly, practitioners of the 'radical triangle' felt more confident in proposing political action as a legitimised method of intervention. The concept of 'neutrality', central to the modernising tool kits, was the first to be deconstructed in the process of social work radicalisation. Radical academics Alayon, Barreix and Cassineri (1971: 58) captured these tensions when they asked:

> If the Alliance for Progress has been a political response to a political problem; if the developmentalist thesis was born in the shadow of this political approach, which crept into the Social Work curricula, then how could social workers develop alternative theoretical models linked to frontline realities and break free from the illusion of neutrality?

In order to break free from the limitations of mainstream community interventions and social services, indignation was not enough. A radical theory combined with radical practice was required and the major contribution of Latin American reconceptualisation was exactly this: it managed to transform anger against structural injustices into a concrete theory of practice. Central to emancipatory theory and practice developed in this period and used extensively by social workers and educators alike was the concept of 'conscientisation' (*conscientização*). This concept, largely influenced by the quest for 'class consciousness', emphasised tangible strategies that social workers and educators could employ in order to: (1) help expose the oppressive social structures that dehumanise people; (2) use dialogue, participatory research and active learning as tools for challenging these structures; and (3) highlight the importance of political mobilisation as a precondition for individual and collective liberation (Crivas, 1999):

> Reconceptualized social work claims for itself activities relating to consciousness-raising, training, organization, and social mobilization, elements of a process through which it is possible to visualize the liberation of man.... The theoretical base of the movement of reconceptualization was viewed as follows: the first stage of development of the theoretical foundation of reconceptualization

rested on a structural-functionalistic base and was known generically as the 'basic method'. The second stage was to implement those actions based on dialectical materialism, and which were consequently known as dialectic. (IASSW, 1977: 104)

Paulo Freire

Paulo Freire (1921–97) was a Brazilian radical educator and political activist whose work heavily influenced progressive theory and practice in social education and social work. Freire suggested that the fields of education and social welfare are never politically neutral. Instead, the perceived neutrality of these institutions only perpetuates a system of inequality and exclusion. According to Freire, educational and social welfare practice can become powerful tools of emancipation only when they work in collaboration with oppressed classes in order to develop a critical understanding of their own social realities and the potential for social action (a process he described as 'conscientisation'). To this end, he developed a creative methodology of practice that focused on critical thinking and action (*praxis*), which is used extensively by progressive social workers and social educators in Latin America and other developing regions. After the 1964 military coup in Brazil, Freire was detained and eventually forced to live in exile for 15 years. Upon his return to Brazil, he supervised one of the most ambitious adult literacy projects in Brazil.

Rise and fall of reconceptualisation

The need for the articulation of alternative theories generated very rich debates within schools of social work. These debates were concurrent and often antagonistic, representing diverse political traditions. The breadth and diversity of these initial debates makes it rather difficult to pinpoint the exact time when social work's political engagement took the form of a more concrete movement. By convention, most social work historians (see Barreix, 2003) would suggest that the first issue of the magazine *Hoy en el Servicio Social* (*Social Services Today*) in 1965 (which, after the fourth issue, was renamed *Hoy en el Trabajo Social* [*Social Work Today*]) should be considered as the first major milestone in the creation of the 'reconceptualisation' movement. This is not to ignore the various events and actions preceding this publication, but, instead, to consider *Social Services Today* as the first systematic effort to coordinate dynamic activities and synthesise ideas towards developing an alternative social work theory and practice.

During the same year, two other major political developments that consolidated 'reconceptualisation' as an emerging movement also took place. The Latin American Social Service Seminar, an annual meeting point for radical social workers, was launched in Porto Alegre. In the same year, the social services undergraduate programme of the University of Uruguay became the first one to officially endorse a curriculum that allowed space for alternative social work theories and practices, followed by the Catholic University of Sao Paulo, which created the 'campo piloto', an unapologetically radical educational project that aimed at connecting social work with popular movements (Raichelis and Rosa, 1982). Social work academics, students and practitioners involved in these campaigns and publications would eventually be considered pioneers of Latin American social work. 'Generation 65' was considered a term synonymous with the reconceptualisation pioneers.

Social Work Today, until it was closed by the military dictatorship in Argentina, remained the most influential medium of communicating radical social work ideas and literature. Initially, most of the people involved in its editorial board had links with the Social Service Institute in Buenos Aires. The declared objective of the editorial board (known as ECRO) was not only to record and document the exciting political developments on the ground, but also to enrich social work theory with the concepts of critical pedagogy, popular culture and the 'philosophy of liberation'.

It needs to be noted that during the first period (1965–69) of reconceptualisation and despite great enthusiasm, the movement went through major theoretical debates and tensions. It was a movement that encompassed a variety of ideological currents and nurtured several strands of Marxism – reflecting the broader debates of the age – the ideas of Mao Zedong, Guevarism, dependency theory and concepts of popular education associated with Paulo Freire, and it was also influenced by variations of Peronism, the works of Althusser, Mounier and Oscar Lewis, and even more radical versions of Christianity (Gloria et al, 2008).

What united the activists involved in the movement at this early stage was their shared frustration at the inefficiency of developmentalist policies and the rejection of technocratic neutrality. The latter, as we discussed earlier, had created a type of practice so anodyne and detached from structural problems that ECRO would routinely describe it as 'aseptic social work practice' (ie 'ideologically sterile'). Despite the loud rejection of mainstream social work, at that early stage, it was totally unclear what could replace 'aseptic social work'. One of the main criticisms about this early period of reconceptualisation is that it tried to confront Western positivism often using the tools of positivism (Alayon and Molina, 2006). Although 'Generation 65' is characterised by evident ideological contradictions, it nonetheless allowed space for the deeper exploration of radical approaches to social work. In this sense, 'Generation 65' acted as a prelude for the much more militant wave of reconceptualisation that formed between 1969 and 1972.

The move towards the second phase of reconceptualisation is evident in the 'Araxa Document', named after the Brazilian city where the Brazilian committee of the International Social Services Conference attempted to summarise and clarify the intellectual contributions of progressive social workers thus far. The Araxa Document is not itself a radical manifesto; its main contribution lies in the fact that it offers a succinct review of scholarship and activities linked to the reconceptualisation movement. Such a systematisation of the rich, yet messy, ideological debates helped expose the limitations of the eclecticism that characterised the early stages of the movement (Barreix, 2003: 28). Such a contradictory mix of determinism with critical theory was evident in the document's list of conclusions, where it called upon social workers:

- to act in the process of creation, reformulation and adjustment of social policies;
- to facilitate public participation in this reformulation and planning process in order to ensure the appreciation of macro-analysis;
- to promote and participate in surveys in order to assess the policies that are being adopted; and
- to work with individuals or groups, providing a corrective, preventive and empowering method (see the Araxa Document, cited in Netto, 1994).

The call for people's involvement in re-imagining social services was a significant departure and helped create space for the consolidation of more radical voices in the reconceptualisation movement. By the end of the 1960s, some of these voices were presenting openly revolutionary arguments for a different social work: they suggested that social work had to not only work towards highlighting the structural inefficiencies of the capitalist system, but propose social work methods that could contribute towards overthrowing capitalism. The second period of reconceptualisation is characterised, ideologically, by a stronger emphasis on 'historical materialism', which allowed the reconceptualisation movement to move beyond the 'limitations of eclecticism' and focus on connecting social work practice with the politics of class liberation. Parra (cited in Servio, 2015) suggests that 'the movement boom between 1969 and 1972 was a consequence of the fact that conservative social workers and technocratic modernisers "resignedly or combatively" accepted the need for a renovation of the profession'.

In reality, the 'resignation of the more conservative voices in the movement' was not a reason for the strengthening of reconceptualisation; rather, it signalled that socialist social workers had won the 'battle of ideas' within the movement. This is the most productive period of reconceptualisation, both intellectually and methodologically. Barreix (2003) and Servio (2015) suggest that during this period, the influence of reconceptualisation was so wide that one could say that radical social work had become the 'new mainstream' across the whole South American cone. By the early 1970s, most major social work schools had adopted curricula influenced by Marxism of one variation or another, as well as the politics of liberation. Such was the intellectual engagement with reconceptualisation in social work schools that within 10 years, the scholarly output of radical social work writings had exceeded the total number of mainstream social work books and articles that existed since the inception of the profession (Alayon and Molina, 2006). Moreover, at a time when most international and regional social work associations were still confined within the Anglo-American zone of influence, the Latin American Association of Social Service Schools (founded in 1965) articulated a combatively anti-colonial approach.

However, as the movement was reaching its height, it was brought to an abrupt halt by the military regimes that seized power across the continent. As an integral part of broader political movements, the radical reconceptualisation movement was crushed by the extraordinary violence of the military dictatorships, which condemned Latin American societies to an extended period of authoritarianism. The US and local ruling classes had become increasingly wary of the influence of progressive and revolutionary politics in Latin America. By the late 1960s, it had become clear that the US strategy of 'soft colonisation' had failed. Social movements had become so powerful and popular that left-wing parties and alliances achieved unprecedented electoral successes. Local ruling classes demanded decisive action against what they perceived as a threat to their interests. To these developments, the US responded with a clandestine plan of intervention that provided intelligence, resources and military support to dictators across the continent (a Central Intelligence Agency (CIA) plan known with the code name 'Condor'). By 1976, democracy was suppressed in the largest part of the Latin American cone, including Brazil, Bolivia, Chile and Argentina. The rest of the continent, although technically not under military rule, also experienced a period of extensive violence and instability.

Social work was among the most demonised and persecuted professions as it was considered to be irreversibly Marxist. Most social work schools closed, several academics and practitioners involved in the reconceptualisation movement were arrested or murdered, and social work students, in the schools that had survived the purge, experienced a prolonged period of censorship and book-burning. In Chile, social work programmes were removed from university education altogether and social work books were banned on campuses (Castañeda and Salamé, 2014).

Conclusion: the legacy and relevance of reconceptualisation

Although 'actually existing' reconceptualisation was short-lived due to the rise of military dictatorships, its legacy has been profound and long-lasting. Never in the global history of the social work profession had a grass-roots political movement influenced so extensively social work theory and practice. Liberation approaches, central to the reconceptualisation movement, have been enormously popular in the Spanish- and Portuguese-speaking world since the 1970s. They are still highly influential to social work education and practice in these countries, where political action is still considered a legitimate social work approach (Saracostti et al, 2012). Its influence and legacy can be witnessed in the Latin American contributions to global social work debates, which are always characterised by their structural and political analysis. One can find direct links between the legacy of reconceptualisation and 'orange tide', the contemporary anti-austerity social work movement in Spain (Ioakimidis et al, 2014). Albeit with some delay and a more modest reach, emancipatory social work theories nurtured in the reconceptualisation movement also inspired sections of North American and non-Spanish-speaking European social work (Belkin Martinez and Fleck-Henderson, 2014).

Reconceptualisation has been the most comprehensive and emphatic example of radical social work that succeeded in moving beyond the mere articulation of an 'alternative' narrative. Latin American social workers successfully created a 'complete' and holistic model, overcoming the division between theory and practice that dominates in much contemporary social work. In this sense, reconceptualisation also disproved arguments which suggest that radical social work is a 'theory without practice' (Servio, 2015).

This was possible through placing emphasis on the concept of 'praxis' as a dynamic intellectual-methodological intervention that is inextricably linked with the objective of liberation from all forms of oppression. Radical social workers in Latin America categorically opposed abstract theoretical schemata that were not informed by concrete front-line experiences. Equally, they were steadfast in rejecting social work models, either mainstream or 'activist', that solely focused on practice. Freire (1972: 156), while discussing the essentials of such holistic practice, highlighted the irreplaceable elements of:

> Consistency between words and practice; boldness, which urges the witnesses [ie facilitators of 'praxis'] to confront existence as a permanent risk; radicalisation (not sectarianism) leading both the witnesses and the ones receiving that witness to increasing action; courage to love, which far from being accommodation to an unjust world, is rather the transformation of that world on behalf of the increasing liberation of human kind; and faith in the people.

What is particularly relevant to current social work debates grappling with postmodern and identity politics is the emphasis of the reconceptualisation movement on a concrete analysis. Despite the fact that reconceptualisation emerged as a diverse dialogue among disillusioned social workers coming from different traditions, it eventually became a movement that managed to synthesise these contributions into a *concrete theory*. This was a 'theory in action', responsive to the diverse experiences from practice but, at the same time, retaining a very clear focus on the broader historical and political context. Gagneten (1986) summarised these elements:

- Social workers should begin from popular culture and rediscover the needs and problematic conditions generated by economic oppression.
- The object of knowledge and innovation in social work should be focusing on unfair structures.
- People should be considered as historical and social beings with capacity to think and transform themselves as the main promoters of their welfare, well-being and history.

The emphasis of reconceptualisation in its latter stage was on the structural-political functions of capitalism and the ways in which this system deprives the oppressed classes of their humanity. Radical social work theory in Latin America allowed space for the rich and diverse experience of the people they worked with (workers, peasants and indigenous communities). Practitioners involved in reconceptualisation insisted that only an analysis that encompasses the shared experience of the oppressed classes and promotes unity in action could be transformed into a truly radical movement: 'To do otherwise is to absolutize and mythologize the relative; alienation then becomes unavoidable' (Freire, 1972: 157).

More than this, the reconceptualisation movement contributed significantly to the disentanglement of radical social work's Gordian knot, that is, progressive practice in the context of a capitalist state. Indeed, the question as to whether social work in a capitalist state was intrinsically and unavoidably oppressive had been of central concern to social workers involved reconceptualisation. As the reconceptualisation movement entered its second phase (1967–71), the period of intellectual maturity, a consensus was achieved that de-professionalising social work and rejecting it as an inherently oppressive profession was a simplistic, under-theorised and harmful approach (Barreix, 2003). Instead, radical social workers had to work with methods that exploited contradictions integral to the capitalist system – and this is what they did.

The fact that state social work had moved beyond the narrowness of philanthropic charity, through the modernisation agenda, meant that the old, religious, middle-class base of the profession was replaced by social workers with a diverse demographic and class background. It was exactly this shift in personnel and demographic that allowed social workers to assert the political identity of the profession. Radical social work analysis exploited this change and highlighted that in this new professional reality, social workers' class interests and life experiences were much closer to the people that they worked with rather than the state institutions that they worked for. Hence, the reconceptualisation movement called for social workers to reverse their political and occupation loyalties. Costa (1987: 120) explained such evolution, suggesting that:

> The professional strategy seems to be, on the one hand the democratisation of the institution [social services] through client or subaltern class pressure and, on the other hand, social workers' conquest of autonomous space in order to ensure a professional practice addresses to the clientele of popular classes.

Moreover, the transition to industrialisation and dynamic change within state institutions seeking new roles and identities allowed social workers to exploit internal contradictions in state policy and achieve extraordinary autonomy. Latin American countries went through tectonic social, cultural and economic changes at the time. The breaking up of old communities in favour of rapid urbanisation was an uncharted territory for governments who required social workers to be in the forefront of dealing with the impact of these changes. Social workers, even when they started becoming 'ideologically unruly', were still very much necessary to the state as their community development projects were, in many cases, the only channel of interaction between the state and the population. The vastness of many Latin American countries, its uneven development and the inability of the state to monitor closely the work of professionals implementing state policies allowed increased autonomy in rural areas.

The 'peak years' of reconceptualisation coincided with the rise of left-wing or populist movements into positions of power, both at the regional and national level. Such an increase in the influence of progressive forces in the state apparatus meant that radical social workers discovered opportunities to directly engage with political action within the state. It is important to remember that Paulo Freire was a senior civil servant in the Ministry of Education when he developed (and practised) his critical pedagogy approaches. Eventually, he even served as a minister of education. In Chile, the electoral success of Salvador Allende allowed significant transformations to happen in social services.

The reconceptualisation movement has been the most important example of radical social work practice globally. Its extraordinary influence, reach and intellectual contribution to social work remains unsurpassed. It bridged the artificial dichotomy between radical theory and practice, demonstrating that meaningful transformation is only possible when social workers and communities are 'united in action'. Crucially, it exposed the ideological function of social services and the futility of neutrality, and proposed a 'preferential option for the poor and the oppressed'. The current resurgence of anti-capitalist movements in many parts of the world and the subsequent re-engagement of social work with radical approaches calls for a careful examination of the lessons and relevance of reconceptualisation. Reclaiming the radical history of our profession is an urgent task, being especially pertinent at a time when mainstream historiographies tend to:

> ignore the conscious or compelled choices the profession made about its ideology goals, methods of interventions and public policy positions. They obscure the role that radical social work played in shaping many of the concepts that the profession and society now take for granted. (Reisch and Andrews, 2002: 4)

The legacy of reconceptualisation in contemporary Latin American social work practice

Decades of paramilitary violence and structural inequalities in Colombia have led to the displacement of approximately 5 million people across Colombia. This has disproportionately affected Afro-Colombians, indigenous people and peasants who have been forced off their land and moved into urban areas, where they face further oppression, violence and lack of opportunities. According to Amnesty International, in 2008 alone, 380,000 people were targeted and forced off their land. The *despalzados* (displaced) live in unacceptable conditions, without documents, jobs, access to electricity or medical care, and Doctors without Borders suggests that these families have borne witness to massacres, detentions and the disappearance of family members or their neighbours. They have been harassed by armed groups, 'taxed' for money and property, and, in some cases, forced to flee to save their children from forced recruitment.

As a result, in early 2011, new displaced communities moved into 'public spaces' in the centre of Bogota, including the large national park, which has been occupied by thousands of *despalzados*. The occupation of the parks served two main purposes: the first one was linked to the practical need to find space for temporary residence; and the second one emphasised on the need for collective political actions.

The response of the central and local governments was predictable and punitive. Police encircled the public areas in order to contain the expansion of camps within the public parks. They constantly harassed the displaced. Moreover, paramilitary groups, functioning as the state's long arm, also targeted indigenous leaders. By and large, the *despalzados*'s leaders adopted a non-violent approach and accepted the involvement of social workers employed by the local council. This was mostly because most of the social workers involved came from Afro-Colombian and indigenous background themselves and they used approaches inspired by the reconceptualisation movement. Their practice focused on the following approaches.

Meeting urgent needs/mediation

Social workers worked with the displaced communities in order to address the urgent needs of the community. Part of the social work engagement was political in the sense that it exposed the state's dereliction of duty and failure to meet their statutory obligations. The state was forced to provide some help in the form of cash benefits, food stamps, shelter and medical care. Most importantly, the campaign in support of the displaced communities mobilised trade unions, students and other groups, who extended their solidarity and provided material support. On several occasions, social workers intervened when police action was threatened and mediated in order to construct the council's evacuation plans.

Trust building/participation and democracy

Despite their ordeal and ongoing tragedy, the *despalzados* have maintained a great sense of community. Large groups of people and families live close to each other, creating small networks of solidarity and self-help (psychological and practical). Social workers worked closely with the community in order to help them facilitate participatory processes, which include the organisation of open assemblies in the parks attended by the displaced and, in some cases, where trusting relationships have been built, representatives of local residential areas. During this process, social workers worked as organisers who attempted to make full use of their institutional capabilities (access to facilities, funds, etc) for the benefit of the community. On several occasions, this was followed by small cultural and sports events co-organised by the practitioners in direct collaboration with the communities. These events were 'owned' by the communities but would not have been organised had social workers not made use of their influence within the state system in order to obtain approval for the events.

Conscientisation and emancipation in social work practice

Social workers did not pretend that they possessed better expertise than the *despalzados*; they accepted that they constantly learn from the interaction with the displaced communities, creating 're-humanising' opportunities for both groups. Through Freirian interventions focusing on dialogue, mutual respect, democratic processes and cultural activities, both social workers and displaced communities work towards understanding the structural causes of their social problems. In doing so, a very important stage in this process is building broader social alliances. Oppression and social inequalities affect not only the groups of people occupying the national parks; all sections of Colombia's peasantry and working class have been affected by the violent conflicts, social inequalities, privatisations and neoliberal policies of recent decades. A number of activities within the parks and the public spaces have attempted to bring together all these groups in an effort to challenge alienation, indifference and individualism. Such active demonstrations of solidarity have had a twofold effect: 'rehumanising' communities that had experienced horrible violence and displacement; and creating a basis for a grass-roots alliance that was eventually transformed into a large, popular pro-peace movement. Eventually, indigenous and Afro-Colombian displaced communities played a key role in the pro-peace movement. In 2016, a peace agreement was ratified by the Colombian Parliament. The peace accord covered most of the demands of the displaced for relocation to their land, collective reparation and agrarian reform.

Source: Hinestroza and Ioakimidis (2011).

SIX

Refugees, migrants and social work

Give me your tired, your poor,
   Your huddled masses yearning to breathe free. (Emma Lazarus, 1883)

Introduction

Social work has a long history of work with and alongside refugees and migrants. Throughout the profession's history, there have been workers who have considered such work as essential and non-controversial – part of the profession's DNA, a reflection of its commitment to human rights and social justice. Equally, there have been practitioners wedded to notions of eugenics, happy to collude in the processing and regulating of vulnerable migrant communities.

   In this chapter, we look at the contemporary 'refugee crisis'. Comprehending the scale and cause of the present crisis is necessary to inform social work theory and practice – and provides the basis for essential policy and practice demands that should be at the heart of any internationalist social work.

Eleanor Rathbone

Support for migrants and refugees has played an important, though often hidden, role in the history of social work activity. The activities of some social work pioneers in this field are worthy of consideration.

Eleanor Rathbone was a Liverpool-based social reformer and early social work pioneer. She was the founding chair of a large voluntary sector organisation called PSS (Person Shaped Support) (which is still active in the city) and was an advocate for women's rights. Support for refugee and asylum causes was an important part of her work. In 1936, she supported the British Provisional Committee for the Defence of Leon Trotsky, and signed a letter to the *Manchester Guardian* defending Trotsky's right to asylum, for example. In 1938, she campaigned for dissident Germans, Austrians and Jews from both countries to gain entry into Britain. Earlier, in 1937, she became a steering committee member of the Basque Children's Committee, which oversaw the transportation, arrival and dispersal of 4,000 Basque children fleeing fascist aggression during the Spanish Civil War. The children were housed across the UK in a number of 'colonies' that met their educational and material needs. An echo of this work can be found today in social work campaigns to support unaccompanied refugee children across much of Europe (Firth, 1986; Benjamin, 2012).

The scale of the contemporary 'refugee crisis'

The last decade witnessed a developing, and unprecedented, refugee crisis across much of the globe. According to the United Nations High Commissioner for Refugees (UNHCR, 2015d), 59.5 million people worldwide were forcibly displaced at the end of 2014, 8.3 million more than the year before. Those who were displaced were overwhelmingly the victims of persecution, war, civil unrest and a range of human rights violations. This figure represented the highest number of displaced people on United Nations (UN) records, though these figures were dwarfed by those from 2015 and 2016. According to the Internal Displacement Monitoring Centre (IDMC), 2014 also saw 38 million people around the world forced to flee their homes by armed conflict and generalised violence, being pushed into internal displacement (moving to an alternative location within the borders of their normal country of residence); this figure is a 15% increase over the previous 12 months (IDMC, 2015). These figures represent the largest number of refugees since just after the end of the Second World War.

This is a crisis that has been fermenting for some time. The second decade of the 21st century witnessed a steady growth in refugee numbers:

> Starting from 10.4 million at the end of 2011, the number increased to 10.5 million in 2012, to 11.7 million in 2013, and finally to 14.4 million by the end of 2014. By mid-2015, it had reached an estimated 15.1 million, its highest level in 20 years. Within three and a half years, then, the global refugee population grew by 4.7 million persons – some 45 per cent. (UNHCR, 2015e: 4)

Faced with this crisis, numerous politicians and much of the media across Europe and the 'advanced' economies of the world have framed the 'refugees and migrants … as a problem, rather than a benefit to host societies' (Berry et al, 2015: 5). Politicians and media outlets have described the refugees as 'economic migrants' (or, in the words of the British Prime Minister at the time, David Cameron, 'a bunch of migrants' [Freedland, 2016]), with the clear inference that they are attempting to enter the European Union (EU) to obtain ('better') work or access to welfare benefits.

Despite such claims, two clear facts stand out. First, in terms of country of origin, the top 10 refugee 'source countries' are those wracked by war, conflict and political unrest; at present, they are (in order) Syria, Afghanistan, Somalia, South Sudan, Sudan, Democratic Republic of Congo, Central African Republic, Myanmar, Eritrea and Iraq. People leave their homes and communities to seek refuge because they have no other reasonable choice. They make the voyage because they are desperate – not to get to Europe, Australia or the US, but to get away from the situation that they are in.

Second, the majority of the world's refugees do not enter Europe, the US, Australia or other parts of the 'economically advanced' world. At the end of 2014, the world's top refugee host was Turkey, followed by Pakistan, Lebanon, Iran, Ethiopia and Jordan. Proportionately, Lebanon hosts by far the largest number of refugees by population, 232 per 1,000 inhabitants. Worldwide, 86% of the refugees under the UNHCR's mandate live in developing countries (UNHCR, 2015d). To take the case of Syrian refugees, by mid-2015, an estimated 4.2 million had fled the country; overwhelmingly, they had moved to neighbouring countries, with Turkey (1.8 million), Lebanon (1.2 million), Jordan (628,800), Iraq (251,300) and Egypt (131,900) being the main hosts (UNHCR, 2015e: 4).

Nevertheless, between 2014 and 2016, much of the focus of the global refugee crisis was on Europe (despite its relatively small share of global refugee numbers). In a sense, the 'refugee crisis' only really started to be interpreted as such because refugees started to come to Europe, whereas for the previous few years, those fleeing Iraq and Syria had stayed in the region and were, to some extent, 'hidden from view'. According to the UNHCR, during 2014–16, Europe faced 'a maritime refugee crisis of historic proportions' (UNHCR, 2015c: 2). They estimate that in the first six months of 2015, 137,000 refugees and migrants attempted to enter the EU, a rise of 83% on the same period in 2014. The International Organisation for Migration argued that in the first two months of 2016, more than 102,547 migrants and refugees arrived in Greece by sea (IOM, 2016).

Arrival in Greece or other parts of Southern Europe is, for most refugees, simply a stage on their travels. Their end destination of choice is often Germany, Austria, Sweden (who, between them, took close to 90% of refugees arriving in Europe in 2015) and, for a small minority, the UK. Greece is part of the 26-country 'Schengen Area', which allows borderless travel between countries who have signed the agreement (Traynor, 2016). Yet, from late autumn 2015, countries started to close their borders, erect barriers and, effectively, suspend the Schengen Area in order to prohibit the movement of refugees. By mid-2016, the EU had entered into an agreement with Turkey to exchange supposedly 'legitimate' refugees from Syria while expelling (presumably 'illegitimate') refugees from other parts of the globe back to Turkey (for further processing) (Rankin, 2016). This was a decision that effectively trampled over internationally recognised refugee rights covered by the UN 1951 Convention and 1967 Protocol on Refugee Status (UNHCR, 1967 [1951]). The UNHRC was unequivocal in their declaration that such border restrictions intensified the refugee crisis (Chappell, 2016) and meant that European countries were unleashing a 'humanitarian crisis, largely of [their] ... own making' (UNHCR, 2016).

The rise in migration across the Mediterranean, often in overcrowded boats, led to a sharp increase in the loss of life. In October 2013, a boat carrying hundreds of refugees and migrants from Libya to Italy sank near the island of Lampedusa, killing 368. Between January and March 2015, it is estimated that 479 refugees drowned or went missing, compared to 15 in the same period the year before (UNHCR, 2015c: 8). In the single month of April 2015, it was estimated that 1,308 refugees and migrants were lost at sea, compared to 42 in the same month the previous year (UNHCR, 2015c: 2): 'During the first six weeks of 2016, 410 people drowned out of the 80,000 people crossing the eastern Mediterranean ... a 35-fold increase year-on-year from 2015' (Procaccini, 2016). In just one week at the end of May 2016, the UNHCR estimated that 'at least 880 people ... died ... as their vessels capsized in the Mediterranean, bringing the total fatalities along the dangerous crossing route to 2,510' in the year to that point (UN News Centre, 2016).

These figures are horrific but, again, deaths at sea do not only occur in the Mediterranean. The UNHCR estimated that almost 70,000 refugees, asylum-seekers and migrants – primarily from Ethiopia and Somalia – reached Yemen by sea in 2015. In the first 10 months of 2015, there were 88 recorded deaths of people travelling by sea between the Horn of Africa and Yemen. In early October 2015, 'a boat with migrants and refugees capsized in the Arabian Sea. Of the 68 passengers, only 33 survived' (UNHCR, 2015b). However, those who arrived in Yemen found themselves in the midst of an ongoing conflict, which led to a significant increase in the number of internally displaced people (IDP). In October 2015, the UNHCR estimated that Yemen's IDP population reached a 'record high' of 2,305,048 (UNHCR, 2015b).

Andreas Needham (2016) reported that mixed maritime movements in South-East Asia were three times more deadly than in the Mediterranean in 2015. Across the region, an estimated 33,600 refugees and migrants took to the sea to travel, including 32,600 in the Bay of Bengal and the Andaman Sea, and an estimated 1,000 who crossed the Straits of Malacca or attempted to get to Australia from Indonesia, Sri Lanka and Vietnam (UNHCR, 2015a). This included large numbers of Rohingya from Myanmar, who have faced state repression and officially sanctioned Islamophobia. According to Graham-Harrison (2015):

> The Rohingya are faced with two options: stay and face annihilation, or flee.... Those who remain suffer destitution, malnutrition and starvation; severe physical and mental illness; restrictions on movement, education, marriage, childbirth, livelihood, land ownership; and the ever-present threat of violence and corruption.

The pace of departures picked up in 2015. It is estimated that up to 25,000 set off from the Bay of Bengal in the first three months of 2015 – double the levels in 2013 and 2014 – but approximately '12 of every 1,000 people who embark on mixed maritime movements from the Bay of Bengal do not survive the boat journey' (UNHCR, 2015a: 4).

Faced with this global crisis, the response of the most powerful states has been to further tighten their border controls. The dominant political model established across Europe, Australia and the US has been one of, what Carr (2012) calls, 'hard borders' against external migrants and refugees.

In Europe, the 'fortress' model has combined the internal liberalisation of movement (via the Schengen Agreement) with hard border controls on the periphery of the region. This has effectively pushed border controls onto the poorer, peripheral regions of the EU. On the EU borders, somewhere in the region of 400,000 border guards deployed through agencies such as Frontex (the European border agency) and Rapid Intervention Border Teams (called RABITs) mix with immigration officials and national police forces to control EU entry points. The EU border is covered by 'Satellite surveillance; naval patrols ... a proliferation of immigration detention centres that extend across the continent and beyond; 'offshore' border controls and neighbourhood partnerships aimed at monitoring and trapping unwanted travellers before they even reach European territory' (Carr, 2012: 23).

Since the early 1990s, the US has built larger and more fortified fences on its Mexican border and has utilised surveillance technologies, border patrols and guards in an attempt to control Mexican and Latin American migrants. Those who are apprehended after crossing the border will be 'returned' to Mexico or held in US detention centres. According to Amnesty International (2009: 3): 'In 1996, immigration authorities had a daily detention capacity of less than 10,000.... Today [ie 2009] more than 30,000 immigrants are detained each day.... More than 300,000 men, women and children are detained by US immigration authorities each year'. The hard border policy in the US has created an atmosphere of growing hostility to migrants. Between 2010 and 2011, 164 anti-immigrant laws were passed by state legislatures across the US – indeed, only seven states (Alaska, Connecticut, Delaware, New Hampshire, Ohio, Wisconsin and Wyoming) did not pass anti-immigration Acts, with some passing as many as six Bills during this period (Gordon and Raja, 2012).

The UNHCR's *Asylum trends* report (2015e) notes that Australia received 8,960 asylum applications in 2014 – about 1% of all global applications. Refugees have attempted to reach Australia on boats from Indonesia, and mostly come from Afghanistan, Sri Lanka, Iraq, Iran or Myanmar (Burma). Hundreds have died making the dangerous journey. Yet, as they approach the Australian waters, they have been sent back out to sea in lifeboats (BBC, 2015a). Australia's 'hard borders' policy has included building offshore detention centres in remote Nauru and the Papua New Guinean island of Manus. In these centres, there have been repeated reports of violence against asylum seekers, including the sexual assault of children and the rape of men and women in detention, as well as other abuses, such as detainees being given out-of-date food and expired medication (Doherty, 2016).

The global refugee crisis and the closing of borders by powerful First World countries to vulnerable people fleeing war, a range of political, economic and environmental crises, and all manifestations of poverty and need pose important questions for social work. Given our strong value base and our commitment to international standards of practice, what can and should we do in the face of this situation? To begin to answer this question, we need to put the present crisis into a longer historical frame.

Social work with refugees and asylum seekers in England

Asylum Link Merseyside is a drop-in support centre for refugees in Liverpool, UK. The centre is supported by more than 90 volunteers. It runs English-language classes and serves lunch to around 220 people a day. There is access to free clothing for the homeless and cheap clothing for those needing support. There is limited housing and food for the destitute. Well Being programmes (bikes, allotments and football) and social events enable networking and solidarity. Individual casework support helps people navigate the complex legislation and UK Border Agency policy that determines refugees' and asylum seekers' rights to assistance.

Qualified social workers and social work students on placement work across the organisation's activities but are key providers of casework support. The work includes supporting people as they apply for help with accommodation or subsistence costs under section 95 of the Immigration and Asylum Act 1999, or help for those refused asylum and left destitute under section 4 of the Act.

The system is dehumanising, isolating and degrading, and destroys both dignity and self-respect. It disperses people around the country without any choice as to location. When they are given financial support, it is at a rate lower than existing benefit levels, sometimes via a 'payment card' that can only be used at certain shops. Using the cards is stigmatising and shaped by social policy responses steeped in notions of 'deterrence'.

Social workers working on section 4 applications have to navigate very strict criteria imposed by the UK Home Office. Applications can take weeks or months to be processed and people are often left homeless and destitute while decisions are made. A recent tactic employed by the state is for decisions to be drawn out, with constant requests for further information, one piece at a time, leading to further frustration and delay. All of this can have hugely damaging effects on individuals and lead to engagement with other areas of service delivery (eg mental health support, drug or alcohol addiction teams, etc).

Assisting people to fight for their liberty is at the heart of the caseworker's role at Asylum Link. They support people to appeal unsuccessful claims and access further statutory assistance. They also look to assist with any housing problems people face and offer to help with access to GPs and other health-care services. The role inevitably involves tapping into other local refugee and asylum support services. Asylum Link works closely with the Merseyside Refugee Support Network, Greater Manchester Immigration Aid Unit, Refugee Action and the British Red Cross to help secure a range of services unavailable at the centre. The charity also works with statutory services, including councils, the Home Office, the police, GPs, MerseyCare and other health providers. However, as an independent agency, Asylum Link also has to challenge the decisions made by statutory agencies where necessary, and, at times, relations can become strained between social workers working in different agency settings. Proposed new legislation will undoubtedly make things worse.

Refugees, migrants and asylum seekers

One of the most pressing issues for social workers is to be clear about the language used around the refugee crisis. The language used to describe migrants, refugees and asylum seekers matters. To emphasise the point, let us take an example from the UK. Figures indicate that just as many UK citizens live outside the UK in the EU as there are EU citizens living in the UK, despite popular perceptions (Rettman, 2014). Just over 1 million people born in Britain live in Spain, 330,000 in France and 329,000 in Ireland. Yet, the British media and politicians never refer to these people as 'migrants' (and certainly not refugees or asylum seekers); they are more often referred to as 'ex-pats' – a term that has few negative connotations.

Political scientist Murray Edelman's (1985 [1964]) work on 'condensation symbols' looks at the way(s) that key words in political discourse become loaded with myth, emotion and symbolism. There is no doubt that the words 'migrant', 'refugee' and 'asylum seeker' are loaded with (often unspoken) meaning. As Carr (2012) notes, in the post-Second World War era, in the context of the Cold War, the term 'refugee' was often viewed positively, referring those fleeing the 'horrors' of the East European 'Communist' (or, in reality, state capitalist) societies. However, by the last quarter of the 20th century, with the ending of the Cold War and increasing numbers of refugees from the Global South seeking protection from wars and political turmoil in the West, the terminology shifted. These people were now increasingly:

> Portrayed by politicians and the media as 'economic migrants' seeking to evade the continent's immigration restrictions. By the end of the Cold War, 'asylum seeker' was firmly enshrined in European political and media discourse as a sub-category of refugee whose legitimacy had yet to be proven and whose claims were often assumed to be suspect. These assumptions were often steeped in racial prejudices in which 'asylum seeker' became a code word for Third World immigrants in general. (Carr, 2012: 22)

Berry et al (2015) undertook a study of media language used to describe refugees entering the EU in 2015. They looked at the press coverage in five countries (German, Sweden, Italy, Spain and the UK). They found that:

> The use of labels (migrant, refugee, immigrant etc.) varied markedly by country. Both Germany (91.0%) and Sweden (75.3%) overwhelmingly used the terms refugee (flüchtling(e)/flykting) or asylum seeker (asylsuchende(r)/asylsokande). In contrast migrant (migrante) was the most used term in Italy (35.8%) and especially the UK (54.2%).... In Spain, the dominant term was immigrant (immigrante) which was used 67.1% of time. (Berry et al, 2015: 7–8)

More recently, developing Carr (2012), we suggest that the terms 'migrant', 'refugee' and 'asylum seeker' are increasingly prefixed with the adjective 'Muslim' (although, in reality, many refugees are not Muslims and do not come from Muslim countries). Thus, the refugee crisis has emerged from and merged with the wars and turmoil created by Western interventions in the Middle East to reinforce Islamophobia and general hostility to *Muslim* migrants and Muslim communities more generally.

Let us look at the formal definitions. A refugee is someone who has fled armed conflict or persecution or who:

> owing to a well-founded fear of being persecuted for reasons of race, religion, nationality, membership of a particular social group or political opinion, is outside the country of his nationality and is unable or, owing to such fear, is unwilling to avail himself of the protection of that country. (1951 UN Convention Relating to the Status of Refugees)

As such, it is recognised that refugees need international protection and are protected under international law by the 1951 Refugee Convention.

Thus, refugees who arrive in countries are subject to international conventions and domestic legislation based on the 1951 Refugee Convention, which 'commits agencies to provide services ranging from housing, health, employment, emergency aid and education' (Robinson, 2013: 2). The convention's basic principle is that refugees should not be expelled or returned to situations where their life and freedom would be under threat. Once someone has been recognised as a refugee, they are supposed to be given access to social housing and welfare benefits and helped to find a job and integrate into society. An asylum seeker is someone who is officially a refugee and has applied for asylum in another country. However, the legal process and assessment has not yet been completed; hence, they are seeking asylum.

A migrant is someone who moves from one place to another in order to live in another country for more than a year: 'It is estimated that some 232 million people or 3 per cent of the world's population live outside their country of birth' (Williams and Graham, 2014: il). Migrants include those who move to work or seek a better life: they may be international students, or those who move for family reasons; some will move to flee war, persecution or the effects of climate change; some will move because of the crushing effects of poverty; and some will move because their skills are in demand – or their personal wealth effectively allows them the freedom to settle where they wish. Of course, it is possible that people move because of a mixture of these reasons – that people fleeing the war in Syria face crushing poverty at home and want to better their own, and their families', prospects elsewhere.

Much popular discussion around the issue of migration assumes that people move through 'free choice'. Of course, some do. However, the overarching conditions shaping human movement are the social conditions created by capitalism and its impacts on our world.

'Popular' social work with refugees in Samos, Greece

The island of Samos, Greece, sits in the eastern Aegean Sea, separated from Turkey by the mile-wide Mycale Strait. Its 'normal' population is 32,977, yet this figure has been significantly increased because the island is one of the 'hot entry' points for refugees and migrants attempting to access 'fortress Europe' (Carr, 2012).

In the summer of 2015, approximately 1,500 refugees were arriving on Samos each day (Lee, 2015). Denied safe passage, they came by night packed in small rubber inflatables. Significant numbers did not make it, turning the sea into a graveyard. The official response to the migrant population processes them like criminals. The police are the main agency responsible. There is little support, minimal food and shelter, and no clothes or material goods on offer to replace those lost at sea or sold to pay for their hazardous journeys. They are housed behind a barbed-wire enclosed purpose-built 'reception centre', where they await papers that permit them to move on to Athens and an uncertain fate.

Faced with state indifference, a group of local activists, former social workers and volunteers formed 'Samos Refugees' to work with, and support, the migrants. Each morning, the group travel the island looking for those who have arrived overnight and pick them up from the beach. Until the arrival of some big non-governmental organisations (NGOs) in November 2015, this small group helped feed, clothe and support around 200–300 refugees a day.

The social work extends to playing with the children and talking to those traumatised by their perilous journey and the destruction of their homelands. They use every opportunity to involve the refugees in the daily tasks and to deepen their solidarities. All of their work is fundamentally informed by the key social work value of respect and an equally precious social work understanding that power and authority is never the friend of the poor and vulnerable.

So, each day, members of the group defy the authorities. They refuse to seek the permission of the police to be humane, and take food and other resources to those held behind the fences and in the police cells. Part of their work is political: involving refugees and migrants in various political events, and listening to the voice of the migrants and taking their advice over policy direction.

Samos Refugees vigorously maintains its independence. They refuse all overtures to collaborate with the 'international aid community'. However, the price of collaboration is high, for it entails keeping silent and making no criticism of the authorities. Finance is also a constant challenge, but through its website, it has so far been successful in securing funds for its work.

The project's commitment to working with and alongside the refugees, to involvement of refugees in decision-making and policy direction, to breaking down and challenging any notion of hierarchy between 'workers', 'volunteers' and 'refugees', marks Samos Refugees out as an example of high-quality popular social work working in this field (Chalalet and Jones, no date).

Migrants, refugees and capitalism

Migration has been part of human history from its earliest times. However, the speed and significance of migratory movements has increased significantly with the spread and development of capitalism.

Capitalism was built on the forced dispersal, enslavement and internal displacement of people from the land to urban centres, or from regional homelands to agribusiness across the 'new world'. The transatlantic slave trade brutally and forcibly transported people to work in enslaved, 'unfree' labour in the plantations of the southern states of the US and the Caribbean (Blackburn, 1997). The trade in humans, in part, provided the wealth that funded the Industrial Revolution in Britain, France and the US, which, in turn, sucked 'free' labour (migrants) into the developing towns and cities from the surrounding rural areas (or, in the case of the US, from other countries), where they worked long, unregulated hours in arduous conditions. Of course, the reality of enslavement was far more barbaric than the brutality of urban life during the Industrial Revolution; nevertheless, both processes were rooted in the drives of capital accumulation in the early phase of capitalist development.

Within capitalism, various forms of 'unfree labour' have always existed (eg slavery or indentured labour) but capitalism is characterised as a system where labour is commodified – people meet their daily needs by selling their ability to work on the labour market – which is considered a system of 'free labour' (Miles, 1990).

The use of the term 'free labour' has two aspects to it. First, it means workers are not tied to any particular employer, they are 'free' to enter a contract to sell their labour power to anyone, and, of course, an employer is 'free' to employ those they consider can best meet their productive needs. Ideologically, this aspect of 'free labour' is utilised to give the impression that the employers and workers meet each other in the labour market as, apparent, equals. It also suggests that we all have a 'free choice' about who we work for, where and when.

However, things are not so straightforward. A second sense of 'free labour' is vitally important: workers within capitalism are also 'freed' of any other means of living or supporting themselves and their families (eg they do not have access to significant land to grow crops or raise animals, or they do not have independent wealth). Thus, they face a major problem: if they do not work, they face desperate poverty. Therefore, alongside their 'freedom' comes 'economic compulsion': their only means of supporting themselves and their dependants is by selling their labour power by undertaking waged labour.

The wage labourer enters a labour market that is dynamic and subject to all manner of changes. Marx and Engels (1848: 13), writing in *The communist manifesto*, describe capitalism as a system that 'constantly revolutionises the forces of production', with, as a result, 'uninterrupted disturbance of all social conditions, everlasting uncertainty... [where] All that is solid melts into air'. Furthermore, this is a system that constantly seeks to expand the 'market for its products' and therefore forces 'the bourgeoisie over the whole surface of the globe. It must nestle everywhere, settle everywhere, establish connexions everywhere' (Marx and Engels, 1848: 13).

What Marx and Engels highlight here is various ongoing tendencies within capitalism, the drive: to expand into new markets; to invest in new machines and technologies of production, in part, to establish cheaper ways of producing commodities; to search out cheaper sources of labour power; and to create new commodities to sell. As a result of these tendencies, the working class is constantly created and recreated – jobs that were once common can disappear, to be replaced with other types of employment and this, in turn, forces people to change jobs, to move location, to retrain or to be left redundant and abandoned to a more or less impoverished future.

Within capitalism, therefore, there are always 'push' and 'pull' factors encouraging some of us to move to look for opportunities to work and engage in the labour market. The 'push' factors vary according to time and place. In the earliest phases of capitalist development, social, economic and political developments forced people away from their traditional homes: land enclosures, famine, religious and political persecution, poverty, and political and economic turmoil forced people off the land and 'pulled' them to work in factories, mines, mills and railways in the newly expanding towns and cities. In the 19th century, some of the 'migrants' may not have moved far geographically (though some moved continents), but the social dislocation that people experienced was significant and traumatic.

The 'push–pull' pattern of 19th-century migration was repeated throughout the 20th century and continues to play a significant part in migratory movements today. In the face of grinding poverty, of disconnection from the land, of environmental catastrophes like flooding or drought, of famine and disease, of economic crisis and unemployment, or of war or political turmoil, people look to migrate. Sometimes they move to the local town or city in search of wage labour, sometimes they move to other parts of the country and sometimes they seek new beginnings in different lands.

Historically, of course, this means that the vast majority of us are migrants or the children of migrants. If we search our family backgrounds, then, at some point, some of our relatives have migrated with the hope that the move would improve their life and that of their dependants.

During much of the 19th century, migrants were viewed as an economic resource who would fuel economic development in the host location. The dominant philosophy of 'free market liberalism' equally applied to the 'free market in labour'. As a result, until the second half of the 19th century, there were few state immigration controls. However, this gradually changed. As the state started to take on a great organising role within society (the growth of what is sometimes referred to as the 'interventionist state'), it took on a more directing role within the economy and within social and political life. The state became more concerned with the organisation of its population, of its education and 'health', and such concerns were often imbued with eugenicist ideas of 'race' and nation: the notion that economic and imperial ambitions could be undermined by 'inferior' human stock – meaning, for example, the poor, the elderly and the disabled at 'home', as well as 'inferior migrants' coming from other lands.

Many of the first controls were introduced to restrict Chinese migration. In the aftermath of the Taiping Rebellion, large numbers of Chinese refugees looked to leave the country and were attracted to the US, Australia and Canada, both to work on the railroads and to participate in the 'gold rushes' of the time. However, the Chinese migrants faced hostility and increasing controls on their movement. Once implemented against Chinese workers, these laws soon spread and were applied to other groups.

In the US, the Page Act 1875 was the first attempt at the federal regulation of Chinese migrants, while the Chinese Exclusion Act was passed in 1882. These exclusions were then generalised and encoded in the Immigration Act 1903, which also included a clause to exclude 'anarchists'. In Australia, the Immigration Restriction Act 1855 targeted Chinese labour, though this was later superseded by the Immigration Restriction Act 1901, which formed the basis of the White Australia policy that sought to exclude all non-Europeans from Australia.

In Canada, the Chinese Immigration Act 1885 introduced a head tax on Chinese migrants and was the first attempt to control immigration to Canada. It was soon to be followed by similar legislation targeting Italians. In the UK, the first immigration controls (the Aliens Act 1905) were implemented to control Jewish migration as Jewish workers and peasants fled Tsarist pogroms in the Pale of Settlement. The legislation was implemented in response to agitation by the racist, anti-Semitic organisation the British Brothers League.

From their onset, then, immigration controls have discriminated on the basis of 'race', ethnicity and national origin; that purpose is built into their very DNA. The idea that it is possible to have immigration controls, controls on the movement of people, which do not reinforce discrimination and prejudice is an oxymoron.

Jane Addams and Ellen Gates Starr

Jane Addams and *Ellen Gates Starr* are well known as the founders of Hull House settlement. They founded Hull House in 1889, where it became an important focal point for newly arrived migrants to Chicago, USA. The settlement became an important centre for Greek, German, Jewish, Irish and Italian migrants, and helped ease the new migrants' integration into the broader Chicago community. According to Addams, the settlement was structured around three principles, known as the three Rs: residence, research and reform. The last of these, 'reform', emphasised a clear commitment to improving the lives of those who the settlement worked with through political reform and campaign work. The settlement offered lectures, educational classes, drama workshops and free meals for children, and engaged in a range of campaign activities in their locality. It is one of the earliest examples of social work with migrant communities (Addams, 1910).

Social work with refugees

On World Social Work Day 2016, the two main international social work organisations (the International Federation of Social Workers and the International Association of Schools of Social Work [IASSW]) released a joint statement about the refugee crisis. The aim was to establish a five-point working plan to:

1. Coordinate social worker action in each of the affected countries to provide better understandings and responses to refugee needs during their journey, transfer and integration in the asylum countries.
2. Provide a focused strategy that supports vulnerable groups such as unaccompanied children and young people, older people, those with health issues, and trafficked persons.
3. Establish a comprehensive political advocacy strategy that reflects a 'ground-up' perspective on refugee needs, aspirations and solutions.
4. Develop social work models that support refugees in isolated or life-threatening situations where other forms of assistance are not available, including that there will be an increasing number of refugees who face closed borders or hostile host communities who will face the critical dilemma of staying where they are not welcome or returning to a war situation that may result in their death.
5. Enhance the skills of social workers working with others to constructively develop inclusive and cohesive societies (IASSW, 2016b).

In addition, the Social Care Institute for Excellence (SCIE, 2015) has established five principles for practice with refugees and asylum seekers, which reflect social work values and a rights-based approach to meeting social care needs. These principles are:

1. A humane, person-centred, rights-based and solution-focused response to the social care needs of asylum seekers and refugees.
2. Respect for cultural identity and the experiences of migration.
3. Non-discrimination and the promotion of equality.
4. Decision-making that is timely and transparent and involves people, or their advocates, as fully as possible in the process.
5. The promotion of social inclusion and independence.

Both the IASSW goals and the SCIE principles are admirable statements – though they perhaps underplay the negative role that *some* social workers play in the processing and assessment of vulnerable refugees (such as their involvement in the age assessment of child migrants [Moran and Gillett, 2014]).

The IASSW (2016b) statement goes on to note that:

> Millions of people caught up in the crisis are working with social workers, some employed by the state or NGOs, and many who are volunteering. They have the skills to work effectively with very traumatised and distressed people. They also act as the catalyst in organising volunteers to welcome and assist the integration of refugees into new areas.

The IASSW makes an important point – one that stretches beyond social work. In the face of the refugee crisis, many in the media and large numbers of politicians emphasised the 'problems of large migratory flows', focusing on issues of control and numbers, and the social tensions that they predicted would 'inevitably' occur. Yet, the plight of refugees and migrants has generated significant levels of support in many countries. As Carr (2015) notes: 'What were once marginal forms of solidarity with refugees and migrants have moved into the public mainstream'. Richardson (2016) discusses the extent of refugee solidarity:

> On 12 September 2015, SUTR [Stand Up To Racism] convened ... a demonstration ... at just two weeks notice. An estimated 80,000 people marched.... Across [Britain] ... people have collected provisions in schools, colleges, workplaces, among faith groups and in local communities.... Across Europe ordinary families have offered refugees a warm welcome. Where the authorities have refused to allow asylum seekers in, activists have risked their own liberty by organising transport to ferry them across the borders.... In Greece ... families cook[ed] extra food in order to provide a hot meal for refugees. Such solidarity has even been on display in some unlikely quarters. Those of us who are football fans are often on the defensive about the macho and offensive behaviour that frequently emanates from the stands. Yet even here the hoardings of football stadia have been draped with banners declaring 'Refugees Welcome Here'. Furthermore, a match between two Greek sides, AEL Larissa and Acharnaikos, was briefly halted when players from both sides sat down in protest at the treatment of Syrian refugees.

Social workers have not been immune to such solidarity drives. As the refugee crisis in Europe erupted in August 2015, large numbers of social workers joined campaigns for refugee rights. The Social Work Action Network (SWAN), drawing on longer traditions of solidarity with refugee struggles going back to networks like International Red Aid, which operated in the late 1920s and 1930s, worked with the UK-based anti-racist organisation Stand Up To Racism to organise convoys taking material aid and solidarity to refugees in both France and Greece. The convoys also joined political campaigns for refugee rights. This included SWAN having an official speaker at a demonstration inside the Calais Jungle demanding that refugees, and unaccompanied child refugees in particular, be allowed into the UK.

The SWAN convoys drew social work students and practitioners from across the UK to go to Calais, France, but it was impractical for many social workers to return to France on a regular basis. Out of the initial convoy, some SWAN supporters in Kent organised to travel back and forth to Calais on a more regular basis. Setting up Social Work First, practitioners travelled to the refugee camps and carried out needs assessments with the children. Schraer (2016) reported on the group's activities by quoting a practitioner who had taken part in the assessment process:

> Our aim was to complete a single assessment on these children. Of course, they're not in the UK so they have no right to a statutory assessment, but we wrote an assessment of their needs ... based on the format we would use at work.

In the camps, the network found that, within the dimensions of a single assessment, not a single need was being met.

Social Work Without Borders was a second network that formed in 2016. Drawing on experience of working in Leros, Greece, the network set itself up to safeguard women and children and challenge hostility to refugees in Europe (Wroe, 2016). As Wroe (2016) argues:

> Inspired by refugee women speaking about the risks they face as they make their journey through Europe, I spent my last week creating a quiet space for women in the camp by converting a storage room into a small lounge. My observation is that it provided a release for women and girls whose presence is often overshadowed in the busy camps. By bringing refugee women together with female volunteers we created an environment in which safeguarding issues relating to these women could be identified, recorded and responded to.

These examples of campaigning social work models grew out of the refugee solidarity movement but established a distinctive role for social workers within it. These campaigns combine a focus on individual support and relationship building with a campaigning edge to address the political causes of the present crisis. In this, they drew on older traditions of radical social work practice in the refugee support field.

Mentona Moser

Mentona Moser was born in 1874 and was brought up in Southern Germany and Switzerland. In 1894, she travelled to London to study, where she came into contact with the Settlement Movement. In 1899, she worked at the Southwark Settlement, where she was confronted by extreme levels of poverty. This, and her growing contact with the workers' movement, had a radicalising impact on Moser. Over the following few years: she worked with disabled people, young women and families; she railed against 'snooping' inspectors and welfare bureaucrats; she went to work for the Swiss Association for Child Protection; and she was involved in setting up 'garden cities', workers' settlements and children's playgrounds in working-class Zurich (Moser, 1985, 1986). In 1919, she joined the Swiss Communist Party (Hering, 2003), and in the 1920s and 1930s, she became heavily involved in International Red Aid (Schilde, 2009). International Red Aid was active across most of Europe in the late 1920s and 1930s. It offered support to refugees and those fleeing political persecution. It was based on the centrality of 'solidarity' to those who were 'victims of the class struggle' (Schilling, 2015).

Practical demands for an internationalist social work

The global definition of social work encapsulates a series of universal values applicable to all people in all societies. It asserts that 'Principles of social justice, human rights, collective responsibility and respect for diversities are central to social work' (IFSW, 2014). The present global refugee crisis poses some very particular questions for radical social workers internationally. We end this chapter by suggesting some practical social work demands that can shape social work intervention in this field.

Safe passage for refugees and migrants

In 2014, the Mare Nostrum operation, run by the Italian navy in the Mediterranean, saved an estimated 100,000 lives. Rather than welcoming the operation, the UK Home Secretary at the time, Theresa May, argued that it actively encouraged 'migrants' to make the perilous journey to Europe. In 2015, the EU cut funding for the Mare Nostrum programme and, as a result, there was, almost immediately, a sharp increase in deaths at sea.

The lives of thousands of vulnerable refugees fleeing war, human rights abuses, poverty and repression continue to be lost, needlessly, at sea, in the back of trucks, during travel on hazardous 'routes to safety' and in makeshift camps where they live in unacceptable conditions. The stretch of the Aegean Sea between Turkey and Greece is among the deadliest routes in the world for refugees and migrants: 'During the first six weeks of 2016, 410 people drowned ... crossing the eastern Mediterranean. This amounts to a 35-fold increase year-on-year from 2015' (IOM, 2016).

As those seeking refuge travel, they are vulnerable to exploitation from those in authority, by border guards and by those who engage in 'people smuggling'. Politicians and media commentators often blame refugee deaths on 'traffickers', but this is too one-sided. Of course, when we see refugees killed in the back of overcrowded trucks or lost at sea after being crammed onto overcrowded and unsafe boats, it is clear that some traffickers are no more than gangsters out to exploit vulnerable people. However, there is a relationship between traffickers and refugees. Refugee networks pass on information about safer routes of passage and people to avoid if possible. Furthermore, there is a level of hypocrisy in governments blaming traffickers for refugee deaths:

> no one would have to rely on traffickers if they were able to get to the places they want to go to by legitimate legal means. It is almost impossible for someone outside Europe to apply for asylum in Europe. The moment they book a flight they are likely to be identified and when they arrive at the airport the plane won't carry them because the carrier might be fined if they do. A few years ago there was a tabloid furore [in the UK] about Mugabe in Zimbabwe and how evil his regime was … most of which is true, but what was the UK government doing? It was making it harder for people who wanted to leave Zimbabwe to get to the UK. And that's what always happens whenever there's a country that seems like it's going to produce a lot of refugees – we simply make it more difficult for these people to obtain visas. (Carr, 2015)

As refugees take their lives in their hands and travel across the Mediterranean on boats that are often overcrowded and unsafe, they travel routes that are served by commercial passenger ships. In Lesbos and Samos, for example, refugees, if they survive the journey, will land on shore near ports where ships disembark passengers who have made the same journey in safety and paid a fraction of the price that refugees will have been charged to make their risky passage. The only way to ensure that the refugee crisis gets no worse, and to control the number of preventable deaths, is by introducing 'safe passage' measures:

- Effective access to coherent asylum procedures and assistance should be provided at entry points along migratory routes.
- Legal migration pathways need to be established.
- Dignified reception conditions must be offered to all.

Against incarceration

Across the so-called advanced world, governments are locking up refugees in detention centres. The UNHCR (2012a: 6, 12) are clear that:

> The rights to liberty and security of person are fundamental human rights, reflected in the international prohibition on arbitrary detention, and supported by the right to freedom of movement.... Every person has the right to seek and enjoy in other countries asylum from persecution, serious human rights violations and other serious harm. Seeking asylum is not, therefore, an unlawful act. Furthermore, the 1951 Convention provides that asylum-seekers shall not be penalised for their illegal entry or stay, provided they present themselves to the authorities without delay and show good cause for their illegal entry or presence.

In 2015, 14,832 asylum seekers were locked up in detention centres in the UK. Approximately half of all asylum seekers find themselves detained during the asylum process, and this includes children, 154 of whom were detained in the UK between 2010 and 2015 (Refugee Council, 2015). In the US, Amnesty International is quite explicit that the government's use of detention centres 'as a tool to combat unauthorized migration falls short of international human rights law' (Amnesty International, 2009: 3), while in Australia, a report by the Australian Human Rights Commission concluded that 'immigration detention in [Australia] is harmful to the health and mental health of young children and youth' (Elliott and Gunasekera, 2016: 3). As such, the following should be recognised:

• Refugees, asylum seekers and migrants are not 'illegal'; they have committed no crime.
• Detention centres should be closed down as a breach of people's fundamental human rights.

Support for unaccompanied minors

Between September 2015 and February 2016, it was estimated that, on average, two children drowned every day trying to cross the Eastern Mediterranean, a figure that, if anything, is likely to be an underestimate given the numbers lost and never found (Procaccini, 2016). In the first five months of 2016, the United Nations Children's Fund (UNICEF) claimed that more than 7,000 unaccompanied children made the crossing from North Africa to Italy (*The Guardian*, 2016), while elsewhere, the UNHCR estimated that children accounted for 36% of those on the move (Procaccini, 2016). Figures from the EU's criminal intelligence agency suggest that at least 10,000 unaccompanied child refugees disappeared after arriving in Europe between 2013 and 2016 (Townsend, 2016).

Unaccompanied asylum-seeking children should have the same rights and entitlements to services as other young children. In the UK:

> Local authorities have a statutory duty under the Children Act (1989) to safeguard and promote the welfare of all children 'in need'.

> Children 'in need' are those whose health and development would suffer without the provision of services. Unaccompanied children and young people, lacking the presence of parents or customary caregivers, are by definition children 'in need'. (Wade et al, 2005: 7)

Central to social work values is the need to protect and safeguard the needs and rights of children:

- Vulnerable, unaccompanied child refugees, 'children in need' as understood in the UK context, should have a right of entry to their country of choice.
- Refugee children should have a right to education, a right to protection and full access to welfare and social service provision.

The right to family reunification

The circumstances in which refugees flee their homes often lead to significant family disruption and separation. Family reunification is an essential part of bringing some form of normality back to refugees' lives. Pursuing the reunification of partners, parents with their children and siblings with each other should be viewed as a central social work task in our work with refugee communities. As the UNHCR (2012b: 3) states:

> The reality for many refugees … is … that they have lost track of their families or have had to leave them behind. The family however plays an essential role to help persons rebuild their lives and can provide critical support to adapt to new and challenging circumstances. Restoring families can also ease the sense of loss that accompanies many refugees who, in addition to family, have lost their country, network and life as they knew it. Family support in this sense goes beyond any traditional and cultural understanding of a family but will include those who rely and depend on each other.

As such:

- Family reunification is a central human right that should be acted upon by governments.

The right to work

Refugee employment rights are enshrined in the 1951 Convention Relating to the Status of Refugees and its 1967 Protocol (referred to collectively as the 1951 Refugee Convention). As the Asylum Access and Refugee Work Rights Coalition (2014: 2) assert, 'access to safe and lawful employment is a fundamental human right ... [which] applies to all persons, including refugees and asylum seekers'. They continue:

> When permitted to engage in safe and lawful work, an individual may fulfil his or her basic survival needs and contribute to the needs of the family, community and the country in which they reside. The realization of the right is the means through which the individual may achieve a range of other civil, political, economic, social and cultural rights, fulfilling the human desire to feel useful, valued and productive. (Asylum Access and Refugee Work Rights Coalition, 2014: 2)

Refugees arrive with many skills and much to offer their host society. Yet, many states, for example, the UK, prohibit refugees from legally entering the labour market until their formal asylum status is established. They are forced into poverty and reliance on benefits, often paid at a rate lower than those offered to indigenous citizens:

• To maintain their human dignity, refugees should have the right to work.

Self-activity

Refugees are often portrayed as 'passive victims' of social and economic processes. Such a portrayal comes from media outlets, politicians, voluntary sector organisations and welfare institutions (Harrel-Bond, 1999). These perspectives deny refugee independence and agency. The ways in which refugees and asylum seekers are perceived as victims or threats has a direct bearing on their access to support, safety and services. Yet, there is a rich history of refugee self-activity and political campaign work that needs to be recognised and celebrated:

• Social workers need to recognise refugee agency and work and campaign alongside refugees in the co-design and co-production of suitable knowledge and practice (Moran and Lavalette, 2016).

No collusion with discriminatory laws

Immigration controls and laws discriminate against people because of their skin colour, religion, place or origin and identification as the 'other'. Non-discriminatory immigration controls are not possible – the concept is an oxymoron. Social work's commitment to anti-oppressive practice demands that the 'virtuous social worker', one who acts in accordance with our value base and system, is one who cannot collude with discriminatory laws and practices:

• Working in detention centres, working and colluding with government border control agencies, and processing refugees and asylum seekers in ways that infringe their human rights bring social workers into conflict with the profession's value base and question their 'fitness to practise'.

Open borders

Teresa Hayter (2000: 163) notes that 'Objections to immigration on economic and welfare grounds have little basis in reality … immigration controls exist mainly because of racism in the countries which apply them'. Here, Hayter makes two central points. First, the evidence of numerous studies is that immigration does not lead to increased unemployment among the 'indigenous population', nor does it undermine wages and working conditions, nor, indeed, does it place a significant strain on the economic system. In fact, refugees and migrants (when allowed to work) are overwhelmingly contributors to tax revenues and economic performance indicators in host nations. Per capita, they use fewer public services and consume fewer public resources than host nation citizens. This is because 'most international migrants are of working age (twenty to sixty-four years) [who] mak[e] up 74 per cent of the total' (Williams and Graham, 2014: il). Furthermore, there is little evidence to support a claim that migrants create unemployment. Indeed, they 'tend to take jobs which are shunned by the natives and therefore provide an essential means of enabling economies to function and expand' (Hayter, 2000: 159).

Hayter's (2000: 165) second point, therefore, is that 'immigration controls are inherently racist', and, indeed, by forcing refugees and asylum seekers into 'illegality', governments further fuel racism and prejudice within their countries. She concludes that 'To deny people the right to migrate is harsh and oppressive, and is leading to unbearable extremes of cruelty' (Hayter, 2000: 172):

*   The solution is for a policy of 'open borders' and 'safe passage' that gives people the freedom of movement to settle anywhere they wish to.

RAPAR

RAPAR (Refugee and Asylum Seeker Participatory Action Research) was formed in 2001 in Manchester, UK (Moran and Lavalette, 2016). It is a social welfare and human rights organisation that brings academics, practitioners and refugees and asylum seekers together (as equal members of the organisation) to work on individual casework and community campaigns, and to undertake relevant research to shine a light on the predicament of forcibly displaced refugees. RAPAR is based on the notion of refugee and asylum-seeker agency. Those that work with the organisation become full and active members of the organisation, fighting for their rights and the rights of others.

There are three central values that shape the organisation's work. The first two are drawn from the work of Friere (1972): anti-assistentialism (the conscious rejection of dependency) and conscientisation (a commitment to transformative learning processes that arise from campaigning and participatory action research). The third, solidarity, is captured in the work of Galeano (2004 [1999]), where, in contrast to the 'vertical', hierarchical support offered by charity, he describes 'horizontal support' for equals that reveals our common humanity.

RAPAR provides basic legal training and support to refugees to fight and campaign on their own behalf, alongside volunteers from the social work, legal and welfare professions. It works with members around campaigns in their local communities for housing, access to education and other welfare services, and the service undertakes participatory action research to provide data to counter dominant ideas about refugees in British society.

Conclusion

In the face of the contemporary 'refugee crisis', social work is faced with a fundamental question: whose side are we on? This is a question that can only be answered politically. The refugee crisis demands that we meet the needs of vulnerable people for social and material support and protection as they flee war, poverty, environmental degradation and oppression. Confronting the refugees, we have powerful states and elites who have imprisoned, impoverished, dehumanised and stigmatised the vulnerable. For a profession committed to social justice, equality and confronting both oppression and inequality, there should be no doubt: we stand with refugees. Our task is to work in solidarity with refugee communities, and, as a profession, we cannot and must not collude with agencies that undermine their social, political and civil rights.

SEVEN

Social work, climate change and the Anthropocene

The six-month period from January to June [2016] was the warmest half-year on NASA's [North American Space Agency's] global temperature record, with an average temperature that was 1.3 degrees Celsius (2.4 degrees Fahrenheit) warmer than the late nineteenth century. This follows 2015, which was the warmest year on record and among the warmest decade on record. The ongoing warming trend – as well as the increasing frequency and severity of high-humidity heat waves – is ultimately driven by rising concentrations of carbon dioxide and other greenhouse gases in the atmosphere. (Voiland, 2016)

Introduction

One of the most pressing problems confronting humanity is the threat posed by human-induced climate change. This is an issue that social work is only slowly starting to address. In some parts of the world, for example, India, Canada and Australia, social workers are engaged in forms of social work for environmental justice. This is occasionally grouped under the rubric of 'green social work' – an eclectic mix of ideas and practices derived from a range of concerns about human impact on the global environment and global ecology.

The international definition of social work includes clear reference to the environment; yet, too often, this is interpreted unidirectionally as the impact of environments on people and their lives. It is increasingly clear that the impact of humans in their environment upon the planetary system is creating significant social problems that social workers will have to face in practice. As such, social work training and education programmes need to develop the professional knowledge base to consider and teach about climate change while developing and learning skills that could be fruitfully adapted to practice. This chapter engages with these important contemporary social work issues. We start by establishing the extent and roots of the crisis we face.

Medha Patkar, Indian social worker, environmental activist

In India, social workers have a long history of engagement in environmental campaigns, such as those to stop villages being flooded to build dams. Central to many of these campaigns has been the work and example of Medha Patkar. Medha Patkar was born in Mumbai, India, in 1954. In 1974, she gained her master's qualification in social work from the Tata Institute of Social Sciences (the providers of the first social work qualification in India in 1936), with a specialisation in community organising (*The Viewspaper*, 2008).

On qualification, she started to work alongside the indigenous peoples of the Narmada Valley. The Narmada river runs through Central and Western India, and in the 1950s and 1960s, the river and valley were identified as key sites for the Indian state's dam-building programme. The valley was to host:

> 30 major dams, 135 medium-sized dams and over 30,000 micro-harvesting (conservation) reservoirs. It was estimated these dams [would] ... lead to direct displacement of 250,000 people living in the Narmada Valley and affect the livelihood of over one million people. (Pawar and Pulla, 2015: 79)

As the dams started to be built, local communities without the appropriate knowledge of their rights were often displaced to inappropriate locations, without adequate compensation and in the face of official indifference to their plight. In this context, Patkar utilised a range of creative and critical social work methods – derived from the Gandhian concepts of '*satyagraha*' and '*asahakar*' – to build a social movement (the Save Narmada Movement [Narmada Bachao Aandolan (NBA)]) in order to represent the indigenous peoples of the Narmada and fight with them for their rights.

Satyagraha is based on the 'power of truth', what Ghandi called a 'truth force'. Here, the idea is that campaigns and individuals search for truth, are prepared to 'speak truth to power' and act in ways that expose truth to the wider world. *Asahakar* means non-cooperation with those in power. Together, *satyagraha* and *asahakar* promote non-violent means of social action.

Patkar initially undertook action research to establish the extent to which people in the Narmada Valley knew about the development plans and their knowledge of their rights. She then used group-work methods to raise consciousness and promote social action (Mayani, 2009). The long-running campaign included: advocacy and rights-based approaches, where local, state and national politicians and civil servants were held to account; non-violent direct action against construction firms, financial institutions and representatives of the global financial institutions funding the projects; and establishing links between various oppressed and dispossessed groups and challenging perceptions of Dalit and indigenous communities.

There were marches and demonstrations, including (in 1991) a proposed 200km march that was stopped by police at the Gujarat–Madhya Pradesh border – leading to a 22-day hunger strike by a number of activists (including Patkar). In 1993, she went on hunger strike again to try and force the government to review the dam project. This strike resulted in her arrest after 14 days of fasting. This was not the only occasion that she was arrested and beaten by police (Jensen, 2004). The Save Narmada Movement that she established became India's largest social movement.

Her vision of social work is of: a value-driven profession committed to social justice, human rights and social change; professionals engaged and active in social movement activity; and the promotion of sustainable development and the protection of the environment as central social work goals. In 1991, Patkar and her NBA colleagues were given the Right Livelihood Award (the 'Alternative Nobel Peace Prize'), and in 1992, she won the Goldman Environmental Prize. Other awards that she has won include the Deena Nath Mangeshkar Award, the Mahatma Phule Award, the Green Ribbon Award for Best International Political Campaigner by the British Broadcasting Corporation (BBC), and the Human Rights Defender's Award from Amnesty International (*The Viewspaper*, 2008). In 2004, she was a keynote speaker at the World Social Forum in Mumbai. She stands out as a social work activist committed to environmental justice.

The climate change problem

We are living in a world where unusual and extreme weather and climatic events are becoming more frequent – with devastating impacts on the environment and on humans caught in the maelstrom. In their end-of-year survey in 2015, the website Ecowatch identified 10 extreme events from the year that 'sounded the alarm' on climate change. In the Arctic, a heatwave in December caused temperatures in the North Pole to spike at 15 degrees Celsius above the norm for the season. In Paraguay, Uruguay, Brazil and Argentina, severe flooding led to the displacement of more than 150,000 people. Heavy rains in the Mississippi delta caused 'historically high' flooding in the US Midwest. A drought in South Africa was the worst in a generation, and the drought conditions across the south of the African continent meant that at least 29 million people faced food insecurity. In Yemen, a powerful and rare cyclone hit in November, impacting upon more than 1.1 million people and displacing 40,000. In the Philippines, a 'mega-typhoon' hit in October, affecting more than 1.2 million people. Across the Middle East, a dramatic heatwave caused temperatures in Iran to soar and temperatures spiked from Egypt to Syria. A deadly heatwave in Pakistan cost at least 2,000 lives while one in neighbouring India killed at least 2,500 people. Climbing temperatures in the Barents Sea, off the coast of Norway and Russia, are causing a poleward shift in fish communities, impacting upon wildlife as well as the indigenous communities that rely on them for their survival. Finally, and most alarming, for the first time in recorded history, global levels of carbon dioxide in the atmosphere averaged more than 400 parts per million (ppm) for an entire month – in March 2015 (Ecowatch, 2016).

The bleak picture continued to unfold in 2016. In May, a destructive wildfire burned through Fort McMurray in Canada. Windy, dry and unseasonably hot conditions created the conditions for the fire to spread and hold (Hansen, 2016). NASA's Goddard Institute for Space Studies (GISS), in their August 2016 review of global temperatures, found that people living in Siberia, the Middle East and

North America faced extreme heatwaves during the summer of 2016. Siberia recorded temperatures more in keeping with the tropics, Kuwait recorded its hottest day ever (54.0 degrees Celsius), and in the US, several cities broke monthly temperature records, with, at one point, 124 million people living under extreme heat warnings (Voiland, 2016). In November, alarm was raised that the Brazilian city of Rio's coastal defences were insufficient to cope with rising water levels as four-meter waves lashed the city's beaches. Such storm surges are frequent; however, 'In the 1990s, storm surge disruptions occurred roughly once a year, but since 2010 they have hit Rio four or five times as frequently. There have already been four this year [2016], including two of the biggest ever seen' (Watts, 2016).

Three other events of note emphasise the range of ecological problems that the earth and its populations are facing. Gradual melting of winter snow helps feed water to farms, cities and ecosystems across much of the world. However, global warming is leading to declining snow accumulations across the globe. In 2015, the snowpack in California, which is suffering an ongoing drought as well as long-term warming, reached its lowest point in 500 years (Mankin et al, 2015). Since the late 19th century, temperatures in the Alps have been steadily rising, from an average yearly temperature of 9.6 degrees Celsius in the late 1800s to today's average of 10.8 degrees Celsius. About 40% of Europe's fresh water originates from the Alps, which stretch from Austria in the East to France in the West, dipping into parts of Italy and Monaco in the South. Climate change is threatening the area's water cycle (European Environment Agency, 2010). In the Himalayas and the Andes, the effects of climate change are working in seemingly opposite directions. In both regions, the glaciers are shrinking; in the Andes, there will be longer dry spells and less water. Current projections suggest a steady decline in water resources – to about a third of current levels – by the midpoint of the century. In the Himalayas, people will have to contend with flooding, with water discharge expected to increase by as much as 70% (Rüegg, 2016).

The 14-year drought (1998–2012) that engulfed the Eastern Mediterranean region (covering Cyprus, Jordan, Lebanon, Palestine, Syria and Turkey) is the worst drought in the region for 900 years. It has caused substantial hardship for poor and rural communities throughout the region (Cook et al, 2016). Satellite measurements have demonstrated that the waters of Australia's Great Barrier Reef have warmed by 0.2 degrees Celsius, on average, over the past 25 years. This warming has led to a decline in the amount of seafloor covered in coral and the 'death' (the complete ecosystem collapse) of much of the Great Barrier Reef (Slezak, 2016b): 'Bleaching caused by climate change has killed almost a quarter of its coral' in 2016 (Slezak, 2016a).

The root cause of all these extreme weather events and ecological changes is increasing global temperatures. The GISS has found that the earth's 2015 surface temperatures were the warmest since modern record keeping began in 1880 and that the planet's average surface temperature has risen about 1.0 degree Celsius since the late 19th century, a change largely driven by increased carbon dioxide and other human-made emissions into the atmosphere. 'Most of the warming', they noted, 'occurred in the past 35 years, with 15 of the 16 warmest years on record occurring since 2001' (GISS, 2016a). September 2016 recorded the hottest recorded September in 136 years, leading GISS (2016b) to note that 'The record-warm September means 11 of the past 12 consecutive months dating back to October 2015 have set new monthly high-temperature records'. Former NASA scientist James Hanson and his colleagues have gone further, arguing that current global temperature has increased to a level not seen for 115,000 years '[Current] Global temperature has just reached a level similar to the mean level in the prior interglacial (Eemian) period, when sea level was several meters higher than today' (Hansen et al, 2016).

Popular social work and Occupy Sandy, USA

In the face of a range of climate change disasters, social workers will have to respond to meet people's essential needs. These are not skills that are offered in most social work education programmes. In creating and establishing a relevant social work knowledge base, we would do well to engage and to learn from, what we have called elsewhere, 'popular social work' responses to disaster and extreme situations (Lavalette and Ioakimidis, 2011a). One such example would be the response of the US Occupy Movement to Hurricane Sandy, which struck the US in 2012.

Occupy Sandy was a grass-roots disaster relief network that emerged in New York in response to the devastation caused by Hurricane Sandy, which hit the area in October 2012 (Feuer, 2012). Its purpose was to provide mutual aid to communities affected by the storm. Occupy Sandy grew directly out of the Occupy Movement that began in Zuccotti Park, New York, in September 2011, itself part of the Global Justice Movement and influenced by such international movements as the Arab Spring and the Indignados movement in Spain.

From the end of 2011 and throughout 2012, Occupy spread across much of the globe, as 'a wave of protests swept across Asia, the Americas and Europe' (Buckley and Donadiooct, 2011). The movement set itself up to protest against the economic and political power of the '1%': the control of the economic and political system by the global elite at the expense of the '99%'. As Matchar (2011) noted:

It [Occupy] wants corporate money out of politics. It wants the widening gap of income inequality to be narrowed substantially. And it wants meaningful solutions to the jobless crisis. In short, it wants a system that works for the 99 percent.

In the immediate aftermath of Hurricane Sandy, the Occupy Movement in New York were among the first groups to respond by providing aid to those who were without electricity, food and essentials. They provided torches and hot food from a base they established in two churches. They then organised their internet networks to place calls for materials, and were soon inundated.

The group divided into hubs. Some worked social media, relaying calls for supplies or people with specialist trades or services that they could offer. Others worked in the distribution centres. Still more walked the streets and neighbourhoods providing aid and ensuring that people were safe. Feuer (2012), from the midst of the relief effort, reported:

> Occupy Wall Street is capable of summoning an army with the posting of a tweet, and many of the volunteers last week were self-identifying veterans of the movement, although many more were not. Given the numbers passing through the churches, both fresh-faced amateurs and the Occupy managerial class – a label it would reject – were in evidence.

The Occupy Movement grew out of a critique of the priorities of global capitalism and a distrust of the state. The speed of its response to the Hurricane, the networks it both established and drew upon, the unconditionality of the support it delivered, and the philosophy of mutuality and solidarity upon which it was based are all significant features that social work should draw upon in thinking about the construction of a social work for environmental justice.

The science of climate change

The basic science of climate change has been known about for a very long time. In the 1860s, John Tyndall found that carbon dioxide could let light through while trapping heat. In 1896, Svante Arrhenius found a link between the amount of carbon dioxide in the air and global temperature. Since then, scientists have gathered vast amounts of data that show how carbon dioxide, methane, water vapour and other 'greenhouse gases' allow radiation from the sun to pass through them but stop radiation from the earth rising back into space. The more greenhouse gases that are emitted into the atmosphere, the more radiation is trapped as heat, and, as a result, the atmosphere and planet warm up.

Without the greenhouse effect, the earth would be a very cold, inhospitable and uninhabitable place. Water makes the biggest contribution to the natural greenhouse effect, but the amount of water vapour is relatively stable and it does not play a great role in modern climate change. The most important greenhouse gases are carbon dioxide (CO_2) and methane (CH_4). There is far less CO_2 than water in the atmosphere, but it is increasing rapidly – and it stays in the atmosphere for a long time (about 200 years). Methane has a much stronger warming effect than CO_2 but it decomposes much more quickly (in about 12 years). Other gases like, Nitrous oxide (N_2O) and a range of industrial gases add to the greenhouse effect but do not last as long.

Scientists have now established that over the last 12,000 years, the amount of CO_2 in the atmosphere has been relatively stable, at between 260 and 280 ppm. However, the extensive, large-scale coal, oil and gas burning started by, and associated with, the Industrial Revolution launched the long–term concentration of greenhouse gases and has been central to the growth of atmospheric CO_2. The US government National Oceanic and Atmospheric Administration have argued 'that carbon dioxide levels will not drop below the symbolic 400 parts per million (ppm) mark in our lifetimes – the highest concentration of CO_2 since the Pliocene era 3m years ago)' (Milman, 2016).

There are significant carbon sinks that can, to some extent, trap the CO_2 and offset the effect of greenhouse gases. The two main sinks are trees/plants and the oceans. However, we now produce more CO_2 than the sinks can absorb and this fact is made worse by deforestation and by melting polar caps, both of which reduce the carbon sinks and result in the release of more of the earth's 'natural' CO_2.

The second most significant greenhouse warming gas is methane. The amount of methane in the atmosphere has more than doubled in the past 250 years. It is estimated that it is responsible for about a fifth of global warming. There are two main sources of methane. Almost all natural gas is methane, which is produced by the fossil fuel industries. As Neale (2008: 16) notes: 'It leaks from coal-mines, oil-fields, gas-fields, gas pipelines and power stations'. Poor maintenance of Russian gas and oil pipelines is thought to be a significant producer, as is burn-off from oil wells and fracking processes (Pearce, 2016). The second source of methane is biological decay: organic waste in landfill sites, decaying plants and trees in wetlands, and as a by-product of intensive farming (eg it is produced in the guts of animals and by flooded paddy fields producing rice). The latest research suggests, however, that methane is also being produced by increasingly wet and warmer climatic conditions (eg melting polar caps releasing methane stores). As Pearce (2016) notes: 'climate change is starting to accelerate the processes that release methane into the atmosphere, potentially triggering a troubling positive feedback in which further warming could produce more methane and yet more warming'.

What Pearce notes here is the impact of 'feedbacks'. As we increase CO_2 and methane levels, we are beginning to run into feedback effects. Two examples will explain how feedbacks work. Rising CO_2 levels are now warming the Arctic. This begins to melt the permanent snow and ice. The snow and ice generally reflect the sun's heat back into the atmosphere (it is not absorbed by the earth's surface), but as they melt, they reveal sea, tundra and trees. These dark surfaces absorb heat and the Arctic warms up even more, causing the snow and ice to melt more quickly, which reveals more tundra, trees and sea, and so the cycle goes on. A second example comes from deforestation. As rainforests are cut back, large stores of carbon are released from the trees, and even more from the soil. The danger is that this will warm the area and cause drought. In turn, this kills more rainforest and the cycle continues. These two examples show that the more we warm the earth, the more we increase the speed of feedbacks, and the more they reinforce each other, creating the threat of 'runaway climate change', where the changes taking place to our climate cause other changes to the earth's environmental and ecological system that cause 'abrupt climate change' (Neale, 2008).

Despite the claims of well-funded 'climate change deniers', climate change is a scientific fact. Cook et al (2013: 1–2), examining 11,944 peer-reviewed academic papers between 1993 and 2011 matching the topics 'global climate change' or 'global warming', found that 'Surveys of climate scientists have found strong agreement (97–98%) regarding AGW [ie human induced global warming] amongst publishing climate experts.... Repeated surveys of scientists found that scientific agreement about AGW steadily increased from 1996 to 2009'.

On the basis of scientific evidence, there is no debate: human-induced climate change is happening now. From the snow-covered mountains of California and the Alps to the Great Barrier Reef, human-induced global warming is causing immense ecological damage and bringing greater numbers of extreme weather events. It means that the climate is getting warmer, more changeable and more extreme. As a result, there are – and will be – more floods, more droughts, more storms and more 'freak' weather episodes. In the next few decades, global warming, and the resultant rise in sea levels, will threaten coastal plains and cities, and some inhabited islands will be lost to the sea. It will lead to the extinction of numerous animal and plant species: 'Global populations of fish, birds, mammals, amphibians and reptiles declined by 58 per cent between 1970 and 2012 [and we are on track for] ... a two-thirds decline in the half-century from 1970 to 2020' (WWF, 2016: 12). Taken together, this will make human life in general harder, and for vulnerable communities, harder still.

Heatwaves and floods

Climate change creates crises for people that require both a social policy and social work response. In *Heat wave*, Klinenberg (2002) looks at the impact of the Chicago heatwave of 1995: 700 people died as a consequence of the heatwave – leading Klinenberg to describe this as a 'silent killer' of a silenced people.

In France in the summer of 2003, an estimated 15,000 people died after a record-breaking heatwave. The period of extreme heat was the warmest for up to 500 years – an additional 5,000 people died across Western Europe during the same period (Met Office, 2003). The heatwave 'led to a shortage of space to store dead bodies in mortuaries. Temporary mortuaries were set up in refrigeration lorries' (Met Office, 2003). People died as a result of heatstroke, dehydration, sunburn, air pollution and drowning (as people tried to keep cool).

In 2014, the UK suffered a series of floods – an increasingly common event that reflects the impact of climate change on the country. The floods posed serious issues for those working in adult social care. Donovan (2014) outlined some of the social work responses in one region that was badly affected. The priority was initially to support vulnerable people. Initially, this meant social workers liaising with the range of social care agencies to assess the scale of need. More generally, as Donovan (2014) notes: 'social workers join[ed] the emergency services and district council housing teams as they went door-to-door in flood-hit areas to find out who needed help'. Social work support was provided in six areas:

1. Round-the-clock monitoring: of the developing environmental crisis and its impact on vulnerable communities.
2. Information provision: helping to provide information to people about sources of support, but also about suggested time-frames for the crisis.
3. Emergency residential care: coordinating with care providers to ensure that people had places of safety to go to.
4. Extra home-care services: support for those who remain in their homes, regular contact and oversight of medical, food, water and heat needs.
5. Emotional/trauma support: social workers played a key role supporting those directly affected – this work carried on after the floods had subsided.
6. Emergency aid: ensuring that people have clean water, food and heat.

However, this bleak picture is, if anything, an underestimation of the ecological crisis that we are facing.

The Anthropocene

Over millions of years, the earth goes through periods of cooling and warming. The periods are caused by geological shifts, by fluctuations in the earth's orbit or by changes in sea movements. Over the last 11,500 years, the temperature of the earth has been relatively stable. This period – or geological epoch – is called the Holocene and the warm, stable climate facilitated the development of agriculture around the world, which, in turn, made possible the flourishing of human civilisation. Of course, during the Holocene (over the last 11,500 years), there have been colder and hotter periods – but the longer-term trends have been remarkably stable and the average global temperature during the whole epoch shows a variance of only 1 degree Celsius. The Holocene, argues Ian Angus (2016), is the only global environment that we are sure is safe for the complex, extensive civilisation that Homo sapiens have constructed. However, scientists are now suggesting that the earth's system is entering a new epoch called the 'Anthropocene' – a period in which human activity is disrupting the earth's system in fundamental ways, setting it on a dangerous and unpredictable trajectory and uncertain future.

The concentration of greenhouse gases that started to develop over 200 years ago is producing levels of atmospheric CO_2 that are pushing global temperatures up significantly. However, many of the world's leading scientists at the International Geosphere Biosphere Programme (IGBP) have argued that this only captures part of the problem. The IGBP was set up in 1988 and brought thousands of scientists from across the globe together on a range of scientific projects linked to understanding the earth system. Gradually, they came to the conclusion that if we analyse physical and social-scientific phenomena separately, we can miss the extent to which each affects and impacts upon the other. The earth, they argue, needs to be studied as an integrated planetary system. As Steffen et al (2004: 1) argue:

> [A] global perspective has begun to emerge in recent years and to form the framework for a growing body of research within the environmental sciences. Crucial to the emergence of this perspective has been the dawning awareness of two aspects of Earth System functioning. First, that the Earth itself is a single system within which the biosphere is an active, essential component. Secondly, that human activities are now so pervasive and profound in their consequences that they affect the Earth at a global scale in complex, interactive and apparently accelerating ways; humans now have the capacity to alter the Earth System in ways that threaten the very processes and components, both biotic and abiotic, upon which the human species depends.

In their path-breaking study *Global change and the earth system* (Steffen et al, 2004: 131, 132), the scientists looked at trends in 12 socio-economic indicators – population growth, gross domestic product (GDP), urban population, primary energy use, large dam construction, water usage, transportation, telecommunications, foreign direct investment, paper production, fertiliser consumption and international tourism – and 12 'earth system' indicators – CO_2, nitrous oxide, methane, stratospheric ozone, surface temperature, marine fish capture, shrimp agriculture, tropical forest loss, domesticated land, coastal nitrogen, ocean acidification and terrestrial biosphere degradation – and found that in each of the 24 indicators, the 1950s marked a 'Great Acceleration' in the intensification and impact of human activity on the earth system:

> [T]he profound transformation of Earth's environment that is now apparent ... [is the result of human activity].... [T]his transformation has undergone a profound acceleration during the second half of the twentieth century. During the last 100 years the population of humans soared from little more than one to six billion and economic activity increased nearly 10-fold between 1950 and 2000.... Half of Earth's land surface has been domesticated for direct human use and nearly all of it is managed by humans in one way or another. Most of the world's fisheries are fully or over-exploited and little pristine coastline exists outside of the high latitudes. The composition of the atmosphere – greenhouse gases, reactive gases, aerosol particles – is now significantly different from what it was a century ago. The Earth's biota is now experiencing the sixth great extinction event, but the first caused by another species: Homo sapiens. The evidence that these changes are affecting the basic functioning of the Earth System, particularly the climate, grows stronger every year. Evidence from several millennia

shows that the magnitude and rates of human-driven changes to the global environment are in many cases unprecedented. There is no previous analogue for the current operation of the Earth System. (Steffen et al, 2004: v)

The IGBP scientists' case is that human activity on the global environment is producing a transformation in the earth's system. They have suggested that it represents: 'The most rapid transformation of the human relationship with the natural world in the history of the species' (Steffen et al, 2004: 131).

The IGBP scientists moved the debate beyond 'simple' climate change to show the variety of ways in which human activity is fundamentally changing the earth system. For example, they note that nearly 50% of the land surface has been transformed by direct human action, with significant consequences for biodiversity, nutrient cycling, soil structure and biology, as well as climate. They argue that more than half of all accessible fresh water is appropriated for human purposes and that coastal wetlands have been significantly affected by human activities, with the loss of 50% of the world's mangrove ecosystems. Additionally, they note that up to 50% of marine fish stocks for which information is available are fully exploited, 15–18% are overexploited and 9–10% have been depleted or are recovering from depletion (Steffen et al, 2004: 258–9).

On the basis of extensive scientific data, the IGBP scientists argue that the earth system moved into a new stage, what they have termed the 'Anthropocene', in the middle of the 20th century. The move from the Holocene to the Anthropocene is very significant. It is not just another stage in human history, or an indicator that humans are having an impact on the world. Rather, the scientists are indicating that the earth has entered a new geological epoch where the dominant conditions on earth have changed significantly. The conclusion for the planet, its species and for humanity is startling. It has created, they argue, a 'planetary emergency' that will, within the next 100 years, see catastrophic ecological impacts on earth and its species move from the bounds of the possible to the probable.

What the scientists are suggesting is that as a result of human activity, the earth has left its natural geological epoch; forces unleashed by contemporary human societies now rival the great forces of nature itself and the planet is entering an unknown future (they call this 'planetary terra incognita'). In a 2015 update of their 2004 report, they concluded that nine out of the 12 'earth system' indicators that they identified had now moved beyond the bounds of Holocene variation, in other words, the data were no longer within the range of variability that we have had for the previous 12,000 years (Angus, 2016: 46). To emphasise the point, Friedrich et al (2016) have argued that 'Global mean surface temperatures are rising in response to anthropogenic greenhouse gas emissions … [to the extent that] … within the 21st century, global mean temperatures will very likely exceed maximum levels reconstructed for the last 784,000 years'. The conclusion, they suggest, is that the earth could be on course for global warming of more than

7 degrees Celsius within a lifetime. This is far higher than any previous estimates of potential global temperatures (Johnston, 2016).

The conclusions for the planet, its species and humanity are frightening. If human activity continues unabated on its present path, by the end of the present century, vast parts of the globe will be too hot to live in, freshwater resources will be depleted, coastal areas of habitation will be flooded by rising oceans and animal and flower species will increasingly die out. As the scientists point out, this is a planetary emergency and a threat to civilisation as we know it.

Water

Social workers in various parts of the world find themselves working in and with communities where access to water is becoming an important issue. According to Gonzalez and Yanes (2015), water is a trillion-dollar industry but – as a result of population growth, industrial production and ecological change – an increasingly scarce one that may well become the source of military and political conflict in the years to come.

In Palestine, for example, social workers in Palestinian villages have been part of campaigns to stop privatised Israeli water companies from diverting supplies away from the communities and farms that the water aquifers have served for centuries. Since the war of 1967, when Israel took control of the Jordan Valley, the River Jordan and the Golan Heights, Gonzalez and Yanes suggest that the 'manipulation of thirst' has been a strategy employed by the Israeli state to heap pressure on the Palestinians of the West Bank and Gaza.

Capitalist ecocide

The scientists at the IGBP rightly identify the impact that human activity has had, and continues to have, on the earth system. However, that human activity does not exist in a vacuum; rather, it exists within a concrete socio–economic system. Our current relationship with the environment and the earth system is shaped by the needs and drives of modern capitalism. As Moore (2015: 2) argues: "'The economy" and "the environment" are not independent of each other. Capitalism is not [simply] an economic system; it is not [only] a social system; it is [also] a way of organizing nature'.

In 1848, Marx and Engels wrote the *Communist manifesto*, where they heap praise on the way in which capitalism had 'revolutionised the forces of production'. Capitalism is a dynamic system of commodity production that has fundamentally altered our relationships to each other and the world around us. It has harnessed many of the forces of nature and utilised them in the relentless drive for profit maximisation. In the process, it has created the potential for us to meet human need in innumerable ways, for example, it is certainly possible for us to eradicate poverty and to ensure that everyone has enough food to eat each day, that people have appropriate living conditions and sound homes, and that everyone has access to appropriate jobs and forms of labour. However, under capitalism, these possibilities remain unfulfilled. The unplanned and chaotic nature of capitalist production is geared to meeting not the needs of the many, but the profits, desires and goals of the few. Furthermore, the drives of capitalist competition mean that the earth's resources are exploited, used and abused – without due consideration to issues of sustainability and ecological destruction – as sources of profit and wealth generation. According to Heede (2014), just 90 global companies have caused two thirds of man-made global warming emissions.

The exploitation of natural resources and the burning of fossil fuels during the earliest phase of industrial capitalism marked the starting point of human-induced climate change. The spread and impact of capitalism across the globe in the post-Second World War era (during the period of the long post-war boom from 1947 to 1971) – often under the label of 'national development' or 'communism' as much as 'free market capitalism' – marked the point where we entered the Anthropocene.

To satisfy its unquenchable thirst for profits, capital has spread across the world – it is now a truly global system – and as part of this process, it has burnt ever-greater quantities of fossil fuels, produced greater quantities of greenhouse gases, dammed waterways, mined and altered water deltas, deforested and domesticated land, pumped chemicals into the soil, altered river flows, and exhausted much of the ocean's fish stocks – all in the interests of profit maximisation. It is also a system that is riven by wars, and as the 20th century progressed, chemical, gas and nuclear weapons – alongside the impact of more traditional weaponry and military equipment – have all left their mark on humans and on the earth system (McCarthy, 2016).

This is not to suggest that capitalist companies have deliberately and consciously set out to inflict such harm on the planet – climate change and the move to the Anthropocene have been the unintended by-product and consequence of the carbon economy within which capitalism is embedded. However, capitalism is a system of 'many competing capitals', of ruthless competition, in which individual units of capital put their interests for profit above all else. This means, however, that any attempt to control, for example, the emission of greenhouse gasses that is perceived to interfere with the process of accumulation is likely to be resisted. This has been referred to as the '*ecological tyranny of the bottom line*: when protecting humanity and plants might reduce profits, corporations will always put profits first' (Angus, 2016: 114).

To emphasise the point, the magazine *Industry Week*, whose strapline is 'advancing the business of manufacturing', produces a regular list of the top 1,000 companies. In 2015, they noted that 'Petroleum & Coal Industries dominate the IndustryWeek 1000 list not only by capturing seven of the top 10 spots, but by landing 135 companies on the list, 45 more than the No. 2 industry' (Panchak and Szilagyi, 2015). The top six global corporations (in terms of revenue) were (in order): (1) China Petroleum and Chemical Corp; (2) Royal Dutch Shell; (3) Exxon Mobile; (4) Petrochina; (5) BP; and (6) Oil and Natural Gas (India) (Panchak and Szilagyi, 2015).

In the term used by Ian Angus (2016: 203), the modern world represents a form of 'capitalist ecocide' – uncontrolled and unregulated capitalism is driving the planet towards a frightening and uncertain ecological and planetary future. This also indicates that unfettered capitalism is a barrier hindering the actions that need to be undertaken to protect the plant. Ultimately, we need to establish a social system that works in harmony with the earth system, but in the short term, we need to bring pressure to bear on governments and corporations to ensure that we can mitigate, to some extent, the worst outcomes of climate change.

If the scientists at the IGBP are right, we have already entered the Anthropocene. That cannot be reversed, but what we do will determine what the Anthropocene is like. As Angus (2016: 207) argues, we need to slow capitalism's 'ecocidal drive', act immediately to drastically cut greenhouse gas emissions, commit to renewable energies and move towards the rapid elimination of industries – such as arms production and factory farming – that create human and planetary harm. He suggests the following six 'essential immediate changes':

• the drastic and enforceable reduction in the emission of greenhouse gases;
• the development of clean energy sources;
• the provision of an extensive free public transport system;
• the progressive replacement of trucks by trains;
• the creation of pollution clean-up programmes; and
• the elimination of nuclear energy and war spending.

These demands are, by necessity, political. However, as a profession committed to human emancipation, human need, human rights and social justice, the social work profession needs to engage with contemporary discussions of climate change, environmental justice and the Anthropocene because they are, at heart, about the fundamental change affecting the lives, needs and demands of people and communities.

Two food projects in the UK: Fareshare and the Food Cycle

In Britain, it is estimated that 3 million tons of food is wasted each year while 8.4 million people, the equivalent of the entire population of London, are struggling to afford to eat (Cafiero et al, 2016). This is a reflection of increasing food prices (between 2005 and 2013, food prices increased by 43.5% in the UK), increases in general household costs, stagnant wages and irregular working, changes to the social security system, and growing poverty and inequality. In response to these developments, two projects in Liverpool, UK, attempt to combine a commitment to issues of food waste, climate change and food poverty into their practice.

Fareshare is a national organisation that saves food destined for waste and sends it to charities and community groups, who transform it into nutritious meals for vulnerable people. The food that is redistributed is fresh, of good quality and 'in date' surplus from the food industry. In 2015, Fareshare redistributed enough food for 18.3 million meals across the UK. They distributed food to breakfast clubs for children in poor areas, to homeless hostels, to community cafes and to domestic violence refuges – places that provide support to vulnerable communities, as well as lunch and dinner.

The Food Cycle in Liverpool is part of a national food waste network that aims to use 'waste food' to serve nutritious three-course meals to those who find themselves in food poverty. The project in Toxteth, Liverpool, is based in a local church (though the organisation has no religious affiliations) and opens as a community cafe one night each week. The group has one full-time worker whose job is to work with local food shops and supermarkets to get access to 'waste food', undertake fundraising and apply for funding, raise awareness about food poverty and the environmental impact of food waste, and work alongside local campaigns to highlight food issues. The cafe opens each Wednesday and is open to all – offering a free three-course meal to those in need.

Social work in the Anthropocene

The international definition of social work continues to identify the profession as one that should work towards 'enhancing human well-being', 'promoting social justice' and 'sustainability', and working with 'people in their environment'. The scale of the environmental crisis discussed earlier means that we are likely to face increasing situations where people's lives will be disrupted by extreme weather events and their communities will be threatened by the impact of pollution, or where they may struggle to find appropriate food and water resources. In these circumstances, more people will be forced to leave their homes and become – for the short or long term – climate refugees (Demirbilek, 2016). Yet, to date, most social work academics and professionals have not fully considered how these environmental justice themes can be embedded within professional practice.

Part of the reason for this, as Gray and Coates (2013: 357) argue, reflects the roots of social work in the Enlightenment philosophies that shaped the modern era:

> social work as a profession began at a time when science was revered and Western societies adhered to notions of a mechanistic universe, industrial and agricultural innovation, and the spread of capitalism. The impact of human actions on the environment was largely beyond consideration within a worldview where people were largely understood to be in control of their own destiny.

While this is true, it is also the case that many early social workers were concerned with the impact of urban environments on poor communities and that community-based approaches to social work have always had a concern with 'environmental issues' such as bad housing, pollution and poor living and urban conditions. Furthermore, in much of the Global South, such concerns have never fully moved off the social work agenda. In India, for example, social workers have a long and honourable history of engagement with communities and social movements fighting for their social and environmental rights in areas designated as ripe for damming (Jensen, 2004). Nevertheless, as more radical and 'structurally oriented' approaches to social work have been marginalised within the profession, so the space for consideration of the impact of global climate change on people and communities has narrowed. Indeed, as Philip and Reisch (2015: 472) argue, social workers 'tend to regard the environment as the context for practice instead of a dynamic component of people's lives'. Such realities have led Hawkins (2010: 68) to point out that:

> Social work must extend [its] ... mission to include environmental justice, the human right to live in a clean, safe, and healthy environment. The world's most poor, vulnerable, and oppressed people often live in the most degraded environments and have no control over resources. The important connections between social work, sustainability, human rights, and environmental justice in our contemporary world need to be more clearly articulated.

Dominelli (2011, 2012) argues that the profession needs to develop its research base because, given its professional framework, it is 'well placed to contribute to climate change policy discussions and interventions' (Dominelli, 2011: 430), while McKinnon (2008: 266) argues that 'social work has the opportunity to be part of the solution rather than an uninvolved bystander to the emerging environmental predicaments'.

In the work of McKinnon (2008), Hawkins (2010), Dominelli (2011, 2012), Gray and Coates (2013), Philip and Reisch (2015) and Demirbilek (2016), we are starting to see social work theorists addressing the social consequences of climate change and theorising over our 'knowledge base that links social work practice with universal human rights, environmental justice, and sustainable development [and that] will help them to envision the world as a more just and humane place' (Hawkins, 2010: 79). However, what might a social work with environmental justice at its heart look like?

Social work in Kasimode (Chennai, India) in the aftermath of tsunami

Kasimode is a large, overcrowded slum that sits as part of the northern dock area of Chennai, the capital of Tamil Nadu, India. It covers 1 square mile and is home to over 20,000 people (Lavalette, 2009). India is a country of vast inequalities. In the suburbs of Chennai, there are large gated communities where English is increasingly the language of choice. The wealth and opulence in these areas is comparable to that which you would see in the affluent parts of any city in the world. Yet, Chennai is also a city dominated by slums, by people sleeping on the streets or at their place of work, and by desperate people begging for survival. The World Bank estimates that 456 million Indians (42% of the total Indian population) now live under the global poverty line of US$1.25 per day. This means that a third of the global poor now reside in India.

In Kasimode, the people travel to work in the city or work on the fishing boats that are based there. Yet, despite the fact that most people work, they live in desperate poverty. The fish are sold for a few rupees on the landing areas before being driven away by 'merchants' to factories and expensive restaurants in the city. Kasimode is a place of immense poverty: the living and sanitary conditions in the slum are desperate; the electricity regularly fails; the streets are rarely swept; there are few government services in the area; and there is one poorly equipped school and one tiny community centre.

Kasimode was hit by the devastating tsunami that struck the Bay of Bengal on 26 December 2004. Although less than 20 people were killed, over half the houses were destroyed and washed away. There is now significant evidence to suggest that both the Indian government and the state authorities of Tamil Nadu knew that the tsunami was approaching on that fateful day – yet they did nothing. Indeed, some harbour suspicions that the authorities hoped that the tsunami would 'deal' with some of their 'problem communities'. The authorities and police force regularly attack slum areas. They destroy houses and turn families out onto the streets. The former slum areas are then handed over to property developers for housing, office or factory development.

In the days that followed the tsunami, the relief efforts in the poorest areas were totally inadequate and large amounts of international aid 'disappeared' before it could get to the front line. In these circumstances, it is not surprising that there is a very deep-seated suspicion of anything to do with the Indian state – for the Indian poor, it is obvious that the state does not work in their interests.

Given the hardship of daily life, you might think that the people of Kasimode would be too consumed with the struggle for survival to engage with political life. However, these are not a defeated people. The slum hosts a range of social and political movements fighting for the rights of slum dwellers – and local social workers are embedded within these campaigns.

In the central community centre, social workers – drawing on broadly Ghandian principles – work to support the community in ways that meet their material needs and support their political campaigns fighting for their rights. Social workers have been: involved in setting up a local food co-op, which brings good-quality food to local residents; supporting the fish workers, who are in the process of setting up their own union co-op to set up a small smoking factory; involved in various campaigns to fight for Dalit rights, the rights of disabled slum residents and of the poor more generally.

Social work for environmental justice in practice

By way of a conclusion to this chapter, this final section looks at some examples from practice where social workers are starting to work with communities to focus on environmental justice issues.

Disasters

As we enter the Anthropocene, we are increasingly likely to face extreme weather and climatic events that will impact on people and their communities. According to Dominelli (2012), social work has an important role to play in the aftermath of a 'natural' disaster or in the aftermath of an extreme weather event as the 'organisers and managers' of aid and relief efforts. There is no doubt that social work skills can, and have been, useful in such situations – as in the flood situations in the UK discussed earlier, for example. She notes examples where social workers have travelled to disaster zones in the aftermath of hurricanes, floods, earthquakes and droughts, where they establish shelters for people who are forced to evacuate their homes,, manage food distribution, address issues of trauma and provide aid. In these circumstances, social workers fill the need for emergency management that focuses on people instead of the needs of insurance companies. There is no doubt that social work skills can play a vital role in such circumstances. Nevertheless, while social workers have some useful skills, these need to be developed and enhanced – and taught on relevant training programmes.

As we think about building our knowledge base in this area, we need to recognise that 'natural disasters' also shine a light onto the kind of society within which we live and force us to address wider issues (Lavalette and Ioakimidis, 2011a). Disasters pose immediate questions: who has been killed and who has been saved? How can we best meet the immediate needs of survivors? Is the existing social and political structure a help or a hindrance to the relief efforts? We should not be surprised to recognise that different groups in society are likely to answer these questions in different ways.

In *The shock doctrine*, Naomi Klein (2007a) offers various examples of where in the face of such 'natural disasters', multinational corporations and powerful economic and political interests see the events as an opportunity to promote 'economic restructuring' and cement their position within the hierarchy of social relations in the society in question. She gives some examples: 'After a Tsunami wipes out the coasts of Southeast Asia, the pristine beaches are auctioned off to tourist resorts.... New Orleans' residents, scattered from Hurricane Katrina, discover that their public housing, hospitals and schools will never be reopened' (Klein, 2007b).

By way of contrast, Rebecca Solnit suggests that in the midst of disasters, we get a glimpse of what she terms a 'paradise built in hell'. She argues that while:

> Disasters are ... terrible, tragic, grievous ... [and] not to be desired ... [they] drag us into emergencies that require that we act, and act altruistically, bravely, and with initiative in order to survive or save neighbours.... The positive emotions that arise in those unpromising circumstances demonstrate that social ties and meaningful work are deeply desired, readily improvised, and intensely rewarding. (Solnit, 2009: 6–7)

There is no simple answer to whether a society suffers a post-disaster 'social shock' or a 'paradise built in hell', but in a range of recent disasters – from Hurricane Katrina (2005), to the Haitian earthquake (2010), to Hurricane Sandy (2012) – social work intervention has been at both the official level (through state agencies and non-governmental organisations [NGOs] working in the relief field) and through the work of popular social work interventions where social movement activists and grass-roots social workers have combined to meet the needs of communities and individuals in the most desperate circumstances (Ioakimidis and Lavalette, 2016). As Herbert-Boyd (2007: 5) notes:

> Crises force individuals and [social work] professionals to examine their role in the social order, and they can be a catalyst for effective community development, progressive social policy and social change. Conversely, they can lead to conservatism, fear and the maintenance of the *status quo*.

As we develop our environmental justice social work practice tools, we will benefit from working closely with, and listening to, social movements and communities as they develop responses to disaster and crisis situations.

Advocacy

Representing individuals and communities and working alongside them to promote their rights is central to advocacy-based models of social work. In April 2016, the Texas-based Energy Transfer Partners initiated a US$3.7 billion project to establish an 11,720-mile pipeline (the Dakota Access pipeline) to transport fracked crude oil from the Bakken oilfield in North Dakota to a refinery near Chicago. It is proposed that the pipeline will carry 470,000 barrels of crude oil per day (Levin, 2016).

Fracked oil threatens the environment in numerous ways and continues to feed the fossil fuel economy and its attachment to greenhouse gas production. The pipeline emphasises the priorities of fossil fuel capitalism and threatens significant environmental and ecological damage. The proposed route went through lands of historical significance to the Standing Rock Lakota Sioux Nation, including sacred burial grounds, and was seen as a direct threat to both the tribe's water supply and the Missouri river. By the end of 2016, 90 Native American nations had converged on Standing Rock and the Native Americans had garnered significant global support for their campaign to stop the fracking, stop the pipeline and protect the Sioux lands and water sites.

The pipeline, therefore, was a threat to the environment, gave further support to the fossil fuel economy and trampled over indigenous rights in North Dakota. The response of the Native American nations was to launch legal challenges, invite the United Nations (UN) to investigate abuses of indigenous people's rights, launch several peace camps and undertake a range of protests to block the construction as it moved towards the sacred burial lands (Levin, 2016; Levin and Woolf, 2016). In response, US federal forces attacked protestors (who called themselves 'water protectors') with dogs, arrested hundreds and imprisoned them in cages.

Social workers and youth workers were involved in the Standing Rock movement. Youth workers were centrally involved in organising the marches and protests (Levin and Woolf, 2016). Social work educators were involved in offering advice regarding legal challenges, and practitioners associated with the Boston Liberation Health Group were on the ground offering support to those affected by the police action and the protest events.

Pollution

According to the United Nations Children's Fund (UNICEF), 300 million children live in areas with 'extreme air pollution', where toxic fumes are six times international guidelines (Rees, 2016). The UNICEF report suggests that these figures contribute to 600,000 child deaths a year, that poor children are most at risk and that the data emphasise that 'climate change threatens the well-being of children' (Rees, 2016: 10).

The increasing volume of cars and attachment to fossil fuels and other greenhouse gases is at the heart of the pollution crisis. In poor parts of the world, communities are often reduced to burning rubbish and waste, which produces 'highly hazardous' toxins. From a children's rights and human rights perspective, dealing with pollution is an essential part of establishing good community and individual health and well-being.

In Kasimode in Chennai, India, social work practitioners work alongside the community to improve living conditions for the community. Kasimode is a large urban slum near the city's docks. The conditions are very poor – housing is overcrowded, water and sanitation facilities are basic or non-existent, and waste and refuge disposal is very haphazard and infrequent. The practitioners are shaped by broadly Gandhian approaches to community engagement. They work through a local community centre on a range of projects to promote the interests of children and families. This includes clean-up campaigns of the local environment and community organising attempts to address waste and sanitation issues. There is a very clear understanding that such campaigns improve people's health, well-being and life expectancy while also improving the environment.

Food

Each year, roughly one third of all the food produced in the world is wasted. This amounts to about 1.3 billion tons of food waste per year. This means that vast resources used in food production are used in vain, and that the greenhouse gas emissions caused by the production of food that gets lost or wasted are also 'emissions in vain'. The per capita food waste by consumers in Europe and North America is 95–115kg/year, while this figure in sub-Saharan Africa and South/South-east Asia is only 6–11kg/year (Gustavsson et al, 2011). As Gustavsson et al (2011: 1) argue:

> The issue of food losses is of high importance in the efforts to combat hunger, raise income and improve food security in the world's poorest countries. Food losses have an impact on food security for poor people, on food quality and safety, on economic development and on the environment.

The Real Junk Food Project is a UK national network of pay-as-you-feel (PAYF) cafes. The community cafes intercept food that would otherwise go to waste from supermarkets, restaurants and a number of other sources, and turn it into healthy meals for anyone and everyone on a PAYF donation. The network self-identifies not as a 'food poverty' network, but as a 'food waste' network. Part of their mission is to engage with communities and raise awareness about the ecological and social costs of food waste.

Water

> Observational records and climate projections provide abundant evidence that freshwater resources are vulnerable and have the potential to be strongly impacted by climate change, with wide-ranging consequences for human societies and ecosystems. (Bates et al, 2008: 3)

Water rights are an issue of growing concern across the globe. Fresh water is drained, dammed, polluted, diverted and fought over, and poor communities often find themselves dealing with the consequences. In 2016, community activists in Flint in the US had to take emergency action to deal with a water crisis. In April 2014, the city authorities began using water from the Flint River without treating it for corrosive pollutants. The result was that lead appeared in the public water supply. Ingesting lead is dangerous for anyone, but it is especially damaging to children and pregnant women, with long-term effects including hearing problems, delayed foetus growth and harm to the brain, kidneys and other essential organs.

Research shows, however, that good nutrition and calcium can help mitigate the impact on children with elevated lead levels. Given this, community activists worked with the local farmers' market to try and ensure that Flint's poor communities were supplied with good-quality fruits and vegetables, and activists from Michigan State University set up cooking classes to teach participants to prepare meals with the lead-fighting foods:

> Various other community groups ... joined the lead-fighting effort ... the market hosted a program sponsored by the National Basketball Players Association (NBPA) and the non-profit FlintNOW. On the last day of school, 8,000 Flint public school children received 'nutrition backpacks' containing a mini basketball, information about nutrition and lead, and three $5 gift certificates to the Flint farmers' market. Additional funding from the Detroit Pistons [the city basketball team] matched each $5 gift certificate with another $5 – bringing the total to $30 worth of free food. (Hardman, 2016)

Conclusion

To date, social work has not paid as much attention to the impact of climate change on the environment and on humanity as it should have. Climate change is creating a range of environmental and social problems that will most significantly impact our most vulnerable communities. Social workers will increasingly have to deal with the consequences of environmental degradation by meeting people's needs in new, complex and unpredictable circumstances. We need to develop our knowledge base, we need to develop our practice skills and we need to embrace the demands of environmental justice in our theory and practice.

Part Three
Debating the politics of social work today

EIGHT

A new politics of social work?

Introduction

Radical social work is often associated with an understanding of society based on Marxist ideas, above all, the idea that we live in a society in which the central division (though clearly not the only division) is class. While that tradition has been important in shaping radical social work theory and practice both in the 1970s and currently, it has not been the only source of critical thinking within social work. Feminist and anti-racist approaches, for example, have also been influential, as have approaches based on identity politics more generally (essentially, the idea that only those experiencing a particular form of oppression can either define it or fight against it). While postmodern and post-structuralist approaches have had less influence in social work than in other academic disciplines, in Australia, Canada and, especially, the US, they have shaped much of the critical social work literature.

In previous publications, we have sought to provide an assessment of different strands of critical social work thought including postmodernism, post-structuralism and identity politics, as well as exploring the roots of oppression and alienation. Rather than repeating the arguments presented there, we would refer readers to these earlier writings (Ferguson and Lavalette, 1999; Ferguson et al, 2002; Ferguson, 2008; Lavalette, 2011). Rather, our intention here is to look at what are often new takes on older questions.

As an example, two prominent social work academics, Mel Gray and Stephen Webb, have suggested that current developments in political theory and political philosophy, notably, the work of Nancy Fraser, Axel Honneth and Alain Badiou, 'have the potential to galvanize a new politics of social work by innovatively reworking agendas on social justice and solidarity, of political possibility, and transformative ideas relating to universal emancipation and freedom' (Gray and Webb, 2013: 4). They go on to provide a list of thinkers whom they see as having a contribution to make to the formation of what they call a 'New Social Work Left', which includes, *inter alia*, Slavoj Zizek, Jacques Ranciere, Chantal Mouffe, Jean-Luc Nancy, Antonio Negri, Peter Hallward, Costas Douzinas, Gianni Vattimo, Susan Buck-Morss, Alberto Toscano, Roberto Esposito and Giorgio Agamben.

Some of these names also pop up in another recent collection of writings that aims to revisit anti-discriminatory and anti-oppressive practice, drawing primarily on the work of Michel Foucault but as the editors also note:

Although the work of Foucault is forefronted, there are a range of other theoreticians manifest in this book including Derrida, Badiou, Butler and even Althusser who, as a Marxist, might have been considered too 'modern' for such a post-structuralist/postmodernist text. This theoretical focus enables theoretical depth, similar to an oil-painting with its many-layered profundity. (Cocker and Hafford-Letchfield, 2014: vii)

There are undoubtedly positive aspects to these developments. First, the insistence of Gray and Webb, among others, that social work is a *political* project is welcome contrast to a mainstream social work literature that frequently eschews politics and presents social work as primarily a therapeutic, practical or technical enterprise. Second, with all their differences, what the thinkers listed share is a spirit of resistance to neoliberal capitalism, a spirit fuelled, in part, by a global anti-capitalist movement that emerged out of the protests against the World Trade Organization in Seattle in 1999 (Held and McGrew, 2002; Callinicos, 2003; George, 2004). Third, engaging with new ideas is crucial if the critical and radical social work tradition is to thrive and develop. Theory and practice cannot be set in stone.

However, these developments are not without difficulties. For a start, rather than 'many-layered profundity', there is, to put it at its mildest, a real danger of eclecticism in lumping together thinkers who often start from very different theoretical and political premises. Gray and Webb, for example, hold up as representative of the new politics a conference that took place in London in 2009 entitled *The idea of communism* (Douzinas and Žižek, 2010). While it is true that all of those involved were united in seeking an alternative to neoliberal capitalism, they did so from very different starting points. They included, for example: Terry Eagleton, a fairly orthodox classical Marxist, one of whose recent publications was entitled *Why Marx was right*; the maverick Slovenian philosopher Slavoj Žižek, whose political positions in recent years have included support for Donald Trump in the 2016 US presidential election and, more recently, a highly ambivalent response to the issue of refugees fleeing war and famine; and Alain Badiou, a leading French philosopher, who began his political life as a Maoist and, despite all the evidence to the contrary, still appears to view the Chinese Cultural Revolution as a key emancipatory event in human history. While these thinkers share some areas in common, their differences are at least as important. While fresh ideas are always to be welcomed, it is difficult to see quite how a 'new politics of social work' that has any coherence or consistency can emerge from such an eclectic (and frequently highly abstract) group of thinkers. That said, insofar as there is a theoretical convergence between them (and, here, thinkers such as David Harvey and Terry Eagleton are notable exceptions), it tends to be around a set of themes sometimes labelled 'post-Marxist'.

Post-Marxism is a current of thought that came into existence in the 1980s, though its origins may be said to lie in the ideas developed in 1970s' France by Jacques Derrida and Michel Foucault. Its founding text, which we shall discuss in some detail later, is often identified as *Hegemony and socialist strategy* by the Argentinian scholar Ernesto Laclau and his partner and collaborator Chantal Mouffe (Laclau and Mouffe, 1985).

It would be inaccurate and unfair to characterise all those included in Gray and Webb's list, let alone many others working in the critical social work tradition, as 'post-Marxist'. Some have never claimed to be Marxist, some continue to see themselves as Marxist, and some left Marxism behind a long time ago. Others, such as Alain Badiou, reject the label but share several of its key assumptions. As his biographer comments:

> If Badiou both rejects any direct articulation of politics with economics and tolerates a degree of reliance on the state, in what sense does his project still merit the Marxist label? Badiou recognizes no single subject of History, no global historical movement, no priority of the mode of production – not even the ultimate political primacy of class struggle per se. (Hallward, 2003: 239)

His conclusion is that 'Badiou's work must figure as part of the "eclectic", antisystemic trend of much Western social and cultural theory since the early 1970s' (Hallward, 2003: 239).

Whatever their differences, some of the themes shared by several of the writers cited earlier – a view of Marxism as essentialist or reductionist; a rejection of any 'privileged' role for the working class; and a search for alternative agents of change, including social movements and intellectuals – are also the core themes of post-Marxism. These ideas also form a kind of 'common sense' among many of those working within the critical social work tradition.

Given the likelihood that many social work practitioners (and many social work academics) will be unfamiliar with these thinkers and their concerns, it is tempting to dismiss these debates as irrelevant to the realities of practice. This is an understandable response and we are certainly not suggesting that the influence of post-Marxist thinking on social work theory and practice is the central issue confronting the social work community at the present time. That said, ideas matter and do filter their way down to the front line of practice, often through social work education or more indirectly. One of us recalls visiting a children and families agency in the east of Scotland some years ago where a social work practice educator confidently informed a student that recent findings in neuroscience had proved beyond doubt that the first three months of a child's life were crucial and that social work intervention with children or parents after that period was largely futile (for a more balanced account of the findings of neuroscience and their implications for social work, see Wastell and White, 2017).

In addition, Laclau and Mouffe's ideas have recently taken on an additional if unexpected political and ideological significance as an important influence on the thinking and strategy of the leaderships of Syriza and Podemos, the new radical Left parties in Greece and Spain (Hancox, 2015). For both of these reasons, these ideas merit our consideration. The first part of this chapter will therefore outline some of the key themes of *Hegemony and socialist strategy*. The second part of the chapter will offer a critique of these ideas, while the final part will assess the extent to which post-Marxist perspectives more generally can provide a firm foundation for a New Social Work Left.

Post-Marxism: key themes

In a recent reassessment of the putative heirs of the Italian Marxist Antonio Gramsci, Perry Anderson has provided a useful outline of the ideas of Laclau and Mouffe, who are among those who claim to be working in the Gramscian tradition:

> Together, in 1985, they published *Hegemony and Socialist Strategy*, bringing post-structuralism boldly to bear on the Marxist tradition, in political sympathy with what had been Eurocommunism, but in theoretical outlook now declaratively post-Marxist. Reviewing the history of the Second and Third Internationals, they concluded that both had remained trapped in the illusion that ideologies corresponded to classes, and historical development led by economic necessity to the triumph of socialism. What neither had been able to resolve was the existence, not only of divisions within the working class as the carrier of this supposed necessity in the shape of the revolutionary subject of history, but also of non-capitalist classes that did not form part of the working class.... The way forward was now to scrap all residues of class essentialism and drop any idea of a war of movement. Rather than interests giving rise to ideologies, discourses created subject-positions, and the goal today should not be socialism but a 'radical democracy', of which socialism would – since capitalism bred relations of undemocratic subordination – remain a dimension, not the other way round.

Here, Anderson provides a succinct summary of some of the key themes of post-Marxism: first, a rejection of what Laclau and Mouffe call 'class essentialism', above all, the notion that the working class has any 'privileged' role as an agent of societal transformation; second, a denial of any link between the dominant ideas in society (eg racist ideas) and material interests and conflicts between classes (instead, there is 'the autonomy of discourse'); and, third, a view that the goal of the progressive Left should not be the total transformation of society in the direction of socialism (however conceived), but rather the radical extension of democracy. Each of these themes will be considered in turn.

Class essentialism

First, there is the rejection of what Laclau and Mouffe refer to as 'classism' or 'class struggle essentialism' and its replacement by antagonisms based around gender, race and other divisions:

> What is now in question is a whole conception of socialism which rests upon the ontological centrality of the working-class, upon the role of the Revolution with a capital 'r', as the founding moment of the transition from one society to another, and upon the illusory prospect of a perfectly unitary and homogeneous collective will that will render pointless the moment of politics. (Laclau and Mouffe, 2014 [1985]: xxii)

The idea that the working class, insofar as it even exists, no longer has any role to play, let alone a central or 'privileged' role, in changing society has been repeated so often over the past four decades, not only by right-wing ideologues, but also by thinkers on the Left such as Eric Hobsbawm and Guy Manning, that it has taken on the status of a truism. In a discussion of agency, Webb and Gray, for example, remark almost in passing that 'This absence of agency is a structural effect conditioned by the disappearance of a politically influential working-class' (Webb and Gray, 2013: 215).

Now, it is undoubtedly true that the shape and composition of the working class has changed considerably in recent decades. It is also true that the level of class struggle in some countries, notably, Britain, is at a historically low level. However, is it really accurate to characterise this as 'disappearance' (Ferguson et al, 2002)? In Britain, for example, the economy has experienced structural change since the end of the Second World War, with a decline in the manufacturing sector and an increase in the service sector. Jobs in the service industries have increased by 45%, from 14.8 million in 1978 to 21.5 million in 2005, while those in manufacturing have fallen 54%, from 6.9 million to 3.2 million over the same period (Smith, 2007).

It is a mistake, however, to see this as a 'decline', let alone a disappearance, in the working class. For one thing, even in Britain, one in seven workers is still employed in manufacturing industry. As Smith (2007) notes:

> These workers often work in large and well-organised workplaces like engineering, car manufacturing and food production. Although their numbers have fallen, those workers who are still employed have become more and more productive and in some senses more powerful. Take, for instance, the UK car industry. Over the last 30 years there has been a huge fall in the numbers of workers employed in the industry. However, car production has barely fallen. At the height of UK car production in the 1970s Britain produced about 1.7 million

cars a year. By 2005 it had only fallen to 1.6 million a year. New technology means that one car worker can produce eight times what their predecessors could 30 years before.

It seems more accurate, then, to talk about a *restructuring* of the working class in response to the needs of capital. For example, the need for a highly skilled and educated workforce in the post-war era has resulted in a massive expansion of education in most West European countries, resulting in the employment of more teachers and lecturers. That investment requires, in turn, a reasonably comprehensive health service to ensure that these workers remain productive. Furthermore, in order to address the social and emotional needs of these workers and their families (as well as ensuring that they do not behave in disruptive or damaging ways), a social work and social care workforce is required – hence the massive growth in the service sector in many countries since the Second World War (Ferguson, 2014).

In turn, this has resulted in what the American Marxist Harry Braverman (1974), in his classic *Labour and monopoly capital*, called 'the degradation of work in the 20th century'. In other words, groups of workers such as civil servants, teachers, lecturers and social workers who, at one time, were seen as 'middle class' and enjoyed both considerable status and autonomy in carrying out their work are increasingly subject to the same working conditions and forms of supervision as other workers (Ferguson and Lavalette, 1999; Harris, 2003). That process has intensified in recent years as a result of the imposition of the New Public Management practices associated with neoliberalism. The consequence is that groups of white-collar workers who previously thought of themselves as being superior to manual workers will now often belong to trade unions and see themselves as part of the working class. So, for example, the British Social Attitudes Survey for 2016 found that the majority of Britons identify as working class even if they have stereotypically middle-class jobs. The survey found that although just 25% of people now work in routine and manual occupations, 60% of Britons regard themselves as working class. Nearly half of people in managerial and professional occupations identify as working class (Butler, 2016).

On a global scale, Filmer's detailed analysis of global employment in the mid-1990s found that out of a total of 2,474 million people who participated in the global non-domestic labour market (and excluding members of 'the new middle class' – managers, supervisors, etc), some 700 million could be defined as workers (working for a wage or salary), with one third employed in manufacturing and two thirds in services (health, education, transport, etc). Taking their dependants and retired workers into account, this suggests a global working class of between 1.5 billion and 2 billion (Harman, 2009: 331–2). In fact, more recent figures suggest that the figure is now around 3 billion (Panitch and Albo, 2014) – hardly a disappearing class!

None of this, of course, is to deny that there are serious and legitimate questions to be asked about the capacity of the working class in the 21st century to play a central role as an agent of social transformation. Nor does it mean that workers will therefore automatically challenge capitalism or even have progressive ideas. In the next section of this chapter, we will explore the relation between people's material position and their ideas. What the preceding discussion suggests, however, is that, on a global scale, far from having disappeared, the working class is now bigger than it has ever been, both geographically and also in including within its ranks millions of white-collar workers who would previously not have considered themselves working class. As Jack Shenker has shown in his eye-witness account of the revolution against Hosni Mubarak's neoliberal Egyptian state in 2011, that class continues to play a central role in the struggle for a different world, even if that struggle is too often marked (as in Egypt) by terrible setbacks as well as by great victories:

> Workers were at the forefront of the days of fighting that had enabled the revolution to reach this point: those killed by Mubarak's troops on the days of rage included a welder, a plumber, a cement factory mechanic, a stone mason, a shoemaker and a microbus driver. The Egyptians most directly afflicted by structural adjustments had brought protest from the margins into the core of the capital. Now, as the eighteen days rumbled on, they swept revolution back out again from Tahrir [Square, in central Cairo] to workplaces up and down the country; on the final days before Mubarak crumbled, workers in the transport, petroleum, steel, fertilizer, cement, textile, printing, military production and many, many other industries came out on strike to apply a final dose of pressure on a broken dictatorship, pressure which sealed Mubarak's fate. (Shenker, 2016: 226)

'All the world is discourse'

In the previous section, we argued that, empirically, not only does the working class exist, but it is also numerically larger than it has ever been in its history. There is, however, a second question that is no less important, namely: even accepting that the working class has not disappeared, is that class capable of becoming a revolutionary force, an agent of social transformation? To what extent, in Marx's own formulation, is the working class as a class *in itself* capable of becoming a class *for itself*? How, in other words, can the working class move from its current non-revolutionary consciousness to a point where a majority – or, at the very least, substantial numbers – of workers see the need to overthrow capitalism?

Within the Marxist tradition, the ideas that people hold are seen as being shaped by two factors: first, their material circumstances and day-to-day experience; and, second, the ideas that are promoted by the ruling class, the main aim of which is to reinforce the status quo, for example, by suggesting that the world we live in is the best of all possible worlds or by diverting discontent onto scapegoats such as minority ethnic groups or homosexuals. The best exploration of this relationship between ideas and class society is contained in Antonio Gramsci's discussion of what he called 'contradictory consciousness', which we shall address more fully later.

Post-Marxists see things very differently. So, not only do Laclau and Mouffe deny any relationship between people's material circumstances and the ideas they hold, but they also appear to deny any reality outside language or discourse. The editors of a recent social work text on anti-discriminatory practice define discourse as meaning 'A body of statements organized in a regular and systematic way which claim to represent the "truth" or promote dominant narratives in order to provide the rationale and justification for following subsequent rules' (Cocker and Hafford-Letchfield, 2014: 75). As the reference to dominant narratives suggests, in practice, the term is often used by writers within the critical social work tradition to explore and critique ideas and practices that maintain forms of oppression, such as the biomedical model or assumptions about the role of women within the family.

While critical discourse analysis can be useful in terms of deconstructing dominant assumptions and terminologies, as well as exposing the assumptions that underpin them (see, eg, Cowden and Singh's [2007] discussion of the language of 'user involvement'), from the perspective of developing an anti-oppressive social work practice – and, more widely, challenging social injustice – it suffers from three main limitations. First, there are philosophical objections, specifically, the question of the relationship between language and material reality. For Marx and Engels, arguing against the idealist philosophers of their own time, material reality was primary. One can abolish the 'idea' of gravity but that will not prevent things from falling down! As we have seen, however, the post-Marxists, like the Young Hegelians almost two centuries earlier, reverse this relationship. Thus, Laclau and Mouffe (2014 [1985], p 93) argue that 'Our analysis rejects the distinction between discursive and nondiscursive practices. It affirms ... that every object is constituted as an object of discourse, insofar as no object is given outside every discursive condition of emergence'.

In his critique of *Hegemony and socialist strategy*, Norman Geras (1987: 66) has demonstrated the absurdity of this kind of thinking:

> However frequently these may be denied, either in high philosophical argument or in popular assertion, a pre-discursive reality and an extra-theoretical objectivity form the irreplaceable basis of all rational enquiry, as well as the condition of meaningful communication across and between differing viewpoints. This foundation once removed, one simply slides into a bottomless, relativist gloom, in which opposed discourses or paradigms are left with no common reference point, uselessly trading blows. The most elementary facts of existence become strictly unthinkable without the aid of more or less elaborate theoretical sophistries. Was not the pre-human world 'an objective field constituted outside of any discursive intervention' – or did it

have to await the appearance of humanity to 'construct' it? And even today, 'several currents of contemporary thought' notwithstanding, are there not realities of nature, both external and human, which are not merely 'given outside' every discourse ... but the material precondition of them all?

John Molyneux makes a similar point in the context of a discussion of 'political correctness' and the overriding emphasis that some sections of the Left place on the use of 'correct' language:

> While it is true that the development of language gave an enormous boost to the development of consciousness and thought, and that the nature of language exercises an important influence on what is thought and what is 'thinkable', it cannot be true that there is no consciousness or thought prior to language or animals would be unable to hunt, cats would not find their way home, chimps could not engage in elementary tool use and babies would not be able to learn language. Nor is it true that language constructs or determines consciousness from nothing. If it were, the project of language reform would itself be inconceivable. There is an ongoing complex interaction between external material conditions, physical and psychological human needs, human social relations and human thought and language. Within this interaction social being – the combination of circumstances, needs and social relations – remains primary. (Molyneux, 1993)

Second, seeing ideas – and politics – as completely autonomous from any class or material base offers no way of understanding where these ideas come from, why particular ideas dominate at particular times or, most importantly, how ideas can change – or, rather, as Geras (1987) observes, it *does* provide a way of understanding but one that is far from new and one that could hardly be further from the Marxist tradition that Laclau and Mouffe claim to be developing:

> The suggestion ... that there is no stronger relation between socialism and the working class than there is between socialism and anybody else is an idealism ... run wild [which displays a] cavalier disregard ... in the name of discourse, for material realities, relationships and needs.

Third, the alternative to what Geras describes as this 'shamefaced idealism' does not need to fall back on vulgar Marxist notions of 'false consciousness', or Stalinist versions of 'banking' models in which ruling-class ideas are simply poured into the heads of workers and passively accepted. A much more nuanced and complex analysis of where ideas come from, how they can be changed and their relationship with material reality was provided by the Italian Marxist Antonio Gramsci in his concept of *contradictory consciousness*. Gramsci distinguished between two different types of consciousness that chaotically coexist in the heads of working-class people. On the one hand, there is what he called 'common sense', based on the ideas that are churned out on a daily basis by the tabloid press and by mainstream politicians. Typical examples would be the idea that excessive welfare spending is the cause of economic crises, or that immigrants are responsible for overcrowded health services. In reality, these are examples of what Marx called 'the ideas of the ruling class', ideas that legitimise the capitalist status quo and divide workers. Alongside these, however, are very different ideas that spring from people's direct experience, particularly in the workplace: the understanding, for example, that it is only by acting collectively that it is possible to stand up to the employer or to gain improvements in working conditions, or learning through the experience of being on strike that the media do not always tell the truth and that the police are not our friends. Gramsci called such ideas 'good sense':

> The active man-in-the-mass has a practical activity, but has no clear theoretical consciousness of his practical activity, which nonetheless involves understanding the world in so far as it transforms it. His theoretical consciousness can indeed be historically in opposition to his activity. One might almost say that he has two theoretical consciousnesses (or one contradictory consciousness): one which is implicit in his activity and which in reality unites him with all his fellow workers in the practical transformation of the real world; and one, superficially explicit or verbal, which he has inherited from the past and uncritically absorbed. (Forgacs, 1998: 333)

Gramsci's primary concern was with how 'good' sense could be purged of the stains of 'common sense', in other words, of how the working class could develop a genuinely collective consciousness free of racist, sexist and other backward ideas. For that to happen, he argued, based on his time as editor of a workers' newspaper during Italy's two 'red years' of 1919–20, two things were required.

The first was the experience of collective struggle, in the course of which, workers would become aware of the role of the media, the employers and the state, on the one hand, and their own collective power, on the other. Such struggles did not automatically lead to a change in ideas, but they created the conditions in which such a change could take place. Second, for political as well as ideological purposes, a revolutionary organisation was necessary, made up not of left-wing academics (though some choose to join), but rather of 'organic intellectuals', workers who through experience, study and discussion had developed a revolutionary worldview that enabled them to act as more effective leaders in their workplace or community.

Many examples could be given of the ways in which, in the course of collective struggle, when so-called ordinary people begin to develop an awareness of their own power, reactionary ideas – sexist, racist and homophobic – begin to change. Here, two will illustrate the point.

The 2014 movie *Pride* is set during the British miners' strike of 1984. It tells the true story of the formation of the first Lesbians and Gays Support the Miners group (LGSM), the relationship they developed with the striking mining community in South Wales, and the national impact they had. LGSM was formed after two gay activists decided to do a collection for the miners at the Gay Pride march in 1984. Having set about raising money, the group tried to make contact with the National Union of Miners but encountered an embarrassed silence. Determined not to be rebuffed, the group randomly chose a mining village in Wales and contacted its strike committee. So began a relationship that culminated in the astonishing and inspirational sight of a Welsh miners' brass band leading Pride in 1985 and the National Union of Miners voting in support of gay rights at the Trade Union Congress and Labour Party conferences the same year.

The second more recent example is from the early stages of the Egyptian revolution (or 'Arab Spring') of 2011 and shows how even the most deeply ingrained prejudices, in this case, religious prejudices, can be broken down when people are involved in a common struggle for a better world. In her eye-witness account, journalist and academic Anne Alexander (2011) described how just weeks after a New Year's Day church bombing rocked the port city of Alexandria, Egypt's religious tensions were set aside as the country's Muslims and Christians joined forces at anti-government protests:

> Making my way to Tahrir Square during the anti-Mubarak protests, a striking piece of graffiti caught my eye. Scrawled on the concrete pillar of a flyover was the symbol of a Muslim crescent embracing the Christian cross and the words: 'We are all against the regime'. During the big 'Day of Departure' protest in Tahrir Square last Friday, Coptic Christian protesters made a human chain around their Muslim brothers and sisters as they performed the noon prayers. Two days later, 'Martyrs' Sunday' was celebrated by Egyptians of both religions as an affirmation of national unity in struggle. On that day, a crowd had gathered in front of a sound system by the Mogamma government building on the eastern side of the square. A man in a jacket began to speak as chanting died away. 'He was someone from the church, a priest,' someone in the crowd told me. I was told: 'We are all in this together. Muslims and Christians.' Other people were listening and nodding. 'One hand, one hand,' the crowd roared.

Such changes in people's ideas and consciousness are not simply fortunate by-products of struggle; rather, as Marx and Engels (1845) recognised in 'The German ideology', they are an essential part of the process through which people become fitted to build a new world:

> Both for the production on a mass scale of this communist consciousness, and for the success of the cause itself, the alteration of

men on a mass scale is necessary, an alteration which can only take place in a practical movement, a revolution; this revolution is necessary, therefore, not only because the ruling class cannot be overthrown in any other way, but also because the class overthrowing it can only in a revolution succeed in ridding itself of all the muck of ages and become fitted to found society anew.

Intersectionality?

As well as the post-Marxist ideas discussed earlier, another important concept that has recently gained some traction in contemporary social work theorisation is the idea of 'intersectionality', a concept explored by Sarah Carr in the collection by Cocker and Hafford-Letchfield (2014). Carr's (2014) piece is primarily a focused critique of bureaucratic, administrative and managerialist approaches to anti-oppressive social work practice. Carr's (2014: 141–3) point is, rightly, that oppression has a detrimental impact on people's lives and cannot be reduced to a functional tick-box exercise carried out as part of the 'proceduralist culture' that shapes the routine of much social work engagement. Carr (2014: 143–4) is also critical of those perspectives that portray oppression as a permanent given or a fixed state – with 'permanent oppressors and perpetual victims'. In contrast, she argues that it can, and must, be challenged and that this must involve those that suffer at the forefront of structures of discrimination and oppression.

On all these points, we have little disagreement with Carr. The second decade of the 21st century has witnessed renewed struggles around the impact of oppression on people's lives, with campaigns against structural racism and police brutality (where key roles have been played by organisations such as Black Lives Matter and Stand Up To Racism), against the impact of austerity (where, in Britain, organisations such as Disabled People Against Cuts and Recovery in the Bin have been central) and for women's equality (with organised Slut Walks, Reclaim the Night marches and a renewed focus on abortion rights). As radical social workers, we celebrate these movements and the challenges they present to social work theory and practice. As we have emphasised in many of our writings over the years, radical social work has much to learn from immersing itself into social movement activity and confronting the issues, problems and dilemmas that such activity generates (eg Ferguson et al, 2005; Lavalette and Ferguson, 2007; Lavalette and Ioakimidis, 2011a).

However, Carr's piece claims that theories of intersectionality can clarify and enhance our understanding of oppression, and this is something that we wish to challenge. Notions of intersectionality have developed out of the work of black feminist writers Kimberle Crenshaw (1989, 1991) and Patricia Hill Collins (2009, 2013). The concept was developed by them as a critique of postmodern approaches to difference and a critique of some white feminist practice that, they argued, ignored and excluded the specific experience of black women in the movement. Audre Lorde (2000: 289), for example, writes that:

> By and large within the women's movement today, white women focus upon their oppression as women and ignore differences of race, sexual preference, class and age. There is a pretence to homogeneity of experience covered by the word sisterhood that does not in fact exist.

The attraction of intersectionality is that it points to a range of oppressions and to a common cause – to build unity against oppressive structures. In the work of Patricia Hill Collins, it also seems (in contrast to postmodern theories) to re-emphasise the importance of the socioeconomic analysis of inequality (Carr, 2014).

At the level of description, it can also usefully describe the reality of the issues that some people face. So, for example, for a social worker, it can be a useful reminder that the needs of a migrant, black, disabled woman for a particular service might be significantly different from other service users who are black but not disabled, for instance. However, the danger here, in the terms that Carr (2014) poses the issue, is that the 'tick-box' approach just becomes further extended within 'proceduralist practice'.

In any case, this descriptive use of intersectionality is not what Crenshaw meant when she used the term. Crenshaw first developed the concept after she used a metaphor of different roads (different oppressions) that 'crashed' when they met at the 'intersections'. In her case, she described her oppression as a woman and as a member of the black community, but at the 'intersection', when the two oppressions crashed into each other, the whole became greater than the sum of the parts. In other words, it was not merely an accumulation of oppressions, layered one upon another. Rather, the intersection produced something more: an integrated and compounded oppression as a black woman (where she was on the receiving end of racism from white women and sexism from black men). This is a powerful reminder that there is no necessary solidarity within oppressed groups – the way in which many French feminists have colluded with the French state's oppression of Muslim hijab-wearing women in their country is perhaps the most obvious recent example.

Here is a demand to consider the impact of class, race, gender, disability, sexuality, poverty and the way these interact to shape people's experiences. However, in its usage, there are two important consequences deriving from this. The first is that, as Carr (2014) notes, this approach often sits within Foucauldian ideas of power and its distribution, where every individual is inescapably part of a multiplicity of oppressive relationships – what Patricia Hill Collins (2013) calls a 'matrix of domination'.

For Foucault, power is not something that is primarily concentrated in the hands of capital or the state (as classical Marxists would argue): 'Neither the caste which governs, nor the groups which control the state apparatus, nor those who make the most important economic decisions direct the entire network of power that functions in a society' (Foucault, 1981: 95). Rather, power is distributed throughout society and exists in all social and interpersonal relationships. This has some very important strategic conclusions. Foucault (1981: 96) argues, for example, that there is, by necessity, a 'multiplicity of points of resistance' and so:

> there is no single locus of great Refusal, no soul of revolt, source of all rebellions, or pure law of the revolutionary. Instead there is a plurality of resistances, each of them a special case ... by definition, they can only exist in the strategic field of power relations.

The consequence is that each of the oppressions and intersections come laden with notions of discrimination, penalty, individual privilege and interpersonal domination. As Patricia Hill Collins (2013: 234) argues: 'each one of us derives varying amounts of penalty and privilege from the multiple systems of oppression that frame our lives'.

However, rather than draw us together, to consider what we have in common and how we can work together collectively to confront and overcome a system of oppression, such perspectives tend to infinite division and separation as 'difference' and micro-relations of power are emphasised at the expense of commonality and solidarity. Here, the collective confrontation of structural inequalities and oppressions is replaced with individual solutions and demands that we each 'check our privilege' that is derived (perhaps unconsciously) for our social position in an intersectional world.

The second theme that comes from the literature on intersectionality is an emphasis on individual 'experience' and subjects' 'lived reality'. Within social work, one of the great advances of recent years has come about from the demands of the service user movements that their voice be heard and given full consideration within social work processes, and that 'knowledge through experience' is a vital source for discovering, tackling and addressing all manner of institutional practices that reinforce discrimination. However, theories of intersectionality remain locked in broadly postmodern concerns with essentialist knowledge that prioritises individual experiences. The problem with this is that it removes our ability to make judgements between competing 'experiences'. Here is one rather extreme example. In 2013, the then Mayor of London (now UK Foreign Secretary) Boris Johnson wrote an article telling us that we should 'stop bashing the rich':

> I neither resent nor disapprove of [London's super-rich] ... quite the reverse.... we should stop bashing the rich.... On the contrary, the latest data suggest that we should be offering them humble and hearty thanks. It is through their restless concupiscent energy and sheer wealth-creating dynamism that we pay for an ever-growing proportion of public services.... And yet they are brow-beaten and bullied and threatened with new taxes, by everyone from the Archbishop of Canterbury to Nick Clegg [at the time the Deputy Prime Minister of the UK]. (Johnson, 2013)

Johnson's rather ludicrous point was that the super-rich were a picked-upon minority – a point not even worth responding to. However, the more serious point in our discussion here is that if the super-rich self-define as a 'picked-upon minority' bashed by government, media and the population at large, how can we disagree if we prioritise individual 'experience' as the key definer of oppression?

In contrast, classical Marxist approaches to oppression see it as rooted in the systems of structured inequality that shape capitalist (and, more generally, class) societies. Thus, individual experiences are important, and shed light on the impact of oppression and discrimination, but this does not, in itself, tell us where that oppression originated, its social function and how it has been 'socially constructed' within the specific context of modern class society. This does not mean that classical Marxism ignores oppression. From the writing of Marx and Engels onwards, the classical Marxist tradition has attempted to offer analysis of the roots of women's oppression, of racism and of disability discrimination, for example, and has tied these theoretical approaches into a political struggle to counter oppression and fight for liberation. It is the question of liberation that brings us back to the question of agency.

'The point is to change it!': the question of agency

Finally, we return to the question of agency. In a world dominated by 'capitalist realism' in which, as Frederic Jameson (2003) has observed, people often find it easier to envisage the end of the word than the end of capitalism, the fact that there is a resurgence of interest in utopian thinking, driven by the idea that 'another world is possible', is to be welcomed. Envisioning a different world, however, is not enough: the key question is how do we get there and what role, if any, can a critical and radical social work play in this process? What force, or forces, in society have the interest, power and capability to challenge the seemingly impregnable citadels of neoliberal capitalism? These are questions that Gray and Webb seek to address in the concluding part of their search for a 'new politics of social work':

> The question of a militant political agent – Foucault's subject of resistance – antagonistic to the supposed inevitability and universality of capitalism – sits at the very centre of this seemingly bleak state of affairs…. The question is just as pressing for social work as it is for any other agency of progressive change. Indeed, any attempt to construct a new politics of social work must confront the question directly. (Gray and Webb, 2013b: 215)

Indeed it must. Unfortunately, their attempts to confront that question do not take us very far. Positively, they are highly critical of the contribution of both postmodernism and identity politics:

Some social work researchers are fascinated and seduced by the aura of postmodernism. Let us be clear, postmodern politics is not the slightest bit concerned with equality, justice and poverty. Postmodernism is not cool. The vagaries found in the postmodern social work literature, and often associated with 'identity politics', celebrations of diversity and the Othering of difference is a self-defeating exercise that can only lead to a political blind alley. (Gray and Webb, 2013b: 218)

Less positively, they offer no real alternative. Thus, the possibility that a radical alternative might inhere in Marxism is dismissed with a 1978 quote from the Polish ex-Marxist philosopher Leszek Kolakowski suggesting that 'Marxist literature, although plentiful in quality, has a depressing air of sterility and helplessness' (cited in Webb and Gray, 2013b, p 218). This is lazy thinking. For a start, Kolakowski's view of Marxism, understandably given his experience of life and persecution under 'actually existing socialism' in both Poland and the Soviet Union, was that brutal Stalinism was the logical outcome of Marxism. In similar fashion, Geras (1987, emphasis in original) notes that, while based on very different experiences, 'Laclau and Mouffe go so far as to conflate the whole of Marxism with its Stalinist, or authoritarian, forms by writing sometimes as though democracy was just *external* to it'.

While the equation of authoritarian Stalinism with Marxism was a standard feature of Cold War thought (and a very convenient one for the ideologues of Western capitalism), in reality, within the classical Marxist tradition, democracy and socialism have been seen as inextricably linked. As Geras (1987) argues in his critique of Laclau and Mouffe, there have always been those on the Left who:

> knew – what the authors have evidently forgotten – and sought to strengthen and extend, the principles and sources within the Marxist tradition which, against both the forms and the pretensions of 'actually existing socialism', spoke insistently of socialist democracy: in Marx, from his earliest philosophical writings to the Paris Commune; in Trotsky, from the pluralist arguments of Our Political Tasks to the fight against Stalinism; in Luxemburg – incandescent – practically everywhere; and in Lenin, and elsewhere besides. The cover of darkness, either intellectual or contemporary political, was not a necessary excuse.

Insofar as they do offer an alternative agency, it seems to be based on a combination of a 'politics of refusal', protest groups, the creation of community spaces and envisioning an alternative to capitalism. All of these are important but they hardly constitute an adequate vehicle for challenging a global system that is threatening to destroy within decades the very conditions for life on this planet (Klein, 2015).

Conclusion: 'Anything goes'

In a brutal assessment of the propositions of Laclau, Mouffe and post-Marxism in general, Perry Anderson (2016) has written:

> The linguistic turn of the theory, in common with its late-twentieth-century vogue in general, proposed a discursive idealism severing significations from any stable connexion with referents. Here the result was to detach ideas and demands so completely from socio-economic moorings that they could in principle be appropriated by any agency for any political construct. Inherently, the range of articulations knows no limit.

Similarly, a philosophy that not only fails to address the material realities of the lives of those who rely on social work services – realities of poverty, inequality and oppression – but also ignores or denies the ways in which these realities shape their lives, their behaviour and their consciousness, is of little value to a social work that is seeking to make sense of these realities in order to change them.

NINE

The case for a social justice-based global social work definition

The social work profession promotes social change, problem solving in human relationships and the empowerment and liberation of people to enhance well-being. Utilising theories of human behaviour and social systems, social work intervenes at the points where people interact with their environments. Principles of human rights and social justice are fundamental to social work. (IFSW, 2002, cited in BASW, 2012)

Social work and social justice: current definitions and debates

Part of the current ideological and political discussion about social work is reflected in the crucial question 'How do we define what we do?'. In fact, the different ways in which international organisations, states and movements have engaged with this debate reveal the ideological tensions that divide the social work project. This is not simply a theoretical or abstract debate: defining social work has an impact on what happens in practice. Prescriptive, 'clinical' or apolitical interpretations of social work have profound effects on the realities on the ground. When they stress individualistic and moralistic interpretations of social work, they tend to reduce social work to a technical activity in the most formal ways. Official definitions that feed into law, academic curricula and job descriptions can create artificial professional boundaries limiting space for relationship-based and politically engaged social work. The 2002 International Federation of Social Work (IFSW) and International Association of Schools of Social Work (IASSW) global definition (see opening quote), in particular, which has been the most widely recognised one, usually results in direct changes in regional and country-specific legislation regarding the nature, description and professional boundaries of social work practice.

Definitions do matter: the experience of social work in Colombia

In 2016, the Colombian Ministry of Education made use of the United Nations Educational, Scientific, and Cultural Organization (UNESCO) definition of social work in order to reclassify social work as a health profession, thus challenging its social science basis and openly demanding that curricula be devoid of sociology and discussions about social movements (Ministerio de Educación Nacional, 2016). Colombian social work has historically been influenced by the tradition of liberation theology, and Colombian practitioners and educators were central to the development of the reconceptualisation movement in Latin America.

Moreover, social work in the country has been important in the development of a peace and social justice movement demanding an end to the decades-long conflict. The decision to reclassify the profession as a technical activity, using the UNESCO definition, aimed at rooting out the most radical and political traditions of social work. After weeks of mobilisation, sit-ins, nationwide protests and an important wave of solidarity from other Latin American countries and the IFSW, the Colombian government backtracked and reinstated the social science basis of social work. The movement developed organically, adopting and quickly uniting most social work departments across the country under the banner 'Mi trabajo es SOCIAL' ('My work is SOCIAL').

In 2014, the IFSW and IASSW adopted an 'updated' global definition after a consultation that lasted for almost five years. We will examine later the political and professional debates that underpinned this change. In our view, the latest definition has been a step backwards in terms of its aspirations for a social justice-based social work as it includes mutually conflicting terms and concepts (see later) that eventually render the definition unworkable and meaningless. The adoption of an eclectic and mixed social work definition has rather obscured the profession's commitments to social justice and can potentially weaken efforts to promote a genuinely anti-oppressive and emancipatory practice.

It is our contention that social work practitioners, service users and students need to engage with this discussion meaningfully and contribute towards a definition of social work that reflects the profession's commitment to social justice. In this chapter, we assess the main aspects of the current debate, focusing on the concepts and contradictions that have informed discussion. In particular, there is an emphasis on the importance of understanding the contested history of social work and the main tension between 'social care' and 'social control' as a way of comprehending the complexity and significance of this debate.

Exposing and challenging the structural causes of personal problems

Social work as an activity is located in a rather unique position: at the point of interaction between the state and the most vulnerable people in society. Therefore, front-line practitioners in much of the world routinely witness some of the most brutal effects of structural inequalities on people who, voluntarily or involuntarily, interact with social services. Despite the fact that social workers deal on a daily basis with the brutality of a socio-political system based on a profoundly illogical and disastrous distribution of wealth, this knowledge and experience has not always fed into our theory and practice. Most importantly, in societies where discussions about poverty and inequality are customarily silenced, speaking truth to power about clients' experiences needs to be the basis of an ethical, value-based and politically engaged social work practice.

Modern capitalist societies are characterised by one of the most overwhelming paradoxes in human history. On the one hand, tremendous advances and innovations in technology, industry and research have made it possible for humanity to generate unparalleled wealth. The global annual output of wealth is nowadays sufficient to feed, educate and provide good standards of life for the whole population on this planet. A research report commissioned by Oxfam (2013) revealed that the annual income of the richest 100 people is enough to end global poverty four times over. On the other hand, the main characteristic – and tragedy – of modern capitalism is the immense concentration of such wealth in the hands of a minuscule minority of individuals and businesses. In 2006, a study by the World Institute for Development Economics Research revealed that the bottom half of the world's population owns almost 1% of all global wealth (Davies et al, 2006), while Oxfam (2013) indicates that this trend is not confined to rich countries:

> In the UK inequality is rapidly returning to levels not seen since the time of Charles Dickens. In China the top 10% now take home nearly 60% of the income. Chinese inequality levels are now similar to those in South Africa, which is now the most unequal country on earth and significantly more unequal than at the end of apartheid. Even in many of the poorest countries, inequality has rapidly grown.

As this report indicates, even though inequality is not a phenomenon unheard of in the history of societies, its extent, pace and ferocity in the age of neoliberal capitalism is unprecedented. Apart from the startlingly unequal distribution of resources at a global level, one has to consider the widening inequalities within individual country contexts.

The impact of structural inequality on individuals and communities alike is nowadays very well documented. Recent epidemiological studies (Wilkinson and Pickett, 2009; Stuckier and Basu, 2013) have confirmed that the more unequal societies are, the more likely it will be for the poorest people to die younger, suffer mental health problems, be affected by chronic illnesses, be exposed to criminal activities, experience racism and face exclusion from education. In short, neoliberal capitalism, a brutal system based on exploitation and the unequal distribution of resources, is responsible for most of the reasons for people to interact – whether voluntarily or involuntarily – with social services. Social work clients arrive at social services not as a result of their own individual inadequacies, weakness or misfortunes. Neither is it because they are idle, malicious and greedy people who want to benefit from an overgenerous 'nanny state' – as the dominant neoliberal rhetoric misleadingly claims. Poverty, inequality and unemployment are unambiguous determinant factors forcing the most vulnerable people into exclusion and alienation. Nevertheless, as we argue later, much of mainstream social work has turned a blind eye towards this reality.

Pathologisation, stigmatisation and surveillance have been the norm rather than the exception in much of the history of top-down welfare (Jones and Novak, 1999). Omitting to highlight the structural causes of 'private ills' leaves space for 'blaming the victims' rather than addressing the roots of the problem. A genuinely non-stigmatising and anti-oppressive social work practice needs to be organically rooted to the principles of social justice. Therefore, it is imperative that the global definition of social work reflects the struggle towards alleviating the structural causes of 'private ills' and does not legitimise the perpetuation of social injustice towards the people we work with. As we explain later, in the history of social work, there has been considerable tension between those social work approaches that have endorsed the need for social justice, on the one hand, and 'top-down' bureaucratic approaches whose main concern has been with the policing of poor families and individuals, on the other.

'Nunca Mas!' ('Never again!'): exposing oppressive practice and the dark history of social work

In 2010, the disciplinary committee of the College of Social Service Professionals in Argentina decided to expel and take legal action against a social work practitioner on the basis of his politically unethical practice during the period of General Videla's military junta in that country (1976–83) (see Alayón, 2010). The practitioner had collaborated with the regime in promoting one of the most horrible examples of oppressive and punitive social work practice. While working at the Central Hospital of Neuquén, he gained access to injured students and other activists who had participated in the movements for democratic change. Under the pretext of professionalism and claiming confidentiality, he 'caseworked' the patients, collecting information about their political actions. He then routinely passed all this sensitive information to the junta's intelligence services (Intelligence Battalion 601). Several of the activists involved in the case were arrested and tortured. The Argentinian Federation of Professional Associations of Social Service Workers (FAAPSS) justified its decision to expel and take legal action against this individual by stating that 'It is important to promote the politics of memory, truth and justice reflecting the commitment of Argentinian social workers to the process of social emancipation for the peoples of Latin America' (Martins, cited in Alayón, 2010). Such swift and powerful action against social workers who had collaborated with the regime and engaged with oppressive practice is part of a broader movement in Argentina that demands justice through the exploration of truth with reference to the 'dark' years of the military junta; the movement has adopted the short but powerful motto 'Nunca Mas!' ('Never again!').

The open debate within Argentinian social work is rather unique in the context of the profession. Social work as a profession has long suffered from 'selective amnesia' (Reisch and Andrews, 2002). Literature about the history of the profession is scarce and shallow, emphasising the almost 'inherent' benevolence of social workers and their sacred commitment to 'do good'. Mainstream histories about the origins of social work are monotonously structured around the brilliance of charitable individuals, known as the 'pioneers', who were committed to developing expertise in order to pull 'dysfunctional' people and families out of their misery (for a critique of this approach, see Lavalette and Ioakimidis, 2011b). These kinds of historiographies are filled with didactic cliches about the kind-hearted 'do-gooders' and the readily available tool kits of social workers that seem appropriate to nearly all known 'dysfunctions' and 'problems'. They hardly ever mention the fact that social work is the direct product of political calculations and that the creation of the profession has always been bound to contradictory and politically opposing ideologies. References to the broader political context, the class nature of the pioneers' activities and the internal contradictions within the profession are almost non-existent (Jones, 2012). Moreover, the existence of a rich radical social work tradition that developed in different parts of the world, and that rejected top-down professionalism in favour of developing social alliances that could bring about social change, is wiped out of most mainstream social work histories. The direct outcome of such selective amnesia seems to be the creation of a distorted, unrealistic and disabling self-imaginary, detached from social realities. Historically, such lack of self-awareness has rendered social work a questionable activity in much of the world.

Tragically, the refusal to understand the political context within which social work operates has led to some of the darkest chapters of the profession's history. Despite the fact that research on the 'dark side' of social work is scarce, the findings available are strong enough to suggest that behind the pretext of 'political neutrality', social work has been involved in some of the most terrible cases of political oppression. The examples that we discussed in Chapter Four of this book are only a few illustrations of social work's systematic involvement in political practices contrary to the ethos of the profession's public declarations and statements. Unless we reflect on our history (even the grimmest chapters of it) and acknowledge the clear political nature of social work activity, we are incapable of developing a global social work distinctly and unconditionally committed to social justice. It is imperative that any global definition of social work reflects this dynamic process of politically repositioning the profession towards social justice and clearly opposes epistemologically vague, abstract or apolitical notions of social work. Otherwise, we risk the possibility of re-experiencing some of the ugliest cases in social work history.

Recognising and protecting practitioners who fight for social justice

Ultimately, it is the behaviour, ideology and practices of front-line practitioners that determine whether social work is a 'worthy' or 'unworthy' activity, 'relevant' or 'irrelevant' to the service users and broader society. Since social work does not operate in a political vacuum, it is the way in which social workers endorse or challenge oppressive and unjust policies that resolves the historic contradiction between 'social care' and 'social control'. In short, the decisive question that social workers often need to answer is 'Which side are you on?'.

Fortunately, alongside the cases of oppression mentioned earlier, social work is entitled to boast some brilliant examples of steadfast commitment to social justice. These examples have been present since the very beginning of social work history, thus forming a long-standing radical tradition. In the UK, in opposition to the elitist and punitive agenda of the Charity Organisation Society – which transformed charitable activity to 'scientific' social work – a reformist tradition emerged around the 'settlement movement' (in the late 19th century). Social workers and volunteers involved in this movement placed emphasis on the material context of poverty and deprivation, hence challenging the elitist belief that the poor are inferior and inherently incapable of leading meaningful lives (Ferguson, 2008). Furthermore, the strengthening of trade unionism in the first three decades of the 20th century and its subsequent suppression by the ruling classes across Europe informed the creation of one of the most extensive networks of grass-roots politically committed social work. The Red Aid was an umbrella organisation that originated in Germany in 1919, and by the Second World War, its operations covered many European countries, including Austria, Poland, France, Greece, Sweden and the UK. The Red Aid not only emphasised the class divisions and inequalities prevalent in the capitalist world, but also adopted a clear militant stance towards alleviating the structural causes of inequality and poverty (Schilde, 2003). Most importantly, it provided support to groups and individuals who suffered from the criminalisation of political activism and were excluded from state-controlled welfare organisations. In practice, the Red Aid tried to combine multilevel support to political prisoners, refugees and their families with mobilising the 'masses' against oppression and injustice. Many of the 'interventions' and methods that mainstream social work discovered nearly 60 years later (such as 'advocacy and legal representation', women's rights and the use of contraceptives, political campaigning, non-judgemental moral and material support, and social education) originated from this radical tradition. These activities were based on class solidarity and were in opposition to the ethos and traditions of ruling-class charity. As Mentona Mosser, the founder of the first social work school in Switzerland and leading member of the Red Aid, explained, 'The bourgeoisie is never so repulsive as in those cases when they are doing charity work, "stinking" charity work' (cited in Hering, 2003: 90), while Clara Zetkin described the social work activities of the Red Aid as 'the aid squad of the class struggle' (cited in Schilde, 2003: 142).

Another large social justice-based tradition that has greatly influenced social work in parts of the world (Latin America in particular) is that of liberation theology. Suffice it to say that this tradition has also been excluded from mainstream social work textbooks and historiographies. Liberation theology emerged in the 1950s, blending the influence of the Christian faith in the region with the optimism for social emancipation of the oppressed embedded in the Marxist tradition (see Gerassi, 1973). In much of Latin America, the old colonial systems were not overthrown after independence, but only replaced by local corrupt and authoritarian elites, manipulated by imperialist powers. As the peoples of Latin America were disillusioned by the perpetuation of inequality, devastation and extensive exploitation, a distinct current of grass-roots social solidarity shook the conservative Catholic Church. This radical current focused its theory and *praxis* on two main elements: (1) the material and spiritual support of the oppressed; and (2) political 'conscientisation', a necessary stage in the process of broad political emancipation. The former was expressed through grass-roots community work, based on genuine class solidarity – not charity – while the latter took the form of open confrontation (often violent) against authoritarian states and large landowners. For liberation theologians, the idea that the poor had to humbly accept the harsh realities of their lives, hoping for spiritual redemption, was simply unacceptable and had to be challenged by any means available. Such an ethos was reflected in the famous 'preferential option for the poor approach' articulated by Gutierez (1971). This revolutionary tradition was tremendously popular in several Latin American countries (including Brazil, El Salvador, Paraguay, Argentina, Colombia and Chile) and led to the political transformation of social work (Norwood-Evans, 1992). The *'reconceptualisation'* movement in these countries is still highly influential and has historically generated powerful examples of genuine anti-oppressive practice, even when a wave of US-sponsored military coups devastated most of Latin America – Brazil (1964), Peru (1968), Bolivia (1971), Chile (1973), Uruguay (1973) and Argentina (1976) (see Allayon, 2005). Radical social work theory and practice in Latin America has emphasised the importance of a holistic view of the challenges that people experience in their lives, the primacy of understanding the material and political context of social work practice (conscientisation), the need to develop social alliances and partnerships based on democratic values and mutual understanding, and, finally, the importance of direct action in order to alleviate the structural causes of oppression. Paulo Freire, the leading educational theorist, specifically advocated for a social work practice based on political action (praxis) rather than professional elitism within social work. His remarks are timely and important in the context of debates around the global definition of social work:

> In this sense, therefore, the social worker, as much as the educator, is not a neutral agent, either in practice or in action. One of the inclinations that we sometimes have – and this is an offense, an illegality, that we imbibe in our technological society – is to think that the social worker is a very specialized person, a technician, who works in a compartmentalized technical area, and who has a sort of protection within this area, a sort of aggregate of rights, as a particular social group, to stand apart from the political battles of society. For me, this is impossible. It is an error. Social workers are compromised if they become convinced that they possess a technical expertise that is more to be defended than is the work of other workers. (Freire, 1990: 5)

At present, in the context of austerity policies across much of Europe, social workers have not only participated *en masse* in demonstrations in defence of the welfare state and social services, but also engaged with acts of direct social activism and political disobedience against government policies that violate human rights (Ioakimidis and Teloni, 2013). In this process, social work networks and national associations opposing the politics of austerity have used the existing definition of social work as a *tool* in their campaigning work. In several cases, the politically progressive content of the definition as well as the 'statement of ethical principles' adopted by the IFSW has provided the necessary justification and legitimisation for activist social workers to pursue radical practice even when they faced criminalisation and intimidation by their employers and the state.

Two notable examples of such practice come – not coincidentally – from countries 'bailed out' by the notorious international Troika of lenders (the European Union [EU], European Central Bank and International Monetary Fund [IMF]). One of the most malicious characteristics of the austerity imposed in several European countries is its absolute disregard of constitutionally protected human rights. Such disregard of the post-war 'social contract' is safeguarded by crude authoritarianism and justified on the basis of the 'law of necessity', often used in extreme circumstances in order to circumvent constitutional processes (see Pillay, 2011). Using such legal argumentation, in 2011, the Hungarian government passed a law making homelessness punishable by a fine or prison (BBC, 2011a). At a time when violent austerity had pushed more than 10,000 Hungarians into homelessness in Budapest alone, the government decided to outlaw poverty rather than dealing with the causes of it. Norbert Ferenzc, a social worker who belonged to a local radical social work network, played an active role in the campaign against state violence targeting the most vulnerable in society. He actively participated in demonstrations against the municipal ordinance that classified 'dumpster diving' as a misdemeanour, linked to the aforementioned law. His involvement in this campaign was considered by the police as 'incitement', a felony punishable by up to three years in prison. Ferenzc was eventually arrested and stood trial (SWAN, 2011b).

His arrest triggered an overwhelming international movement of solidarity among social workers. Thousands of practitioners, students and academics signed a petition demanding his immediate release. At this point, it is critical to highlight that legal and ethical justification of both Ferenzc's action and the international campaign in his support was based on the mandate to social justice stated in official documents of international social work organisations. The IFSW/IASSW definition and the Code of Ethics were effectively utilised in order to demonstrate that Ferenzc acted appropriately and in accordance with the guidelines of international social work organisations. The solidarity petition that was initiated by the Social Work Action Network and was signed by thousands of social workers stated that:

As a social worker, Norbert was following the International Federation of Social Work's definition of social work as an activist occupation that confronts social injustices. The Hungarian Code of Ethics for Social Workers also makes it clear that practitioners have a duty and a responsibility to inform the public of the growth of poverty and inequality and the state's responsibility to address these problems. We demand that all charges against Mr. Norbert Ferencz are dropped, as he was merely following his professional Code of Ethics. The Code states that 'social workers [should] facilitate change through their activities and professional stance' (Point 11) and that 'it is the social workers' responsibility, as well as a right and duty of the undersigned professional organizations, to call the attention of decision makers and the general public to their respective responsibility for the emergence of poverty and suffering as well as for their obstruction of the alleviation thereof'. (SWAN, 2011b)

Such arguments proved effective and the Hungarian Supreme Court eventually acquitted Norbert Ferenzc, in a case that clearly demonstrated the importance of using a social justice-based social work definition as a tool for defending social workers who fight injustices and work in partnership with service users.

Another similar case emerged in Greece almost a year after the arrest of Norbert Ferenzc. In December 2011, the Greek government, desperate to raise necessary funding for the recapitalisation of the banking sector (through a bailout), circulated a decree introducing a draconian 'urgent' property tax payable through electricity bills (Ioakimidis and Teloni, 2013). At a time of vast unemployment, such a tax particularly targeted the most vulnerable and those living below the breadline unable to pay any further taxes. This tax was flat and variations in income were not taken into consideration: even people on benefits had to pay. The fact that it was payable through an electricity bill guaranteed that people unable to afford this tax would face electricity cut-offs. The government, realising that the law was clearly unconstitutional and would be dropped at the Supreme Court, decided to use social workers to sugar-coat this measure. Social work practitioners were thus instructed to participate in committees that would 'assess' poor households in order to decide whether access to electricity should be cut off or not. In reality, the already-set targets in the national budget ensured that there was no space for meaningful assessments. Such an unethical use of social workers was met with fierce opposition. The Greek Association of Social Workers expressed opposition to this law (GASW, 2011), while the Greek Social Work Action Network (SWAN-Greece) and the trade union of local authority workers (POE-OTA) called for social workers to disobey the decree and consciously refuse to participate in these committees (Ioakimidis and Teloni, 2013). Once again, the global definition of social work and the IFSW ethical statement were utilised by social workers in order to justify their, potentially punishable, acts of civil disobedience against unethical and oppressive policies. The Greek Association of Social Workers circulated a statement vehemently rejecting the government's instructions while making reference to the global commitment of social work to social justice, 'the importance of the campaigning role under austerity and the profession's commitment to social change, social justices and universal social welfare' (GASW, 2011). Likewise, SWAN-Greece (2011; emphasis added) explained that:

> the international social work codes of ethics, recognizing that human suffering is constructed upon socially unjust policies and acknowledging that the idea of 'political neutrality' within social work is deceptive, *clearly define* the ethical commitment of social workers towards exposing and fighting against socially unjust policies and practices.

After the coordinated response of local authority social workers and the POE-OTA trade union, the government was forced to retreat. Even though the urgent tax went ahead, the idea of 'assessment committees' invoking social workers as means of implementing this policy was scrapped.

Across Europe, while similar examples of political action against the dismantlement of social services have occurred, the largest movement in defence of universal social welfare has emerged in Spain. Known as the Orange Tide and popularising the slogan 'No Cuts! Don't Shut Up!', the Orange Tide brings together thousands of social workers, welfare officers and service users. Once again, striking social workers based their struggle on their obligation to defend human rights and dignity, which derives, *inter alia*, from the current definition of social work (IFSW-Europe, 2012). The cases presented in this section clearly suggest that a withdrawal of a global definition unconditionally committed to social justice will not only weaken the profile of the profession, but also harm front-line social workers who experience prosecution due to their ethical and value-based practice.

Supporting indigenous movements and challenging the conservatism of cultural relativism

In the run-up to the Global Social Work Congress in Australia in 2014 that ratified the revised definition of social work, heated debate took place within the IASSW board. In one of these meetings, board members placed particular emphasis on a sentence stating that 'Underpinned by theories of social work, social sciences, humanities and indigenous knowledges, social work engages people and structures to address life challenges and enhance well-being'. While most members of the board – which is dominated by North American and European delegates – celebrated the innovation of acknowledging the 'importance of indigenous knowledges', some African board members seemed baffled and clearly thought otherwise. One of them stood up and in a state of frustration and disbelief asked the following question: 'So, what you are trying to say …

is that *you* represent the social sciences and *I* am the indigenous knowledge?'. This anecdote provides a striking example of the hugely paradoxical nature of the '*indigenisation question*' within social work. The epistemological and political complexity of this debate has allowed for the emergence and reproduction of some very conservative and patronising arguments masked by the obscurity of the fashionable term 'indigenisation'.

In recent years, there has been a resurgence of interest around this theme, mostly deriving from the broad region defined in the IASSW as the 'Asia-Pacific' (see, eg, Gray et al, 2008; Yunong and Xiong, 2008). Historically, the indigenisation paradigm originated from national liberation movements and the concept of 'Third Worldism', which gained momentum in international politics in the early 1970s (Atal, 1981). Much of the debate revolved around the issue of professionalisation and, in particular, concentrated on the question of 'transferability'. With the notable exception of Midgley (1981), who provided a groundbreaking analysis of the imperialist nature of international social work, mainstream literature at the time followed a largely developmentalist approach, attempting to provide narrow technical answers to the rather political question of 'transferability' (Shawky, 1972; Resnick, 1976; Walton and Abo El Nasr, 1988).

In the early 2000s, the domination of postmodern theories in the social sciences reinvigorated the indigenisation debate. Aided by the obscurantism of postmodern theorising, the 21st-century debate on indigenisation placed an almost exclusive emphasis on the centrality of culture. As Gray et al (2008: 8) suggest: 'Not only is social work itself a cultural construction but whenever we are attempting to make social work responsive to local contexts we are fashioning it in a cloth that is culturally embedded'.

One of the main deceptions of the indigenisation debate is its use of a language of 'resistance' even though, in reality, it promotes an implicitly conservative agenda. On the one hand, indigenisation seems to be dismissing nearly everything that derived from 'modernity' or that originated from the West, thus heavy-handedly conflating mainstream social work, for example, with the radical tradition of resistance and social movements – equating, in other words, modernity with oppression and exploitation. On the other hand, the unconditional glorification of local indigenous traditions and systems often presupposes the acceptance of rigidly unequal and oppressive hierarchies. Significantly, even though China and Japan (whose representatives appear to be active proponents of the indigenisation agenda) account for almost half of the IASSW membership base, the presence of Latin American schools is nearly non-existent. Consequently, the region with the richest history of the mobilisation of the indigenous population seems to be excluded from the current debates. One reason for that may be that the Latin American approach to liberation of indigenous peoples is diametrically opposite to the conservatism of the 'Asia–Pacific'. This is clearly reflected in the manifesto of the EZLN, the iconic indigenous organisation of the Chiapas, which instead of prioritising 'cultural differences' argues for the development of critical alliances and common struggles with the other oppressed groups in Mexican society:

> We are going to continue fighting for the Indian peoples of Mexico, but now not just for them and not with only them, but for all the exploited and dispossessed of Mexico … we are going to go about building, along with those people … a program of struggle, but a program which will be clearly of the left, or anti-capitalist, or anti-neoliberal, or for justice, democracy and liberty for the Mexican people. (EZLN, 2005)

Furthermore, the official 'Asia-Pacific' line of argumentation seems to undermine the importance of 'social change and social justice', focusing on the need for 'stability of society, harmony in relations, unique culture and traditions, responsibility' (Angten and Paulsen, 2008). Some have gone so far as to anecdotally claim that the concepts of social justice and human rights do not even translate into local languages (such as Mandarin) and others prioritise spirituality. Henrickson (cited in Angten and Paulsen, 2008) explains that 'We have agreed that spirituality needs to be part of the way social work understands itself and its purpose'.

These approaches are, in essence, conservative and seem to be representing an elitist understanding of social work in the context of Asia-Pacific. Their conservatism derives from the fact that they: (1) prioritise idealist understandings of the material context that affects the lives of individuals and communities, masking in this way the fierce inequalities and oppression that exists in the Asia-Pacific countries; and (2) do not seem to be representative of popular indigenous movements that struggle to transform these oppressive structures *in unison* with other social groups (like the indigenous movements in Latin America).

The question of spirituality is a complex one and, indeed, within specific contexts, bears relevance to influential faith-based approaches. It is worth focusing, however, on the cases of China and Japan, whose large membership base in international social work organisations allows them to elevate the idea of 'harmony and stability' over 'social change and justice'.

Over the last decade, the rapid development of the Chinese economy and the gradual endorsement of an 'open market' economy did relatively little to alleviate poverty and inequality in the country. In fact, urbanisation has led to massive waves of internal migration readily available to be used as cheap labour. By 2002, the number of rural–urban migrants exceeded 100 million and the emergence of a new rich entrepreneurial class, largely benefiting from cronyism and corruption, provided an excellent case study of the various processes that generate wealth inequality (Knight, 2013). While urban China experiences considerable wealth generation – fuelling a sharp rise in inequality – rural China is still trapped in poverty. The World Bank (2010) estimated that in 2010, almost 486 million people lived on less than US$2.5 a day. The recent natural disasters that affected rural China exposed the extent of poverty and underdevelopment, and forced the local press to recognise that 'The poverty and fragility that the earthquake has revealed are still pressing problems in China's rural areas and show that the country needs to expend more efforts to reach its target' (see: http://english. people.com.cn/90882/8222866.html).

Mainstream social work in China seems to be developing rapidly following a 'top-down' bureaucratic approach. The creation of social work has been effectively decided and designed at the higher levels of the state apparatus rather than demanded by the poorest and most vulnerable in society. According to Wang (2012), it was the 6th Plenary session of the Chinese CP [Communist Party] central committee that decided to construct 'a large strong team of social work professionals', the purpose of which was to ensure stability and harmony in society. Here, the concept of stability is presented in opposition to the popular struggles for social transformation towards a socially just society. In a country where poverty and inequality are still rife and past efforts to promote social change have been violently crushed, invoking the concepts of harmony and 'spirituality' in order to mask existing class tensions is inextricably linked to the effort to develop a depoliticised, government-controlled social work.

Interestingly, although never mentioned in mainstream social work platforms, let alone the international social work organisations, in China and Hong Kong, a dynamic current of radical social work practitioners and academics already exists, reflecting the class divisions and tensions of Chinese society. Their power and militancy was well represented when, during the 2010 Global Social Work Conference in Hong Kong, striking social workers and trade unionists formed picket lines near the conference venue and, concurrently with the main conference, organised a well-attended counter-conference entitled 'Reclaiming Progressive Social Work' (Ferguson and Lavalette, 2012). Afterwards, the group of radical social workers involved in this conference produced a manifesto stating that:

> we must launch a campaign for progressive social work and social welfare, and insist upon protecting the spirit of social work that is to promote human rights, justice, democracy and equality. We must resist any oppression against social welfare and its service users in order to establish a society that respects human rights and secures social justice. (PSWN, 2011)

Similarly, in Japan, an ESRC-funded series of seminars in 2009–10 found that:

> In contrast to some recent influential British literature which has portrayed Japan as a more equal, and therefore 'happier' society, Japanese colleagues highlighted the wide range of social problems to which neoliberal policies have contributed including very high suicide rates, family breakdown, social isolation and withdrawal. (Ferguson et al, 2011)

Moreover, the same report highlighted the impact of neoliberalism and managerialism on Japanese social work, with colleagues explaining that recent reforms have led to the erosion of social workers' autonomy, marking a significant turn towards neoliberalism.

There is much evidence to suggest that despite the fanfare that surrounds the primacy of harmony in the 'Asia-Pacific' region, scratching the surface would reveal a similar context of structural problems, class divisions and political contradictions rife in social work across the globe. A global definition that neutralises the commitment of social work to social change, emancipation and social justice will harm and disarm social work practitioners in this region in ways very similar to those of the 'West'.

Concluding remarks

The evolution of the definition debates throughout the history of the profession accurately reflects social work's ideological tensions and varying political agendas. The Global Definition adopted by the IFSW/IASSW in 2014 (see the following box), with its new emphasis on 'social cohesion', 'indigenous knowledges' and a let-out clause at the end that allows the definition to be 'expanded' as appropriate, is clearly intended as a compromise, generating an eclectic definition that can be interpreted in various 'convenient' ways. The current debate is reflective of political contradictions embedded in social work throughout its history. This chapter has focused on the contrasting political traditions and histories of social work and rejects the argument that social work can be a politically neutral activity. In fact, the history of social work suggests that in times of fierce inequality and sharp class divisions, 'neutrality' is, in fact, a conscious political stance: that of siding with the oppressors. Consequently, in the current climate of neoliberal domination and the erosion of civil rights, the adoption of a social justice-based definition could have provided front-line practitioners with the necessary tools and protection in order to defend the values and ethical commitments of the profession.

Different traditions, contrasting definitions

The following two definitions represent very different political traditions, scope and aspirations. The first one is the current global definition adopted in 2014. As we suggest in this chapter, the theoretical eclecticism underpinning this definition intentionally obscures the political dimension of social work. In contrast, the definition proposed by the Latin American Association for Teaching and Research in Social Work emphasises the importance of the 'social question' and the 'socio-historical' context of social work.

Global definition of social work (IFSW, 2014)

Social work is a practice-based profession and an academic discipline that promotes social change and development, social cohesion, and the empowerment and liberation of people. Principles of social justice, human rights, collective responsibility and respect for diversities are central to social work. Underpinned by theories of social work, social sciences, humanities and indigenous knowledge, social work engages people and structures to address life challenges and enhance wellbeing.

The above definition may be amplified at national and/or regional levels.

Definition proposed by the Latin American Association for Teaching and Research in Social Work, with the Brazilian Association of Teaching and Research in Social Work (2012–)

Social Work as a profession is positioned within the context of citizens and their interaction with the State; [these relationships] are shaped by the different socio-historical settings of the professional activity. It develops a social praxis and a set of socio-educational actions that focus on life's material and social reproduction from the perspective of social transformation. It is committed to democracy and the fight against social inequalities, by strengthening autonomy, participation and the safeguarding of citizenship for the achievement of human rights and social justice.

Conclusions: 'Making history'

In consideration of all these qualities, I would speak about one last quality of an intellectual and political nature that progressive social workers ought to cultivate, to develop, to perfect, in their practice and that is an understanding of what is historically possible. As I perceive history, it is not something that happens necessarily but something that will be made, can be made, that one can make or refrain from making. I recognize, therefore, the role of the subjective in the process of making or of being made by history. And this then gives me a critical optimism that has nothing to do with, on the one hand, a critical pessimism and an immobilizing fatalism; and on the other hand, nothing to do with history marching on without men, without women, that considers history outside. No, history is not this; history is made by us and we make it, we are made and remade by it. (Freire, 1988)

Introduction

In this book, we have explored the ways in which the roles and activities of social workers have been shaped by political and economic forces. Too often, such shaping has been a top-down process driven by political actors with their own interests and agendas and in opposition to the core values of the profession. What is also the case, however, is that there have been periods when social workers, often in alliance with wider social movements, have sought to create new forms of theory and practice based on opposition to oppression and to the economic and social forces that constrain people's lives. The radical social work movement that emerged in several different parts of the world in the early 1970s was one example. The reconceptualisation movement in Latin America, discussed in Chapter Five of this book, was another, in which the ideas of Paulo Freire, quoted earlier, played an important role.

Freire's injunction to 'make history' is particularly important for social workers at the present time. We began this book by noting some of the similarities between the world of the 1930s and the world today. These similarities, and particularly the rise of extreme right-wing political forces across much of Europe, should fuel a sense of urgency on the part of all those opposed to racism and xenophobia. However, our purpose in noting these similarities is not to create what Freire calls an 'immobilizing fatalism'; rather, it is to argue that this time round, the outcome can be different, depending on how we respond.

In 2004, two of us were involved in writing *Social work and social justice: A manifesto for a new engaged practice* (Jones et al, 2004). Our aim in writing the manifesto was to challenge the increasing influence of neoliberalism on social work practice and to begin to identify the 'resources of hope' out of which a new and more politically engaged social work could be created. More than a decade later and against the background of the political developments referred to earlier, the position of social work is, in some respects, more difficult and more challenging than it was back in 2004. However, what is also true is that the resources of hope are still there if only we look for them. It is still the case that out of the opposition to the dogmas and the priorities of neoliberal capitalism, a new social work radicalism is emerging. Practitioners across the globe are forging new forms of theory and practice that, though still fragile, contain the seeds of a different kind of social work. Here, we shall discuss some examples of these new developments.

Boston Health Liberation Group

The US has a long, if often neglected, history of social work radicalism, which suffered during the Reagan–Thatcher years in the same way as did radical social work elsewhere (Reisch and Andrews, 2002). In response to the inequality and scapegoating of the poor that have characterised the neoliberal era, however, and shaped by a range of social movements, from the post-Seattle anti-capitalist movement to Occupy Wall Street, the past few years have seen a revival of radical social work theory and practice in the US. One of the best examples of this is the Boston Liberation Health Group. In addition to campaigning activity, the Group has developed a model of practice and documented its use across a range of social work settings (Martinez and Fleck-Henderson, 2014). Its guiding principles are summarised by Dawn Belken Martinez as being:

- Holistic: situating individuals in their full matrix of personal structural, ideological and institutional determinants.
- Critical: refusing to accept neoliberalism and refusing to accept the notion that social work ought to subordinate itself to its social agenda.
- Empowering: seeking to liberate clients and social workers from the confusing belief that current conditions are inevitable and beyond our power to change, and seeking to support their becoming active allies of individuals and movements working for social change.
- Hopeful: rescuing memory of and valuing 'the collective human capacity to create change' (Reisch, 2013: 68; see also Martinez and Fleck-Henderson, 2014).

The Social Work Action Network

Founded at a 300-strong conference at Liverpool University in 2006, the Social Work Action Network's (SWAN's) activities have taken four main forms. First, as one recent mainstream historian of social work has noted, 'SWAN has held some very successful annual conferences, attracting numbers far beyond the reach of the

British Association of Social Workers or the College of Social Work' (Bamford, 2015). These conferences, held each year in different universities across the UK, have provided the main forum for discussing and debating national policy responses to issues affecting social work, such as austerity, privatisation and racism. They are typically attended by between 300 and 400 people, with a key feature being the role played by service users, both as platform speakers and as delegates. The conference also hosts the SWAN annual general meeting, which elects a national steering committee to coordinate activities between conferences.

Second, SWAN has been involved in a number of campaigns at both national and local levels. Nationally, these have included challenging the scapegoating in 2008 of social workers involved in the case of Baby P (Peter Connelly), a small child who died at the hands of his carers (Ferguson and Lavalette, 2009; Jones, 2014). More recently, SWAN has played an important role in critiquing the proposed 'reforms' of social work education by the current Conservative government, reforms that would undermine both the academic and ethical bases of the profession and would lead to the creation of a social work elite, an 'officer corps' more well-disposed to privatisation (SWAN, 2014). Locally, SWAN groups have engaged in a range of campaigns, including the defence of asylum seekers, opposition to the privatisation of children's services and challenging cuts to mental health services.

Third, 2013 saw the launch of *Critical and Radical Social Work: An International Journal*, published by an academic publisher. Although not formally linked to SWAN, the fact that the two co-editors were also founder members of SWAN and that many members of the Editorial Board are leading SWAN activists means that, in practice, the links are close. The journal has now established a wide readership and is providing a forum for the development of new thinking in critical and radical social work, with contributions from every continent, including Latin America.

Finally, one of the most exciting developments since 2006 has been the creation of SWAN groups in several countries other than the UK. There are now active SWAN groups in Ireland, Northern Ireland, Greece, Japan, Canada and, most recently, Denmark. Members of the Greek group have played a very active role in Patras and on various Greek islands supporting refugees during the current crisis, while in 2015, SWAN-Ireland members successfully challenged government attempts to reduce pay and conditions for newly qualified workers. SWAN activists have contributed to crucial global debates and intervened in international conferences and events. Most notably, during the Global Conference in 2014, SWAN members successfully moved a historical motion emphasising the Right of Return for Palestinian refugees. During the 2016 Global Social Work Conference in Korea, radical social workers were instrumental in supporting direct action from the Korean Solidarity Against Disability Discrimination group, who were violently removed from the stage in the opening ceremony. The intervention of SWAN activists helped ensure that the service user campaigning group was given space to address the conference and shed light on the impact of neoliberalism on disabled people in Korea (SWAN, 2016).

Sweden

As discussed in an earlier chapter, neither the Swedish welfare system nor Swedish social work has been immune from the impact of neoliberalism. A recent study of 'rationalization, responsibility and resistance' among social workers in that country begins by quoting one experienced worker as saying:

> Those of us who've been around for a while and know how we used to work, we keep getting into conflicts with social workers of this new dawn.... [T]oday, if I allow myself to categorize, you may divide social workers into occupational professionals and organizational professionals. And it's the organizational professionals who are rewarded. Because they follow rules, guidelines and never go outside the box ... you do your documentation and shut up. (Lauri, 2016: 1)

What is less known outside Sweden, however, is the level of resistance that there appears to have been to these developments. According to Lauri, during 2011 and 2012, several different networks of critical social workers were formed, including Critical Organized Social Workers (KAOSA), Social Workers for Social Action (SFSA) and Breaking the Silence (NBVT). He uses the latter as an example of these new networks:

> Founded in Stockholm, this group voiced protest over the disintegration of the social security system, and the deteriorating situation for clients that they were witnessing. They also pointed to a problematic organization of social work, lack of resources and untenable working conditions. Moreover, in the summer of 2012, hundreds of social workers gathered in the city of Gothenburg to hand over a manifesto to local politicians, *Calling for Social Welfare*, protesting against the heavy workloads and recurring budget cuts that they were experiencing, claiming that under current circumstances they could not deliver qualitative help, nor ensure their clients' legal rights. (Lauri, 2016: 1)

According to Lauri, there were media reports of similar protests in several other Swedish cities.

The New Approach Group, Hungary

On Friday, 4 November 2011, Hungarian social worker Norbert Ferencz was sentenced to three years' probation for charges of 'incitement against the public peace and a call for general dissent'. His 'crime' was to participate in a demonstration of social workers aimed specifically against a Budapest municipal ordinance that classified taking food from rubbish bins ('dumpster diving') as a misdemeanour.

Ferencz's defence was that he was simply following the Hungarian social work Code of Ethics, which stipulates that social workers have a responsibility, right and a duty to call to the attention of decision-makers and the general public the emergence of poverty and any obstruction of the alleviation thereof. The judge did consider this as a mitigating circumstance in the case.

What emerged during the campaign was that Ferencz was also a member of a group called New Approach, whose aims and objectives are remarkably similar to those of SWAN. According to the group's manifesto:

> The New Approach to community work and radical social work is based on the idea of combining workshops and action groups, and also the renewal of social work codes of ethics.
>   This dual function is located in a long-term goal:
>
> • Workshops: we want to provide space for discussing issues concerning the social sphere, development of action strategies.
> • As an action group we are committed to the profession and the public's attention is drawn to the situation of those excluded. We seek to be a professional community that is not afraid to stand up for those in need. (New Approach, 2011)

A European-wide campaign led by both SWAN and the European Federation of Social Workers in defence of Ferencz succeeded in averting a custodial sentence and also led to links being established between New Approach and radical social work organisations elsewhere in Europe.

The Progressive Welfare Network, Hong Kong

Another group of front-line workers that has been particularly active in social movements in recent years and has played an important role in developing more radical forms of practice is located in Hong Kong and linked to the Progressive Social Work Network. These workers played an important role both in the Occupy Hong Kong movement in 2011 and an even more central role in the Umbrella democracy movement of 2014/15. In 2010, they organised a well-attended Progressive Social Welfare Conference, which was addressed by SWAN activists, and in 2014, they organised the first-ever South East Asian Progressive Social Work Conference, with delegates from Hong Kong, Taiwan, Mainland China and Japan. Once again, the flavour of their approach is captured in their manifesto for progressive social welfare, published in 2014:

For a decade, social welfare in Hong Kong has been severely challenged. The government's neoliberal approach to welfare has led it to adopt a residualist welfare system, thereby undermining social welfare as a powerful tool for securing human rights and justice. Without long-term planning, welfare spending has been steadily decreasing. The so-called flexible planning and funding mechanism has rendered social welfare to a sporadic, ad hoc services [sic]. As a result, there is a widening rich–poor gap, intensifying social stratification, and worsening of [sic] quality of life for the grassroots. As the important role of Hong Kong's social welfare system is undermined, autonomy of social services, the core values of promoting social justice in social work have also been challenged to an unprecedented degree [sic]. (SWAN, 2011a)

The Orange Tide, Spain

Better known, in part, because of its active support by IFSW General Secretary Rory Truell, and the fact that its leaders have won international awards, is the Orange Tide, a movement in Spain combining social workers and the people who use services. Across Spain, they regularly gather in orange T-shirts on the streets with music and dance to the message of 'No Cuts to Social Services'. Spanish newspapers and television have widely reported on this social action and the Orange Tide has become a part of mainstream media. While the government clearly has a programme of cutting social services at a time when they are needed, the cuts are arguably not as drastic as they would otherwise have been because of the visibility of the Orange Tide (Truell, 2014).

South Africa

Indignation over the impact of austerity and deteriorating working conditions for social workers culminated in one of the most inspiring social work mobilisations in Africa in 2016. In September that year, over 20,000 South African social work practitioners, educators and students took to the streets of Pretoria, demanding better working conditions and more resources available for social services. In a direct reference to historical struggles of the South African people and the development of the more recent student movement, social workers were dressed in white T-shirts and exclusively sung political songs such as 'Senzeni Na' and 'Thupa'. The demonstrators reached the Union Buildings in Pretoria and handed in a list of demands to the government. This demonstration has been among the largest social work mobilisations in the history of the profession worldwide (Nathane and Smith, forthcoming).

Peace movement: Colombia and Cyprus

Radical social workers have been at the forefront of the struggle for social justice and peace in countries experiencing war or post-conflict transitions. The most notable examples in recent years include practitioners from Colombia and Cyprus. Colombian social workers, influenced by the principles of liberation theology and the reconceptualisation movement, have been working directly with indigenous and peasant communities affected by state and paramilitary violence. These practitioners and academics have not only engaged with grass-roots community work supporting the victims of violence, but, most importantly, joined the political movements that emphasise the need for agrarian reform, collective reparations, autonomy for indigenous communities, social justice and amnesty for guerrilla fighters as a prerequisite for peace (IASSW, 2016a).

In recent years, progressive social work academics and practitioners from both sides of the Cypriot separation line have worked towards breaking free from the sectarian and nationalist politics of the profession and demanding the reunification of the island. Greek Cypriot and Turkish Cypriot social workers have organised meetings in the United Nations (UN)-controlled buffer zones, organised discussions with victims of the conflict and families of missing persons, and, through events and mobilisations, highlighted the importance of raising the 'social question' as an integral part of the peace process. These practitioners have expressed their concern about the lack of attention that has been given to the importance of social justice and universal welfare as means of achieving viable peace, and have declared that:

> in the current conjuncture, we need to address the long-standing issue passed on from generation to generation: the issues of past violence, such as disappearances and other forms of violence, requires immediate attention at a moment where Social Services are facing the combination of major social questions in society (poverty, new psychological and mental problems and social ills), and austerity-based recipes that curb various social programs and downsize social services departments in time of increasing need. We must simultaneously address the shape of a future social policies and welfare state of a reunited Cyprus in a manner properly connects this to the broader issues of the ongoing and future struggles for equality. (SSCC, 2016)

This statement was followed by concrete actions, including bi-communal meetings, participation in pro-peace mobilisations and the inclusion of trade unions in their discussions about the role of social work and the welfare state in post-solution Cyprus.

To this list, we could add the Green Social Work network in Australia, which is developing social work theory, practice and campaigns around environmental and climate change issues, and the Rebel Social Work group in

New Zealand/Aotearoa, which is actively campaigning against cuts to services. These are just a few examples of the types of radical social work initiatives that have developed over the past decade which emphasise that radical social work remains a 'living' and 'viable' set of ideas and practices that focus on creating 'another social work'.

The new social work radicalism – key elements

So, what, then, are some of the common features of this new radicalism?

Against the market in social work – people before profit

As John Harris (2014: 7) has noted:

> In many countries, neoliberalism continues to strive for unquestioned acceptance of the superior wisdom of the private sector, its first-rate way of doing things and the transferability of knowledge to other contexts, despite the financial and economic crash of 2008 and subsequent austerity politics.

In reality, as we have argued throughout this book, the three processes that Harris identifies as underpinning neoliberal social work – marketisation, managerialisation and consumerisation – have been responsible for much of what has gone wrong over the past two decades, with social workers from Scotland to Japan complaining that 'what we're doing is not social work' (ESRC, 2011).

Opposition to the market in social work is therefore rooted in two factors: first, a value-based belief that social work policy and practice should primarily be concerned with addressing human need rather than being driven by market considerations of competition, efficiency and profit; and, second, an awareness that neoliberal forms of social work, including their domination by computer-based assessment and recording processes (White et al, 2009), have seriously undermined much of what would be universally recognised as good practice.

As we argued in Chapter Two, however, a rejection of market forces in social work does not entail an uncritical acceptance of state-provided services. Rather, we need to fight for social services that are publicly funded but are also accountable, democratic and based on the views and wishes of those who use them.

Reclaiming relationships

One casualty of neoliberalism has been relationship-based social work. While it is undoubtedly the case that an overemphasis on the worker–client relationship in the past sometimes became a way of *not* addressing the structural factors shaping the lives of social work clients (for examples, see Mayer and Timms, 1970; see also, therefore, *Case Con*, the title of the magazine of radical social workers in the UK in the 1970s), one strength of the personal social services at their best is that they can provide a space where people can explore past or present harms or losses in the context of a supportive relationship – or as the Hungarian social worker George Konrad put it at the end of his great novel *The Case Worker*: 'Let all those come who want to: one of us will talk, the other will listen; at least we shall be together' (Konrad, 1970: 172).

That involves time, space to think and reflect, and also good supervision – all casualties of excessive caseloads, cuts to services, the neoliberal drive for efficiency and productivity, and the undermining of workplace-based union organisation.

Reclaiming community development

Another casualty of neoliberal social work in the UK and elsewhere has been community development, once a key part of social work responses to poverty and deprivation in Britain and the US. Within social work education in other countries, however, such as South Africa and Brazil, community work continues to form part of the curriculum. Community development approaches, particularly those that emphasise community self-help and 'pulling yourself up by your own bootstraps', can, of course, be at least as conservative as individualised approaches. However, more radical forms of community work, as well as community work placements for students that involve direct involvement with social movements, offer real possibilities for addressing structural inequalities and for highlighting the link between private troubles and public issues (Smith and Ferguson, 2016).

Developing radical theory for radical practice

The claim that social work is a purely practical activity that 'anyone can do' and that requires little theoretical input is one that is heard all too frequently, usually from the mouths of mainstream politicians who are irritated by social workers' insistence on talking about such uncomfortable issues as poverty and oppression. Social work is, of course, a practical activity; having a sophisticated understanding of the roots of capitalist exploitation is of little value if one is unable to relate effectively to the small child experiencing abuse at the hands of her parents or the young man terrified of the voices that he is hearing in his head. However, what these examples point to is precisely the *complexity* of the social work task: the need to fuse an understanding of 'what is going on' in a particular situation, based on good relationship and assessment skills, with skills of intervention and use of self. Similarly, if we are to avoid joining in the general scapegoating of disabled people, people on benefits or the Muslim community, we need a theoretical understanding of racism, disablism and ideology more generally That is why we need to insist on the importance of maintaining the social science base of social work education. It is also why publications such as the journal *Critical and Radical Social Work* are crucial as a means of deepening the critical-theoretical base of the profession. That said, radical and critical social work theory cannot

177

and should not be developed in isolation from the experience, knowledge and practice wisdom of workers and service users; rather, it should seek to inform and generalise from that experience. 'Pure theory' of the type advocated by some adherents of the post–Marxist approaches discussed in Chapter Nine has little to contribute to a critical understanding of the role that social workers can play in challenging oppression.

Building coalitions of workers, academics, service users, movement activists and trade unions

Against those who would deny that social workers have any role to play in the struggle against oppression and for a more equal society, in this book, we have emphasised their capacity and potentiality to do so. Clearly, however, given the strength of the forces ranged against all of us who seek to build a better world (or simply to defend existing welfare states), no one should be under any illusions regarding the nature of the contribution that a rather weak and disorganised profession can make – all the more important, then, that social workers form alliances with trade unions, other campaigning organisations and organisations of disabled people and service users to defend existing services and to promote alternatives. As an example, in the UK, SWAN has linked in with the British Association of Social Workers, Disabled People Against Cuts and the service user organisation Shaping Our Lives to form Social Workers and Service Users Against Cuts in order to campaign more effectively against the effects of austerity policies.

A global movement

A limitation of the radical social work movement of the 1970s is that it was mainly confined to English-speaking countries, notably, Britain, Canada and Australia. The new movement is much more global, for three reasons. First, the rise of the Internet and various forms of social media have made it much easier to gain an awareness of what is happening in other countries, to share information and to maintain contact across continents. Second, international social work organisations are playing a much more prominent role than was previously the case, with conferences such as the biennial International Association of Schools of Social Work (IASSW) conference offering opportunities for international networking. As an example, a meeting to launch the new journal *Critical and Radical Social Work* at the IASSW conference in Stockholm in 2012 was attended by around 70 delegates from many different countries, including a large delegation from Latin America. Third, and most importantly, the global dominance of neoliberal ideology and economic policy for three decades and the subordination of welfare services to market requirements has meant that the issues facing social workers across the globe are often very similar. The similarities between the experience of social workers in the UK and those in Japan as a result of the imposition of care management approaches was one of the main findings of an Economic and Social Research Council-funded seminar series in 2011.

Strengthening these global networks and learning from the experience of practitioners, academics, students, service users and campaigners in other countries (including the examples of 'popular social work' that we discussed in Chapter Six) is a priority. However, this is not just about sharing information; it is also about showing solidarity. We all benefit from showing solidarity. Social workers in Britain and Greece who have been involved in supporting and welcoming asylum seekers have found that their colleagues and the wider public are often grateful for the opportunity to sign petitions, give clothes or contribute money to help asylum seekers and refugees. One poll in the UK, for example, found that in the period following the widely publicised death of a three-year-old Syrian-Kurdish refugee child, Aylan Kurdi, on a Greek beach in September 2015 as he and his family crossed the Mediterranean to seek sanctuary in Europe, more than a third of people in the UK had supported refugees in one or other of the forms mentioned earlier.

That is why we should re-inscribe solidarity as a core social work value. Reasserting our common humanity is not only the most effective way of challenging the racists and xenophobes who would divide us; it also challenges the narrow selfish individualism that is at the cold heart of neoliberalism and provides a basis for a different kind of social work. In a discussion of the ways in which the individualism that neoliberalism creates has created an epidemic of loneliness and mental ill-health in many countries, the British journalist George Monbiot has argued:

> This does not require a policy response. It requires something much bigger: the reappraisal of an entire worldview. Of all the fantasies human beings entertain, the idea that we can go it alone is the most absurd and perhaps the most dangerous. We stand together or we fall apart. (Monbiot, 2016)

A social work that emphasises our *social* nature as human beings and our basic need for connectedness, that finds new ways to translate that into practical ways of working, and that challenges the political, social and economic forces that would isolate us and turn us against each other has a part to play in developing that new worldview. That means, in the words of our Hungarian colleagues quoted earlier, becoming 'a professional community that is not afraid to stand up for those in need'.

References

Addams, J. (1910) *Twenty years at Hull-House: With autobiographical notes*, New York, NY: Macmillan.

Alayón, N. (ed) (2005) *Trabajo Social Latinoamericano a 40 años de la Reconceptualización*, Editorial Espacio, Buenos Aires: Argentina.

Alayón, N. (2010) 'La etica professional y la memoria'. Available at: www.margen. org/wp/?p=960 (accessed May 2016).

Alayón, N. and Molina, M.L. (2006) 'La desigualdad social: desarrollo y desafios del Trabajo Social desde la Reconceptualización en América Latina', *Perpectivas*, 17(43): 65

Alayón, N., Barreix, J. and Cassineri, E. (1971) *ABC del Trabajo Social latinoamericano*, Buenos Aires: Ecro.

Alexander, A. (2011) 'Egypt's Muslims and Christians join hands in protest'. Available at: http://www.bbc.co.uk/news/world-middle-east-12407793 (accessed 21 December 2016).

Alexander, P., Lekgowa, T., Mmope, B., Sinwell, L. and Xezwi, B. (2012) *Marikana: A view from the mountain and a case to answer*, South Africa: Jacana.

Amnesty International (2009) 'USA: Jailed without justice: immigration detention in the USA'. Available at: http://www.amnestyusa.org/pdfs/ JailedWithoutJustice.pdf (accessed 21 December 2016).

Anastas, J. (2011) 'Social work and eugenics', National Association of Social Workers. Available at: http://www.socialworkblog.org/pressroom/2011/11/ social-work-and-eugenics/ (accessed 14 June 2016).

Anderson, P. (2016) 'The heirs of Gramsci', *New Left Review*, II(100). Available at: https://newleftreview.org/II/100/perry-anderson-the-heirs-of-gramsci (accessed 21 December 2016).

Angten, J. and Paulsen, P. (2008) 'Review of the international definition of social work', paper presented in Nairobi (29/06/11).

Angus, I. (2016) *Facing the Anthropocene: Fossil capitalism and the crisis of the earth system*, New York, NY: Monthly Review Press.

Asylum Access and the Refugee Work Rights Coalition (2014) *Global refugee work rights report*, Oakland, CA: Asylum Access. Available at: http://asylumaccess. org/wp-content/uploads/2014/09/FINAL_Global-Refugee-Work-Rights-Report-2014_Interactive.pdf (accessed 21 December 2016).

Atal, Y. (1981) 'The call for indigenization', *International Social Science Journal*, 33(1): 189–97.

Bailey, R. and Brake, M. (eds) (1975) *Radical social work*, London: Edward Arnold.

Bamford, T. (2015) *A contemporary history of social work: Learning from the past*, Bristol: The Policy Press.

Barr, B. (2015) 'The mental health impact of recession and welfare reform in England between 2008 and 2013', unpublished PhD Thesis, University of Liverpool.

Barreix, J. (2003) 'La Reconceptualización Hoy. Trabajo Social como utopía de la esperanza', Universidad Nacional de Mar del Plata.

BASW (British Association of Social Workers) (2012) The code of ethics for social work: Statement of principles, http://cdn.basw.co.uk/upload/basw_112315-7.pdf

Bates, B., Kundzewicz, Z., Wu, S. and Palutikof, J. (eds) (2008) 'Climate change and water', IPCC Technical Paper VI (Geneva IPCC Secretariat). Available at: https://www.ipcc.ch/pdf/technical-papers/climate-change-water-en.pdf (accessed 21 December 2016).

BBC (British Broadcasting Corporation) (2006) 'British children deported to Australia', Inside out, 6 March. Available at: http://www.bbc.co.uk/insideout/eastmidlands/series9/week_nine.shtml (accessed 21 April 2017).

BBC (2011a) 'Hungary outlaws homeless in move condemned by charities'. Available at: http://www.bbc.co.uk/news/world-europe-15982882 (accessed 18 December 2016).

BBC (2011b) 'Spain's stolen babies and the families who lived a lie'. Available at: http://www.bbc.com/news/magazine-15335899 (accessed 21 December 2016).

BBC (2014) 'Dutch firm Abellio wins ScotRail franchise from FirstGroup'. Available at: http://www.bbc.co.uk/news/uk-scotland-29531099 (accessed 21 December 2016).

BBC (2015a) 'Australia asylum: why is it controversial?', BBC News, 9 November. Available at: http://www.bbc.co.uk/news/world-asia-28189608 (accessed 21 December 2016).

BBC (2015b) 'The children taken from home for a social experiment'. Available at: http://www.bbc.com/news/magazine-33060450 (accessed 11 May 2016).

Bean, P. and Melville, J. (1989) Lost children of empire: The untold story of Britain's child migrants, London: Unwin and Hyman.

Belkin Martinez, D. and Fleck-Henderson, A. (eds) (2014) Social justice in clinical practice: A liberation health framework for social work, New York, NY: Routledge.

Benjamin, N. (2012) 'Researching the Basque children', paper presented on 21 April at a Day School at Rewley House, Oxford, on the Basque children refugees. Available at: http://www.basquechildren.org/-/docs/articles/gen007 (accessed 21 December 2016).

Beresford, P. (2014) Personalisation, Bristol: The Policy Press.

Beresford, P. (2016) All our welfare: Towards participatory social policy, Bristol: Policy Press.

Berry, M., Garcia-Blanco, I. and Moore, K. (2015) 'Press coverage of the refugee and migrant crisis in the EU: a content analysis of five European countries', report prepared for the United Nations High Commission for Refugees, December. Available at: http://www.unhcr.org/cgi-bin/texis/vtx/home/opendocPDFViewer.html?docid=56bb369c9&query=media%20coverage%20of%20refugee%20crisis (accessed 21 December 2016).

Bevan, A. (1952) In place of fear, London: Heineman.

Blackburn, R. (1997) The making of new world slavery, London: Verso.

Boggs, B. (2014) 'For the public good: the shameful history of forced sterilization in the US'. Available at: https://blog.longreads.com/2014/11/19/for-the-public-good/ (accessed 3 May 2016).

Bond, P., Galvin, M., Jara, M. and Ngwane, T. (2006) 'Problematising civil society: on what terrain does xenophobia flourish?'. Available at: http://www.atlanticphilanthropies.org/app/uploads/2010/07/6_Problematising_c.pdf (accessed 21 December 2016).

Braverman, H. (1974) *Labour and monopoly capital*, New York, NY: Monthly Review Press.

Buckley, C. and Donadiooct, R. (2011) 'Buoyed by Wall St. protests, rallies sweep the globe', *New York Times*, 15 October. Available at: http://www.nytimes.com/2011/10/16/world/occupy-wall-street-protests-worldwide.html?hp=&pagewanted=all (accessed 21 December 2016).

Burns, D., Cowie, L., Earle, J., Folkman, P., Froud, J., Hyde, P., Johal, S., Jones, I., Killett, A. and Williams, K. (2016) 'Where does the money go? Financialised chains and the crisis in residential care', Centre for Research in Social and Cultural Change

Butler, P. (2016) 'Most Britons now regard themselves as working-class, survey finds', *Guardian*, 29 June. Available at: https://www.theguardian.com/society/2016/jun/29/most-brits-regard-themselves-as-working-class-survey-finds (accessed 21 December 2016).

Cafiero, C., Nord, M., Viviani, S., Del Grossi, M.E., Ballard, T., Kepple, A., Miller, M. and Nwosu, C. (2016) *Voices of the hungry*, Rome: UN Food and Agriculture Organisation. Available at: http://www.fao.org/3/a-i4830e.pdf (accessed 21 December 2016).

Callinicos, A. (2003) *An anti-capitalist manifesto*, London: Polity.

Callinicos, A. (2009) *Imperialism and global political economy*, London: Polity.

Cameron, D. (2013) 'Speech at the Lord Mayor's Banquet'. Available at: http://www.telegraph.co.uk/finance/economics/10442263/David-Camerons-Lord-Mayors-Banquest-speech-in-full.html (accessed 21 December 2016).

Carney, M. (2016) 'The spectre of monetarism'. Available at: http://www.bankofengland.co.uk/publications/Documents/speeches/2016/speech946.pdf (accessed 21 December 2016).

Carr, M. (2012) *Fortress Europe: Inside the war against immigration*, London: Hurst.

Carr, M. (2015) 'Battering down the fortress', *Socialist Review*, November. Available at: http://socialistreview.org.uk/407/battering-down-fortress (accessed 21 December 2016).

Carr, S. (2014) 'Critical perspectives on intersectionality', in C. Clocker and T. Hafford-Letchfield (eds) *Rethinking anti-discriminatory and anti-oppressive theories for social work practice*, Basingstoke: Palgrave Macmillan, pp 140–53.

Castañeda, P. and Salamé, M. (2014) 'Trabajo social chileno y dictadura militar. Memoria profesional predictatorial Período 1960-1973. Agentes de cambio social y trauma profesional', *Rumbo*, TS 9, 8–25.

Castro Villacanas, A. (1948) *La Hora*, 14 May.

Chakrabortty, A. (2014) 'Outsourced and unaccountable: this is the future of local government'. Available at: https://www.theguardian.com/commentisfree/2014/dec/15/local-services-barnet-council-town-hall (accessed 21 December 2016).

Chalalet, S.A. and Jones, C. (no date) 'Austerity: resistence and reality'. Available at: https://www.samoschronicles.wordpress.com/ (accessed 21 December 2016).

Chappell, S. (2016) 'UNHCR despairs over Europe's lack of solidarity in handling refugee crisis', *Euronews*, 24 February. Available at: http://www.euronews.com/2016/02/24/unhcr-despairs-over-lack-of-solidarity-in-europe-in-handling-refugee-crisis/ (accessed 21 December 2016).

Chenery, S. (2011) 'I can still hear the kids' screams', *The Sydney Morning Herald*, 12 June. Available at: http://www.smh.com.au/national/i-can-still-hear-the-kids-screams-20110611-1fyap.html (accessed 21 April 2017).

Choonara, J. (2009) *Unravelling capitalism*, London: Bookmarks.

Choonara, J. (2016) 'Is this the end f the neoliberal consensus?'. Available at: http://socialistreview.org.uk/419/end-neoliberal-consensus (accessed 21 December 2016).

Cliff, T. (2000) *Marxism at the millennium*, London: Bookmarks.

Cliff. T. and Gluckstein, D. (1998) *The Labour Party: A Marxist analysis*, London: Bookmarks.

Cocker, C. and Hafford-Letchfield, T. (2014) *Rethinking anti-discriminatory and anti-oppressive theories for social work practice*, Basingstoke: Palgrave Macmillan.

Colegio de Asistentes Sociales de Chile (2008) 'Trabajadores sociales asesinados durante la dictadura militar de Pinochet', Centro de Estudios Miguel Enríquez. Available at: http://www.archivochile.com/Derechos_humanos/doc_gen_ddhh/hhdddocgen0018.pdf (accessed 21 December 2016).

Collins, P.H. (2009) *Black feminist thought: Knowledge, consciousness and the politics of empowerment*, London and New York, NY: Routledge.

Collins, P.H. (2013) 'Towards a new vision: race, class and gender as categories of analysis and connection', in M.S. Kimmel and A. Ferber (eds) *Privilege: A reader* (3rd edn), Boulder, CO: Westview Press.

Connolly, K. (2007) 'I'm no hero, says woman who saved 2,500 ghetto children', *The Guardian*, 15 March. Available at: http://www.theguardian.com/world/2007/mar/15/secondworldwar.poland (accessed 21 December 2016).

Cook, B.I., Anchukaitis, K.J., Touchan, R., Meko, D.M. and Cook, E.R. (2016) 'Spatiotemporal drought variability in the Mediterranean over the last 900 years', *Journal of Geophysical Research: Atmospheres*, 121(5): 2060–74. Available at: http://onlinelibrary.wiley.com/doi/10.1002/2015JD023929/abstract;jsessionid=F314061614D7C5C48FF5FF271A9C1ECD.f02t02 (accessed 21 December 2016).

Cook, J., Nuccitelli, D., Green, S.A., Richardson, M., Winkler, B., Painting, R., Way, R., Jacobs, P. and Skuce, A. (2013) 'Quantifying the consensus on anthropogenic global warming in the scientific literature', Environmental Research Letters. Available at: http://iopscience.iop.org/article/10.1088/1748-9326/8/2/024024/meta;jsessionid=E85277BB22CAF9B1E63253219AFD6BF1.c5.iopscience.cld.iop.org (accessed 21 December 2016).

Costa, M. das Dores (1987) 'Current influences on social work in Brazil: practice and education', *International Social Work*, 30(2): 115–28.

Cowden, S. and Singh, G. (2007) 'The "user": Friend, foe or fetish? A critical exploration of user involvement in health and social care', *Critical Social Policy*, 27(1): 5–23.

CQC (Care Quality Commission) (2012) 'Learning disability services: national overview', CQC.

CQC (2014) *The state of health care and adult social care in England*, HMSO. Available at: http://webarchive.nationalarchives.gov.uk/20151103121342/http://www.cqc.org.uk/content/state-care-201415

Crenshaw, K. (1989) 'Demarginalizing the intersection of race and sex: a black feminist critique of antidiscrimination doctrine, feminist theory and antiracist politics', *University of Chicago Legal Forum*, 1: Article 8. Available at: http://chicagounbound.uchicago.edu/cgi/viewcontent.cgi?article=1052&context=uclf (accessed 2 January 2017).

Crenshaw, K. (1991) 'Mapping the margins: intersectionality, identity politics, and violence against women of color', *Stanford Law Review*, 43(6): 1241–99.

Crivas, S. (1999) *Fundamentals of pedagogy*, Athens: Smyrniotakis.

Crosland, A. (1956/2006) *The future of socialism*, London: Constable.

Crouch, C. (2011) *The strange non-death of neo-liberalism*, London: Polity.

Cunningham, I. (2008) 'A race to the bottom? Exploring variations in employment conditions in the voluntary sector', *Public Administration*, 86(4): 1033–53.

Curtis, P. (2011) https://www.theguardian.com/politics/reality-check-with-polly-curtis/2011/sep/12/reality-check-banking-bailout (accessed 21 December 2016).

Davies, J.B., Sandström, S., Shorrocks, A. and Wolff, E.N. (2006) 'The world distribution of household wealth', Foreign Press Association, London, and UN Secretariat, New York.

Demirbilek, M (2016) 'Environment, environmental refugees and green social work', *International Journal of Social Sciences and Education Research*, 2(3): 1118–30. Available at: http://dergipark.ulakbim.gov.tr/ijsser/article/view/5000185018/5000163492 (accessed 21 December 2016).

Doherty, B. (2016) '"Let them stay": backlash in Australia against plans to send asylum seekers to detention camps', *The Guardian*, 10 February. Available at: http://www.theguardian.com/australia-news/2016/feb/10/let-them-stay-australia-backlash-267-asylum-seekers-island-detention-camps (accessed 21 December 2016).

Dominelli, L. (2011) 'Climate change: social workers' roles and contributions to policy debates and interventions', *International Journal of Social Welfare*, 20(4): 430–8.

Dominelli, L. (2012) *Green social work*, Cambridge: Polity.

Donovan, T. (2014) 'Social care and the floods: finding a safe haven for the vulnerable', *Community Care*, 17 February. Available at: http://www.communitycare.co.uk/2014/02/17/social-care-floods/#.Ux2jaefV-zA (accessed 21 December 2016).

Douzinas, C. and Žižek, S. (eds) (2010) *The idea of communism*, London: Verso.

Ecowatch (2016) '10 extreme weather events in 2015 that sound the alarm on climate chaos', 2 January. Available at: http://www.ecowatch.com/10-extreme-weather-events-in-2015-that-sound-the-alarm-on-climate-chao-1882141451.html (accessed 21 December 2016).

Edelman, M. (1985 [1964]) *The symbolic uses of politics*, Urbana, IL: University of Illinois Press.

Edigheji, O. (2006) *The discourse of the developmental state and a 'people's contract' in South Africa*, Johannesburg: Centre for Policy Studies. Available at: http://citeseerx.ist.psu.edu/viewdoc/download?doi=10.1.1.494.4647&rep=rep1&type=pdf (accessed 21 December 2016).

El Diario Dela Republica (2014) 'Revelador testimonio por el crimen de Luis María Früm'. Available at: http://www.eldiariodelarepublica.com/provincia/-Revelador-testimonio-por-el-crimen-de-Luis-Maria-Frum-20140405-0010.html (accessed 13 May 2016).

Elliott, E. and Gunasekera, H. (2016) 'The health and well-being of children in immigration detention', report to the Australian Human Rights Commission Monitoring Visit to Wickham Point Detention Centre, Darwin, NT. Available at: https://www.humanrights.gov.au/sites/default/files/document/publication/Health%20and%20well-being%20of%20children%20in%20immigration%20detention%20report.pdf (accessed 21 December 2016).

Esping-Andersen, G. (1989) *The three worlds of welfare capitalism*, London: Polity.

ESRC (Economic and Social Research Council) (2011), www.researchcatalogue.esrc.ac.uk/grants/RES-805-26-0005/read

European Environment Agency (2010) 'Alps – the impacts of climate change in Europe today', 17 March. Available at: http://www.eea.europa.eu/signals/signals-2010/alps (accessed 21 December 2016).

EZLN (2005) 'Sixth declaration of the Selva Lacandona'. Available at: http://enlacezapatista.ezln.org.mx/sdsl-en/ (accessed 10 February 2013).

Ferguson, I. (2008) *Reclaiming social work: Challenging neo-liberalism and promoting social justice*, London: Sage.

Ferguson, I. (2012) 'The politics of social work', in M. Gray, J. Midgley and S. Webb (eds) *The Sage handbook of social work*, London: Sage.

Ferguson, I. (2014) 'Can the Tories abolish the welfare state?', *International Social Journal*, 141. Available at: http://isj.org.uk/can-the-tories-abolish-the-welfare-state/ (accessed 21 December 2016).

Ferguson, I. and Lavalette, M. (1999) 'Social work, postmodernism, and Marxism', *European Journal of Social Work*, 2(1): 27-40.

Ferguson, I. and Lavalette, M. (2009) *Social work after Baby P*, Liverpool: Liverpool Hope.

Ferguson, I. and Lavalette, M. (2012) 'Critical and radical social work: An introduction', https://policypress.wordpress.com/2013/04/22/critical-and-radical-social-work-an-introduction/

Ferguson, I. and Lavalette, M. (2014) *Adult social care*, Bristol: The Policy Press.

Ferguson, I. and Smith, L. (2012) 'Education for change: student placements in campaigning organisations and social movements in South Africa'. *British Journal of Social Work*, 42(5): 974–94.

Ferguson, I., Lavalette, M. and Mooney, G. (2002) *Rethinking welfare*, London: Sage.

Ferguson, I., Lavalette, M. and Whitmore, E. (eds) (2005) *Globalisation, global justice and social work*, London: Routledge.

Ferguson, I., Woodward, R., Baldwin, M. and Lavalette, M. (2011) 'The impact of New Public Management policies and perspectives on professional social work: a comparison of British and Japanese experiences', ESRC. Available at: http://www.researchcatalogue.esrc.ac.uk/grants/RES-805-26-0005/outputs/read/f218d3dc-0dfb-4896-aad3-8a9afa2b5aba (accessed 21 December 2016).

Feuer, A. (2012) 'Occupy Sandy: a movement moves to relief', *New York Times*, 9 November. Available at: http://www.nytimes.com/2012/11/11/nyregion/where-fema-fell-short-occupy-sandy-was-there.html (accessed 21 December 2016).

Fine, B. (1999) 'Privatisation: theory and lessons for the United Kingdom and South Africa', in A. Vlachou (ed) *Contemporary economic theory: Radical critiques of neoliberalism*, Basingstoke: Macmillan.

Fine, B. and Saad-Filho, A. (2010) *Marx's 'Capital'* (5th edn), London: Pluto Press.

Firth, J. (1986) *The signal was Spain: The Aid Spain movement in Britain 1936–39*, London: Lawrence and Wishart.

Forgacs, D. (ed) (1998) *The Antonio Gramsci reader*, London: Lawrence and Wishart.

Foucault, M. (1981) *The will to knowledge: The history of sexuality, volume 1*, Harmondsworth: Penguin.

Freedland, J. (2016) 'For Cameron to speak of a "bunch of migrants" is beneath him', *The Guardian*, 27 January. Available at: http://www.theguardian.com/commentisfree/2016/jan/27/cameron-bunch-of-migrants-calais-pmqs-holocaust-memorial-day (accessed 21 December 2016).

Freidli, L. and Stearn, R. (2015) 'Positive affect as coercive strategy: conditionality, activation and the role of psychology in UK government workfare programmes', Available at: http://mh.bmj.com/content/41/1/40

Freire, P. (1972) *The pedagogy of the oppressed*, London: Penguin.

Freire, P. (1988) Speech to the International Federation of Social Workers conference, June, Stockholm. Available at: http://acervo.paulofreire.org:8080/xmlui/bitstream/handle/7891/1046/FPF_OPF_06_024.pdf (accessed 21 December 2016).

Freire, P. (1990) 'A critical understanding of social work', *Journal of Progressive Social Services*, 1(1): 1–10.

Friedrich, T., Timmermann, A., Tigchelaar, M., Timm, O.E. and Ganopolski, A. (2016) 'Nonlinear climate sensitivity and its implications for future greenhouse warming', *Science Advances*, 2(11). Available at: http://advances.sciencemag.org/content/2/11/e1501923.full (accessed 21 December 2016).

Früm, L. (1971) 'Introducción al tema ideología y Trabajo Social', *Revista Hoy en Trabajo Social*, 22(2).

Gagneten, M. (1986) *Hacia una metodologia de sistematizacion de la practica*, Buenos Aires: Humanitas.

Galeano, E. (1998) *Open veins of Latin America: Five centuries of the pillage of a continent*, London: Latin America Bureau.

Galeano, E. (2004 [1999]) 'Interview with Savid Barsamian', in D. Barsamian (ed) *Louder the bombs: Interviews from the Progressive magazine*, Cambridge, MA: Southend Press.

Galeano, E. (2009) *Open veins of Latin America: Five centuries of the pillage of a continent* (25th anniversary edn), New York, NY: Monthly Review Press.

GASW (Greek Association of Social Workers) (1968) 'Our profession's development', *Koinoniki Ergasia*, 29: 1–8.

GASW (2011) 'Press release: GASW campaign against the electricity cut-offs'. Available at: http://www.skle.gr/index.php?option=com_content&view=article&id=207:%CE%A0%CE%B1%CF%81%CE%AD%CE%BC%CE%B2%CE%B1%CF%83%CE%B7-%CE%A3%CE%9A%CE%9B%CE%95

George, S. (2004) *Another world is possible if …*, London: Verso.

Geras, N. (1987) 'Post-Marxism?', *New Left Review*, I(163). Available at: https://newleftreview.org/I/163/norman-geras-post-marxism (accessed 21 December 2016).

Gerassi, J. (ed) (1973) *Camilo Torres; revolutionary priest: His complete writings and messages*, Middlesex: Penguin Books.

Giles, G. (1992) 'The most unkindest cut of all: castration, homosexuality and Nazi justice', *Journal of Contemporary History*, 27(1): 41-6.

GISS (Goddard Institute for Space Studies) (2016a) 'NASA, NOAA analyses reveal record-shattering global warm temperatures in 2015', 20 January. Available at: http://www.giss.nasa.gov/research/news/20160120/ (accessed 21 December 2016).

GISS (2016b) 'NASA analysis finds warmest September on record by narrow margin', 17 October. Available at: http://data.giss.nasa.gov/gistemp/news/20161017/ (accessed 21 December 2016).

Gloria, E., Leal, L. and Édgar Malagón, B. (2008) 'Historia del trabajo social latinoamericano. Estado del arte', *Trabajo Social*, 1(8).

Gómez, F.G. and Buendía, F.H. (2009) 'The development of social work education in Spain', *European Journal of Social Work*, 12 (1): 113–17.

Gonzales, M. and Yanes, M. (2015) *The last drop: The politics of water*, London: Pluto.

González Duro, E. (2008) *Los psiquiatras de Franco. Los rojos no estaban locos*, Barcelona: Península.

Gordon, I. and Raja, T. (2012) '164 anti-immigration laws passed since 2010: a MoJo analysis', Mother Jones, March/April. Available at: http://www.motherjones.com/politics/2012/03/anti-immigration-law-database (accessed 21 December 2016).

Gosling, P. (2011) The rise of the 'public service industry', London: UNISON.

Gove, M. (2013) 'Michael Gove speech to the NSPCC: getting it right for children in need'. Available at: https://www.gov.uk/government/speeches/getting-it-right-for-children-in-need-speech-to-the-nspcc (accessed 21 December 2016).

Government of Canada (2016) 'Home children, 1869–1932', Library and Archives Canada. Available at: http://www.bac-lac.gc.ca/eng/discover/immigration/immigration-records/home-children-1869-1930/Pages/home-children.aspx (accessed 21 April 2017).

Graham-Harrison, E. (2015) 'Burma's boatpeople "faced choice of annihilation or risking their lives at sea"', The Observer, 17 May. Available at: http://www.theguardian.com/world/2015/may/17/rohingya-burma-refugees-boat-migrants (accessed 21 December 2016).

Gray, M. and Coates, J. (2013) 'Changing values and valuing change: toward an ecospiritual perspective in social work', International Social Work, 56(3): 356–68.

Gray, M. and Webb, S. (eds) (2013) The new politics of social work, Basingstoke: Palgrave Macmillan.

Gray, M., Coates, J. and Yellow Bird, M. (eds) (2008) Indigenous social work around the world: Towards culturally relevant education and practice, Aldershot: Ashgate, pp 13–29.

Gustavsson, J., Cederberg, C., Sonesson, U., Van Otterdijk, R. and Meybeck, A. (2011) Global food losses and food waste: Extent, causes and prevention, Rome: UN Food and Agriculture Organisation. Available at: http://www.fao.org/docrep/014/mb060e/mb060e.pdf (accessed 21 December 2016).

Gutierrez, G. (1971) A theology of liberation: History, politics and salvation, New York: Orbis.

Hallward, P. (2003) Badiou: A subject to truth, Minneapolis, MN: UMP.

Hancox, D. (2015) 'Why Ernesto Laclau is the intellectual figurehead for Syriza and Podemos', Guardian, 9 February. Available at: https://www.theguardian.com/commentisfree/2015/feb/09/ernesto-laclau-intellectual-figurehead-syriza-podemos (accessed 21 December 2016).

Hansen, J., Sato, M., Kharecha, P., Von Schuckmann, K., Beerling, D.J., Cao, J., Marcott, S., Masson-Delmotte, V., Prather, M.J., Rohling, E.J., Shakun, J. and Smith, P. (2016) 'Young people's burden: requirement of negative CO2 emissions', Earth System Dynamics. Available at: http://www.earth-syst-dynam-discuss.net/esd-2016-42/esd-2016-42.pdf (accessed 21 December 2016).

Hansen, K. (2016) 'Heat fuels fire at Fort McMurray', NASA Earth Observatory, 7 May, National Aeronautics and Space Administration, Goddard Institute for Space Studies. Available at: http://www.giss.nasa.gov/research/features/201605_fires/ (accessed 21 December 2016).

Hardman, C. (2016) 'How Flint is using good food to combat lead poisoning', 24 October, Civileats. Available at: http://civileats.com/2016/10/24/how-flint-is-using-good-food-to-combat-lead-poisoning/ (accessed 21 December 2016).

Harman, C. (2007) 'Theorising neoliberalism', *International Socialism Journal*, 117. Available at: http://isj.org.uk/theorising-neoliberalism/ (accessed 21 December 2016).

Harman, C. (2009) *Zombie capitalism*, London: Bookmarks.

Harrel-Bond, B. (1999) 'The experience of refugees as recipients of aid', in A.Ager (ed) *Refugees: Perspectives on the experience of forced migration*, New York: Continuum, pp 136-68.

Harris, J. (2003) *The social work business*, London: Routledge.

Harris, J. (2008) 'State social work: constructing the present from moments in the past', *British Journal of Social Work*, 38(4): 662–79.

Harris, J. (2014) '(Against) Neoliberal social work', *Critical and Radical Social Work*, 2(1): 7–22.

Harvey, D. (2004) 'The "new" imperialism: accumulation by dispossession', *Socialist Register*, 40: 63–87.

Harvey, D. (2005) *The new imperialism*, Oxford: Oxford University Press.

Harvey, D. (2014) *Seventeen contradictions and the end of capitalism*, London: Profile Books.

Haste, C. (2001) *Nazi women: Hitler's seduction of a nation*, London and Oxford: Fourth Estate.

Hawkins, C. (2010) 'Sustainability, human rights, and environmental justice: critical connections for contemporary social work', *Critical Social Work*, 11(3): 68–81.

Hayter, T. (2000) *Open borders: The case against immigration controls*, London: Pluto.

Heede, R. (2014) 'Access tracing anthropogenic carbon dioxide and methane emissions to fossil fuel and cement producers, 1854–2010', *Climatic Change*, 122(1/2): 229–41.

Held, D. and McGrew, A. (2002) *Globalization and anti-globalization*, London: Polity.

Henley, J. (2013) 'Recession can hurt but austerity kills'. Available at: https://www.theguardian.com/society/2013/may/15/recessions-hurt-but-austerity-kills (accessed 21 December 2016).

Henley, J. (2015) 'Greece's solidarity movement', *The Guardian*, 23 January. Available at: https://www.theguardian.com/world/2015/jan/23/greece-solidarity-movement-cooperatives-syriza (accessed 21 December 2016).

Herbert-Boyd, M. (2007) *Enriched by catastrophe: Social work and social conflict after the Halifax explosion*, Nova Scotia: Fernwood Publishing.

Hering, S. (2003) 'A soldier of the 3rd International; the social activities of the Swiss communist Mentona Moser', in S. Hering and B. Waaldijk (eds) *History of social work in Europe (1900–1960): Female pioneers and their influence on the development of international social organizations*, Opladen: Soziale Arbeit.

Hinestroza, C. and Ioakimidis, V. (2011) 'In search of emancipatory social work practice in contemporary Colombia; working with the internally displaced in Bogota', in M. Lavalette and V. Ioakimidis (eds) *Social work in extremis: Lessons for social work internationally*, Bristol: The Policy Press.

Hobsbawm, E. (1987) *The age of empire: 1875–1914*, London: George, Weidenfeld and Nicolson.

Hobsbawm, E.J. (1994) *The age of extremes: The short twentieth century, 1914–1991*, New York, NY: Abacus.

Humphries, M. (2011) *Empty cradles*, London: Corgi Books.

IASSW (International Association of Schools of Social Work) (1977) *'Latin America', in social realities and the social work responses*, New York, NY: IASSW.

IASSW (2016a) 'IASSW statement on the peace agreement in Colombia'. Available at: https://www.iassw-aiets.org/2016/09/30/iassw-statement-peace-agreement-colombia/ (accessed 2 January 2017).

IASSW (2016b) 'IASSW supports the IFSW statement: responding to the refugee crisis', 15 March. Available at: https://www.iassw-aiets.org/2016/03/13/851/ (accessed 19 December 2016).

IDMC (Internal Displacement Monitoring Centre) (2015) 'Global overview 2015 people internally displaced by conflict and violence', May. Available at: http://www.internal-displacement.org/assets/library/Media/201505-Global-Overview-2015/20150506-global-overview-2015-en.pdf (accessed 19 December 2016).

IFSW (International Federation of Social Work) (2014) 'Global definition of social work'. Available at: http://ifsw.org/policies/definition-of-social-work/ (accessed 19 December 2016).

IFSW-Europe (2012) 'Newsletter from Spain'. Available at: http://ifsweurope-ifsweurope.blogspot.com/2012/11/spain-newsletter-november-2012-of.html (accessed 18 December 2016).

Ioakimidis, V. (2011) 'Expanding imperialism, exporting expertise: international social work and the Greek project (1946–1974)', *International Social Work*, 54(4): 505–19.

Ioakimidis, V. and Lavalette, M. (2016) '"Popular" social work in extremis: two case studies on collective welfare responses to social crisis situations', *Social Theory, Empirics, Policy and Practice*, 13(2): 117–32.

Ioakimidis, V. and Teloni, D. (2013) 'Greek social work and the never-ending crisis of the welfare state', *Critical and Radical Social Work*, 1(1): 31–49. Available at: www.ingentaconnect.com/content/tpp/crsw/2013/00000001/00000001/art00003 (accessed 21 December 2016).

Ioakimidis, V., Cruz Santos, C. and Martinez Herrero, I. (2014) 'Reconceptualizing social work in times of crisis: an examination of the cases of Greece, Spain and Portugal', *International Social Work*, 57(4): 285–300.

IOM (International Organisation for Migration) (2016) 'With increasing child deaths at sea, IOM and UN partner agencies urge greater protection for migrants and refugees', 22 February. Available at: http://unitedkingdom.iom. int/increasing-child-deaths-sea-iom-and-un-partner-agencies-urge-greater-protection-migrants-and (accessed 19 December 2016).

Jameson, F. (2003) 'Future city', *New Left Review*, II: 21. Available at: https:// newleftreview.org/II/21/fredric-jameson-future-city (accessed 19 December 2016).

Jensen, R. (2004) 'Damn the dams: an interview with Medha Patkar', Alternet, 24 February. Available at: http://www.alternet.org/story/17954/damn_the_dams%3A_an_interview_with_medha_patkar (accessed 19 December 2016).

Jessop, B. (2015) *The state: Past, present and future*, London: Polity.

Johnson, B. (2013) 'We should be humbly thanking the super-rich, not bashing them', *The Telegraph*, 17 November. Available at: http://www.telegraph.co.uk/comment/columnists/borisjohnson/10456202/We-should-be-humbly-thanking-the-super-rich-not-bashing-them.html (accessed 3 January 2017).

Johnson, S. and Moorhead, B. (2011) 'Social eugenics practices with children in Hitler's Nazi Germany and the role of social workers: lessons for current practices', *Journal of Social Work Values & Ethics*. Available at: http://www.socialworker.com/jswve (accessed 23 June 2016).

Johnston, I. (2016) 'Climate change may be escalating so fast it could be "game over", scientists warn', *The Independent*, 11 November. Available at: http://www.independent.co.uk/news/science/climate-change-game-over-global-warming-climate-sensitivity-seven-degrees-a7407881.html (accessed 19 December 2016).

Jones, C. (1983) *State social work and the working class*, Basingstoke: Macmillan.

Jones, C. (2001) 'Voices from the front line: state social work under New Labour', *British Journal of Social Work*, 31: 547–62.

Jones, C. (2012) 'Social work transformed; the British model', in V. Ioakimidis (ed) *Social work for social justice*, Athens: Ion.

Jones, C. and Lavalette, M. (2013) 'The two souls of social sork: exploring the roots of "popular social work"', *Critical and Radical Social Work*, 1(2): 147–65.

Jones, C. and Novak, T. (1999) *Poverty, welfare and the disciplinary state*, London: Routledge.

Jones, C., Lavalette, M., Ferguson, I. and Penketh, L. (2004) 'Social work and social justice: a manifesto for a new engaged practice'. Available at: http://www.socialworkfuture.org/articles-resources/uk-articles/103-social-work-and-social-justice-a-manifesto-for-a-new-engaged-practice (accessed 19 December 2016).

Jones, R. (2014) *The story of Baby P*, Bristol: Policy Press.

Jonsson, J. (2015) 'The contested field of social work in a retreating welfare state: the case of Sweden', *Critical and Radical Social Work*, 3(3): 357–74.

Jordan, B. (1984) *Invitation to social work*, Oxford: Basil Blackwell.

Jordan, B. and Jordan, C. (2000) *Social work and the Third Way: Tough love as social policy*, London: Sage.

Kentikelenis, A., Karanikolos, M., Reeves, A., McKee, M. and Stuckler, D. (2014) 'Greece's health crisis: from austerity to denialism'. Available at: http://www.kentikelenis.net/uploads/3/1/8/9/31894609/kentikelenis2014-greeces_health_crisis_from_austerity_to_denialism.pdf (accessed 21 December 2016).

Kershaw, R. and Sacks, J. (2008) *New lives for old: The story of Britain's child migrants*, London: New Archives Press.

Kidron, M. (1968) *Western capitalism since the War*, London: Penguin.

Kiernan, R. (2016) 'Kamikaze council declares war on Glasgow's workers', *Socialist Worker*, 15 November. Available at: https://socialistworker.co.uk/art/43699/Kamikaze+council+declares+war+on+Glasgows+workers (accessed 19 December 2016).

Klein, N. (2007a) *The shock doctrine: The rise of disaster capitalism*, London: Allen Lane.

Klein, N. (2007b) 'Information is shock resistant: arm yourself – the shock doctrine'. Available at: http://www.naomiklein.org/shock-doctrine (accessed 19 December 2016).

Klein, N. (2015) *This changes everything: Capitalism vs. the climate*, London: Penguin.

Klinenberg, E. (2002) *Heat wave: A social autopsy of disaster in Chicago*, Chicago: University of Chicago Press.

Knight, J. (2013) 'Inequality in China: an overview', World Bank, Capacity Building Unit, June.

Konrad, G. (1970) *The case worker*, London: Hutchinson.

Krugman, P. (2008) *The return of depression economics and the crisis of 2008*, London: Penguin.

Kunstreich, T. (2003) 'Social welfare in Nazi Germany: selection and exclusion', *Journal of Progressive Human Services*, 14(2): 23–52.

Laclau, E. and Mouffe, C. (2014 [1985]) *Hegemony and socialist strategy: Towards a radical democratic politics* (2nd edn), London: Verso.

LaingBuisson (2015) *Care of elderly people UK market report*.

Lauri, M. (2016) 'Narratives of governing: rationalization, responsibility and resistance in social work', Umea University.

Lavalette, M. (2009) 'Indian "village" people demand change', *Socialist Worker*, 1 September. Available at: https://socialistworker.co.uk/art/18542/Indian+village+people+demand+change (accessed 19 December 2016).

Lavalette, M. (ed) (2011) *Radical social work today*, Bristol: The Policy Press.

Lavalette, M. and Ferguson, I. (eds) (2007) *International social work and the radical tradition*, Birmingham: Venture Press.

Lavalette, M. and Ioakimidis, V. (2011a) *Social work in extremis: Lessons for social work internationally*, Bristol: The Policy Press.

Lavalette, M. and Ioakimidis, V. (2011b) 'International social work or social work internationalism?', in M. Lavalette (ed) *Radical social work in the 21st century*, Bristol: The Policy Press.

Lavinas, L. (2013) '21st century welfare', *New Left Review*, 84, November–December: 5–40.

Lazarus, E. (1883) 'The New Colossus', https://www.poetryfoundation.org/poems/46550/the-new-colossus

Lee, G. (2015) 'Inside Europe blog: migrants face grief and illness on Greek island of Samos', BBC News, 24 October. Available at: http://www.bbc.co.uk/news/blogs-eu-34620829 (accessed 19 December 2016).

Levin, S. (2016) 'Dakota Access pipeline: the who, what and why of the Standing Rock protests', The Guardian, 3 November. Available at: https://www.theguardian.com/us-news/2016/nov/03/north-dakota-access-oil-pipeline-protests-explainer (accessed 19 December 2016).

Levin, S. and Woolf, N. (2016) 'Police ordered to arrest Dakota pipeline protesters and destroy bridge they built', The Guardian, 2 November. Available at: https://www.theguardian.com/us-news/2016/nov/02/dakota-access-pipeline-protest-arrests-standing-rock

LEWRG (London Edinburgh Weekend Return Group) (1979) In and against the state, London: Pluto Press.

Lorde, A. (2000) 'Age, race, class and sex: women redefining women', in W. Komar and F. Bartkowski (eds) Feminist theory: A reader, New York: Mayfield.

Lorenz, W. (2004) Towards a European paradigm of social work; studies in the history of modes of social work and social policy in Europe, Dresden: Technischen Universität.

Lorenz, W. (2006) Perspectives on European social work: From the birth of the nation state to the impact of globalisation, Leverkusen: Barbara Budrich Publishers.

Löwy, M. (2005) Fire alarm: Reading Walter Benjamin's 'On the concept of history', London: Verso.

Mankin, J.S., Viviroli, D., Singh, D., Hoekstra, A.Y. and Diffenbaugh, N.S. (2015) 'The potential for snow to supply human water demand in the present and future', Environmental Research Letters, 10(11): 114–16.

Martinez, D.B. and Fleck-Henderson, A. (eds) (2014) Social justice in clinical practice, London: Routledge.

Martinez, I. (2017) 'Human rights and social justice in social work education: a critical realist comparative study of England and Spain', unpublished PhD thesis, Durham University, Durham.

Marx, K. and Engels, F. (1845) 'The German ideology'. Available at: https://www.marxists.org/archive/marx/works/1845/german-ideology/ (accessed 19 December 2016).

Marx, K. and Engels, F. (1848) The communist manifesto. Available at: https://www.marxists.org/archive/marx/works/download/pdf/Manifesto.pdf.

Matchar, E. (2011) 'Will Occupy Wall Street's spark reshape our politics?', The Washington Post, 24 February. Available at: https://www.washingtonpost.com/opinions/will-occupy-wall-streets-spark-reshape-our-politics/2011/10/10/gIQArPJjcL_story.html?utm_term=.4c9d21877955 (accessed 19 December 2016).

Mayani, V. (2009) 'An interview with Medha Patkar', Khabar, July. Available at: http://www.khabar.com/magazine/features/an_interview_with_medha_patkar.aspx (accessed 19 December 2016).

Mayer, J. and Timms, N. (1970) *The client speaks: Working class impressions of casework*, London: Routledge and Kegan Paul.

Mayo, M. (1975) 'Community development: a radical alternative?', in R. Bailey and M. Brake (eds) *Radical social work*, London: Edward Arnold, pp 129–43.

Mazower, M. and Dalianis, M. (2000) 'Children in turmoil during the civil war: today's adults', in M. Mazower (ed) *After the war was over: Reconstructing the family, nation and state in Greece, 1943–1960*, Princeton, NJ: Princeton University Press.

McCarthy, M. (2016) 'War is hell – for the natural world too', *The Guardian*, 1 November. Available at: https://www.theguardian.com/commentisfree/2016/nov/01/war-hell-for-natural-world-battle-atlantic-guillemot-population-95-per-cent?CMP=share_btn_tw (accessed 19 December 2016).

McDonald, C. (2006) *Challenging social work*, Basingstoke: Palgrave Macmillan.

McKinnon, J. (2008) 'Exploring the nexus between social work and the environment', *Australian Social Work*, 61(3): 256–68.

Met Office (2003) 'The heatwave of 2003'. Available at: http://www.metoffice.gov.uk/learning/learn-about-the-weather/weather-phenomena/case-studies/heatwave (accessed 19 December 2016).

Midgley, J. (1981) *Professional imperialism: Social work in the Third World*, London: Heinemann Educational Books.

Miles, R. (1990) *Capitalism and unfree Labour*, London: RKP.

Miliband, R. (2009) *Parliamentary socialism: A study in the politics of labour*, London: Merlin Press.

Milman, O. (2016) 'Planet at its hottest in 115,000 years thanks to climate change, experts say', *The Guardian*, 4 October. Available at: https://www.theguardian.com/environment/2016/oct/03/global-temperature-climate-change-highest-115000-years (accessed 19 December 2016).

Ministerio de Educación (1984) *Informe de la Comisión Nacional sobre la desaparición de personas*, Buenos Aires: Editorial Eudeba. Available at: http://www.ts.ucr.ac.cr/html/reconceptualizacion/reco-12.htm (accessed 4 April 2016).

Ministerio de Educación Nacional (2016) 'Trabajo Social en la Clasificación Internacional Normalizada de la Educación Adaptada para Colombia'. Available at: http://www.mineducacion.gov.co/1759/w3-printer-358493.html (accessed 18 December 2016).

Ministry of Finance (2016) 'Growth, employment and redistribution: A macroeconomic strategy'. Available at: http://www.treasury.gov.za/publications/other/gear/chapters.pdf

Molyneux, J. (1993) 'The "politically correct" controversy', *International Socialism Journal*, 2(81). Available at: https://www.marxists.org/history/etol/writers/molyneux/1993/xx/polcorr.htm (accessed 19 December 2016).

Monbiot, G. (2000) *Captive state: The corporate takeover of Britain*, Basingstoke: Macmillan.

Monbiot, G. (2016) 'Neoliberalism is creating loneliness. That's what's wrenching society apart'. Available at: https://www.theguardian.com/commentisfree/2016/oct/12/neoliberalism-creating-loneliness-wrenching-society-apart (accessed 19 December 2016).

Moore, J.W. (2015) *Capitalism in the web of life: Ecology and the accumulation of capital*, London: Verso.

Moran, R. and Gillett, S. (2014) 'Twenty-first century eugenics? A case study about the Merton Test', in M. Lavalette and L. Penketh (eds) *Race, racism and social work*, Bristol: Policy Press.

Moran, R. and Lavalette, M. (2016) 'Co-Production: working alongside refugees and asylum seekers: "popular" social work in action in Britain', in C. Williams and M.J. Graham (eds) *Social work in a diverse society: Transformative practice with black and ethnic minority individuals and communities*, Bristol: Policy Press.

Moriarty, J., Manthorpe, J., Hussein, S., Cornes, M., Stevens, M. and Harris, J. (2014) *Privatisation and outsourcing in social care*. Available at: https://www.kcl.ac.uk/sspp/policy-institute/scwru/pubs/2014/conf/moriarty14jul14.pdf

Moser, M. (1985) *Unter den Dachern von Morcote: Meine Lebensgeschichte* (ed I. Schiel), Berlin: Dietz.

Moser, M. (1986) *Ich habe gelebt*, Zurich: Limmat.

Motlalepule, N. and Smith, L.H. (2017) 'Hashtag Fees must fall', *Critical and Radical Social Work*, 5(1): 115–18.

Murphy, T. (2016) 'The Frontline programme: Conservative ideology and the creation of a social work officer class', *Critical and Radical Social Work*, 4(2): 279–88.

Nathane, M. and Smith, L.H. (forthcoming) '#FEESMUSTFALL #DECOLONISEDEDUCATION FRONTLINE', *Critical and Radical Social Work*, (5)1.

Neale, J. (2008) *Stop global warming: Change the World*, London: Bookmarks.

Needham, A. (2016) 'UNHCR calls for safer alternatives to deadly Bay of Bengal voyages', 23 February. Available at: http://www.unhcr.org/56cc51c76.html (accessed 19 December 2016).

Needham, C. and Glasby, J. (ed) (2014) *Debates in personalisation*, Bristol: The Policy Press.

Netto, P. (1994) *Ditadura e serviço social. Uma análise do serviço social no Brasil pós-64*, São Pablo: Cortez.

New Approach (2011), http://annyit.blog.hu/2011/03/12/uj_szemlelet_a_radikalis_szocialis_munka_megjelenese_magyarorszagon

NISATSIC (National Inquiry into the Separation of Aboriginal and Torres Strait Islander Children from their Families) (1997) *Bringing them home; report of the National Inquiry into the Separation of Aboriginal and Torres Strait Islander Children from their Families*, Sydney: Human Rights and Equal Opportunities Commission.

Norwood-Evans, E. (1992) 'Liberation theology, empowerment theory and social work practice with the oppressed', *International Social Work*, 35(3): 135.

O'Connor, J. (1991 [1973]) *The fiscal crisis of the state*, New Jersey, NJ: Transaction Books.

OECD (Organisation for Economic Co-operation and Development) (2015) 'OECD income inequality data update: Sweden'. Available at: https://www.oecd.org/els/soc/OECD-Income-Inequality-Sweden.pdf (accessed 19 December 2016).

O'Hara, M. (2014) *Austerity bites*, Bristol: Policy Press.

Ovenden, K. (2015) *Syriza*, London: Penguin.

Oxfam (2013) 'The cost of inequality; how wealth and income extremes hurt us all', Media Briefing, 18/1/2013, Ref: 02/2013. Available at: http://www.oxfam.org/sites/www.oxfam.org/files/cost-of-inequality-oxfam-mb180113.pdf8 (accessed 18 December 2016).

Oxfam (2016) 'An economy for the one percent'. Available at: https://www.oxfam.org/sites/www.oxfam.org/files/file_attachments/bp210-economy-one-percent-tax-havens-180116-en_0.pdf (accessed 21 December 2016).

Pai, H.-H. (2012) *Scattered sand: The story of China's rural migrants*, London: Verso.

Panchak, P. and Szilagyi, B. (2015) 'Who's who among the top industries on the IndustryWeek 1000', *Industry Week: Advancing the Business of Manufacturing*, 9 September. Available at: http://www.industryweek.com/industryweek-1000/who-s-who-among-top-industries-industryweek-1000#slide-1-field_images-176431 (accessed 19 December 2016).

Panitch, L. and Albo, G. (2014) 'Registering class: Socialist Register 2014', Merlin Press.

Patel, L. (2005) *Social welfare and social development in South Africa*, Oxford: Oxford University Press.

Pawar, M. and Pulla, V. (2015) 'Medha Patkar's environmental activism and professional social work in India: mass legitimacy and myopic structures', in N. Yu and D. Mandell (eds) *Subversive action: Extralegal practices for social justice*, Ontario: Wilfrid Laurier University Press.

Pearce, F. (2016) 'What is causing the rapid rise in methane emissions?', *The Guardian*, 26 October. Available at: https://www.theguardian.com/environment/2016/oct/26/what-is-causing-the-rapid-rise-in-methane-emissions?CMP=share_btn_tw (accessed 19 December 2016).

Pearson, C. and Ridley, J. (2014) *Self-directed support: Personalisation, choice and control*, Edinburgh: Dunedin Press

Philip, D. and Reisch, M. (2015) 'Rethinking social work's interpretation of environmental justice: from local to global', *Social Work Education*, 34(5): 471–83.

Piketty, T. (2014) *Capital in the 21st century*, Harvard, MA: Harvard University Press.

Pillay, N. (2011) 'Press conference by UN High Commissioner for Human Rights', press release, Geneva, 18 October.

Post-Crash Economics Society (2014) *Economics, education and unlearning: Economics education at the University of Manchester*, Manchester: University of Manchester, pp 25-26.

Procaccini, M. (2016) 'Two children drown every day on average trying to reach safety in Europe', UNHCR, 19 February. Available at: http://www.unhcr.org/56c707d66.html (accessed 19 December 2016).

PSWN (Progressive Social Work Network) (2011) 'Manifesto'. Available at: http://www.socialworkfuture.org/articles-resources/international-articles/260-progressive-social-work-manifesto (accessed 21 December 2016).

Raichelis, R. and Rosa, C.M.M. (1982) 'Considerações a respeito da prática do serviço social em movimentos sociais – fragmentos de uma experiência', in *Serviço Social e Sociedade*, São Paulo: Cortez.

Rangel, M.C.M (2005) 'Social work in Mexico: towards a different practice', in I. Ferguson, M. Lavalette and E. Whitmore (eds) *Globalisation, global justice and social work*, London: Routledge.

Rankin, J. (2016) 'Turkey and EU agree outline of "one in, one out" deal over Syria refugee crisis', *The Guardian*, 8 March. Available at: http://www.theguardian.com/world/2016/mar/08/european-leaders-agree-outlines-of-refugee-deal-with-turkey (accessed 19 December 2016).

Rees, N. (2016) *Clear the air for children: The impact of air pollution*, New York, NY: UNICEF. Available at: http://www.unicef.org/publications/files/UNICEF_Clear_the_Air_for_Children_30_Oct_2016.pdf (accessed 19 December 2016).

Refugee Council (2015) 'The truth about asylum: the facts about asylum'. Available at: http://www.refugeecouncil.org.uk/policy_research/the_truth_about_asylum/facts_about_asylum_-_page_5 (accessed 19 December 2016).

Reisch, M. (2013) 'What is the future of social work?', *Critical and Radical Social Work*, 1(1): 67–85.

Reisch, M. and Andrews, J. (2002) *The road not taken: A history of radical social work in the United States*, New York, NY: Brunner-Routledge.

Resnick, R.P. (1976) 'Conscientization: an indigenous approach to international social work', *International Social Work*, 19(2): 21–9.

Rettman, A. (2014) 'Two million British people emigrated to EU, figures show', *euobserver*, 10 February. Available at: https://euobserver.com/social/123066 (accessed 19 December 2016).

Richardson, B. (2016) 'Stand up and be counted', *Socialist Review*, March. Available at: http://socialistreview.org.uk/411/stand-and-be-counted (accessed 19 December 2016).

Roberts, M. (2012). Available at: https://thenextrecession.wordpress.com/2012/10/17/the-dilemma-of-the-mainstream/ (accessed 21 December 2016).

Roberts, M. (2015). Available at: https://thenextrecession.wordpress.com/2015/02/08/the-causes-of-recovery-austerity-qe-and-the-spending-multiplier/ (accessed 21 December 2016).

Roberts, M. (2016) *The long depression*, Chicago, IL: Haymarket.

Robinson, K. (2013) 'Voices from the front line: social work with refugees and asylum seekers in Australia and the UK', *British Journal of Social Work*, advanced access 4 March, pp 1–19. Available at: http://bjsw.oxfordjournals.org/content/early/2013/03/04/bjsw.bct040.full.pdf+html (accessed 19 December 2016).

Roubini, N. (2008) 'Public losses for private gain'. Available at: https://www.theguardian.com/commentisfree/2008/sep/18/marketturmoil.creditcrunch (accessed 21 December 2016).

RSA (Republic of South Africa) (1997) 'White Paper for social welfare'. Available at: http://www.gov.za/sites/www.gov.za/files/White_Paper_on_Social_Welfare_0.pdf (accessed 21 December 2016).

Rüegg, P. (2016) 'Himalayas and Andes face opposite challenges', Mountains ETH Zurich. Available at: http://www.futurity.org/himalayas-andes-1216752/ (accessed 19 December 2016).

Ryan, F. (2016) 'The right to choose your own care is the latest casualty of council cuts'. Available at: https://www.theguardian.com/society/2016/dec/07/personal-budget-disabled-funding-cuts-social-care (accessed 19 December 2016).

Sanz Cintora, Á. (2001) 'Acción social y Trabajo Social en España: una revisión histórica', *Acciones e investigaciones socials*, 13: 5–42.

Saracostti, M., Reininger, T. and Parada, H. (2012) 'Social work in Latin America', in K. Lyons, K. Hokenstad, M. Pawar, N. Huegler and N. Hall (eds) *The SAGE handbook of international social work*, London: SAGE, pp 466–80.

Saville, J. (1957) 'The welfare state: an historical approach', *The New Reasoner*, 3. Available at: http://banmarchive.org.uk/collections/nr/03_05.pdf (accessed 21 December 2016).

Saville, J. (1957), https://www.marxists.org/archive/saville/1957/xx/welfare.htm

Schilde, K. (2003) 'First aid squad in the class struggle', in S. Hering and B. Waaldijk (eds) *History of social work in Europe (1900–1960): Female pioneers and their influence on the development of international social organizations*, Opladen: Soziale Arbeit.

Schilde, K. (2009) 'Oppressed today – the winners of tomorrow. The ways and works of International Red Aid: A communist world organisation in the force field between governmental oppression and social work for political prisoners', in G. Hauss and D. Schulte (eds) *Amid social contradictions: Towards a history of social work in Europe*, Farmington Hills, MI: Barbara Budrich.

Schilling, S. (2015) 'Mentona Mosser (1874–1971): the battle for a more just society', *Critical and Radical Social Work*, 3(3): 433–54.

Schraer, R. (2016) 'Social work in a refugee camp: "All we can do is bear witness to people's trauma"', *Community Care*, 8 February. Available at: http://www.communitycare.co.uk/2016/02/08/social-work-refugee-camp-can-bear-witness-peoples-trauma/ (accessed 19 December 2016).

SCIE (Social Care Institute for Excellence) (2015) *Good practice in social care for refugees and asylum seekers*, SCIE Guide 37. Available at: https://www.scie.org.uk/publications/guides/guide37-good-practice-in-social-care-with-refugees-and-asylum-seekers/

Servio, M. (2015) 'The Latin American reconceptualisation movement', *Critical and Radical Social Work*, 2(2): 193–201.

Sewpaul, V. (2012) 'How social work in South Africa entered a new era', *The Guardian*, 5 July. Available at: https://www.theguardian.com/social-care-network/2012/jul/05/social-work-south-africa-nasw (accessed 21 December 2016).

Sewpaul, V. (2013) 'Neoliberalism and social work in South Africa', *Critical and Radical Social Work*, 1(1): 15–30.

Shanks, E., Lundstrom, T. and Wiklund, S. (2015) 'Middle managers in social work: professional identity and management in a marketised welfare state', *British Journal of Social Work*, 45(6): 1871–87.

Shawky, A. (1972) 'Social work education in Africa', *International Social Work*, 15(1): 3–16.

Shenker, J. (2016) *The Egyptians*, London: Penguin Random House.

Sigley, G. (2016) 'From socialism to social work: social workers, professionalism and community governance in contemporary urban China', in D. Braye and E. Jeffries (eds) *New mentalities of government in China*, London: Routledge.

Simpkin, M. (1983) *Trapped within welfare* (2nd edn), Basingstoke: Macmillan.

Skidelsky, R. (2016) 'Trumpism could be a solution to the crisis of neoliberalism'. Available at: https://www.theguardian.com/business/2016/nov/15/trumpism-solution-crisis-neoliberalism-robert-skidelsky (accessed 21 December 2016).

Slezak, M. (2016a) 'The Great Barrier Reef: a catastrophe laid bare', *The Guardian*, 7 June. Available at: https://www.theguardian.com/environment/2016/jun/07/the-great-barrier-reef-a-catastrophe-laid-bare (accessed 19 December 2016).

Slezak, M. (2016b) 'Sections of Great Barrier Reef suffering from "complete ecosystem collapse"', *The Guardian*, 21 July. Available at: https://www.theguardian.com/environment/2016/jul/21/sections-of-great-barrier-reef-suffering-from-complete-ecosystem-collapse (accessed 19 December 2016).

Smith, L. (2014) 'Historiography of South African social work: challenging dominant discourses', *Social work (Stellenbosch. Online)*, 50(2): 305–31.

Smith, L. and Ferguson, I. (2016) 'Practice learning: challenging neoliberalism in a turbulent world', in I. Taylor, M. Bogo, M. Lefevre and B. Teater (eds) *Routledge international handbook of social work education*, London: Routledge, pp 197–208.

Smith, M. (2007) 'The shape of the working-class', *International Socialism Journal*, 113. Available at: http://isj.org.uk/the-shape-of-the-working-class/ (accessed 19 December 2016).

Solnit, R. (2009) *A paradise built in hell*, New York, NY: Viking.

SSCC (Social Services in the Context of Conflict) (2016) 'Nicosia conference concept note'. Available at: http://www.ssccnetwork.org/cyprus-conference (accessed 2 January 2017).

Steffen, W., Sanderson, A., Tyson, P.D., Jäger, J., Matson, P.A., Moore, B., III, Oldfield, F., Richardson, K., Schellnhuber, H.J., Turner, B.L., II and Wasson, R.J. (2004) *Global change and the earth system: A planet under pressure*, Berlin: Springer. Available at: http://www.igbp.net/download/18.56b5e28e137d8d 8c09380001694/1376383141875/SpringerIGBPSynthesisSteffenetal2004_web. pdf (accessed 19 December 2016).

Stiglitz, J. (2003) *Globalization and its discontents*, London: Penguin.

Stiglitz, J. (2013) *The price of inequality*, London: Penguin.

Stuckier, D. and Basu, S. (2013) *The body economics: Why austerity kills*, London: Allen Lane.

SWAN (Social Work Action Network) (2011a) 'Progressive social work manifesto', Hong Kong. Available at: http://www.socialworkfuture.org/ articles-resources/international-articles/260-progressive-social-work-manifesto (accessed 19 December 2016).

SWAN (2011b) 'Defend Norbert Ferencz Campaign'. Available at: http://www. socialworkfuture.org/index.php/articles-and-analysis/news/170-defend-norbert

SWAN (2014) *Against Michael Gove: In defence of social work*, Liverpool: Social Work Action Network.

SWAN (2016) 'Thought-provoking events at the SWSD Conference 2016'. Available at: http://www.socialworkfuture.org/articles-resources/international- articles/502-thought-provoking-events-at-the-swsd-conference-2016 (accessed 2 January 2017).

SWAN-Greece (2011a) 'Announcement with regards to the Ministry of Economics circular on property tax'. Available at: http://socialworkaction. wordpress.com/2011/12/04/185/ (accessed 18 December 2016).

SWAN-Greece (2011b) 'IFSW's list of detained and persecuted social workers'. Available at: https://socialworkaction.wordpress.com/2011/03/14/15-μαρτίου- παγκόσμια-ημέρα-κοινωνικής-ε/#more-112 (accessed June 2016).

The Aboriginal Justice Implementation Commission (1999) 'The justice system and Aboriginal people', Government of Manitoba. Available at: http://www. ajic.mb.ca/reports/final_toc.html (accessed 15 May 2016).

The Guardian (2016) 'Thousands of children travelling alone from Africa to Europe, says Unicef', 14 June. Available at: http://www.theguardian.com/ global-development/2016/jun/14/thousands-of-migrant-refugee-children- travelling-alone-from-africa-to-europe-says-unicef?CMP=share_btn_link (accessed 21 December 2016).

The Independent (2016) 'Child poverty rises by 200,000 on previous year, official figures show'. Available at: http://www.independent.co.uk/news/uk/politics/ child-poverty-increase-tories-200000-per-cent-2014-2015-official-figures- dwp-stephen-crabb-a7107306.html (accessed 21 December 2016).

The Viewspaper (2008) 'Interview with Medha Patkar', 10 November. Available at: http://theviewspaper.net/audio-interview/ (accessed 18 December 2016).

Townsend, M. (2016) '10,000 refugee children are missing, says Europol', *The Observer*, 30 January. Available at: http://www.theguardian.com/world/2016/jan/30/fears-for-missing-child-refugees (accessed 19 December 2016).

Toynbee, P. (2014) 'Now troubled children are an investment opportunity'. Available at: https://www.theguardian.com/commentisfree/2014/may/13/troubled-children-investment-extreme-britain-outsourcing-care (accessed 19 December 2016).

Traynor, I. (2016) 'EU migration crisis: Greece threatened with Schengen area expulsion', *The Guardian*, 25 January. Available at: http://www.theguardian.com/world/2016/jan/25/greece-under-growing-pressure-to-stem-flow-of-refugees-and-migrants-into-eu (accessed 19 December 2016).

Truell, R. (2014) 'Spanish social work leader wins award for "inspirational" anti-cuts movement'. Available at: https://www.theguardian.com/social-care-network/2014/jul/12/spanish-social-work-leader-wins-award-for-inspirational-anti-cuts-movement (accessed 19 December 2016).

UN (United Nations) News Centre (2016) 'As Mediterranean death toll soars, Ban urges collective response to large refugee and migrant movements'. Available at: http://www.un.org/apps/news/story.asp?NewsID=54092#.V06z-4QrIdU (accessed 19 December 2016).

UNHCR (United Nations High Commissioner for Refugees) (1967 [1951]) 'Convention and protocol relating to the status of refugees'. Available at: http://www.unhcr.org/3b66c2aa10.pdf (accessed 19 December 2016).

UNHCR (2012a) 'Detention guidelines: guidelines on the applicable criteria and standards relating to the detention of asylum-seekers and alternatives to detention'. Available at: http://www.unhcr.org/505b10ee9.html (accessed 19 December 2016).

UNHCR (2012b) 'Refugee family reunification: UNHCR's response to the European Commission Green Paper on the right to family reunification of third country nationals living in the European Union (Directive 2003/86/EC)'. Available at: http://www.refworld.org/docid/4f55e1cf2.html (accessed 18 December 2016).

UNHCR (2015a) 'Mixed maritime movements in South-East Asia in 2015'. Available at: http://reporting.unhcr.org/sites/default/files/regionalupdates/UNHCR%20-%20Mixed%20Maritime%20Movements%20in%20South-East%20Asia%20-%202015.pdf#_ga=1.201670673.1486879546.1456746102 (accessed 18 December 2016).

UNHCR (2015b) 'Refugees continue to reach Yemen by sea despite conflict', 27 October. Available at: http://www.unhcr.org/562f882b9.html (accessed 18 December 2016).

UNHCR (2015c) 'The sea route to Europe: the Mediterranean passage in the age of refugees', 1 July. Available at: http://www.unhcr.org/5592bd059.html (accessed 18 December 2016).

UNHCR (2015d) 'UNHCR global trends report: world at war: forced displacement in 2014'. Available at: http://unhcr.org/556725e69.html (accessed 18 December 2016).

UNHCR (2015e) 'Mid-year trends 2015'. Available at: http://www.unhcr.org/56701b969.html#_ga=1.134873138.290722120.1456829431 (accessed 18 December 2016).

UNHCR (2016) 'UNHCR warns of imminent humanitarian crisis in Greece'. Available at: http://www.unhcr.org.uk/news-and-views/news-list/news-detail/article/unhcr-warns-of-imminent-humanitarian-crisis-in-greece.html (accessed 18 December 2016).

Varoufakis, Y. (2016) 'Why we must save the EU', *The Guardian*, 5 April. Available at: https://www.theguardian.com/world/2016/apr/05/yanis-varoufakis-why-we-must-save-the-eu (accessed 21 December 2016).

Vázquez, J.M. (1970) *Situación del Servicio Social en España: Estudio Sociológico*, Madrid: Instituto de Sociología Aplicada.

Vervenioti, T. (2002) 'Charity and nationalism: the Greek civil war and the entrance of right wing women into politics', in P. Bacchetta and M. Power (eds) *Right wing women: From conservatives to extremists around the world*, London: Routledge.

Voiland, A. (2016) 'Extreme heat for an extreme year', NASA Earth Observatory, 11 August, National Aeronautics and Space Administration, Goddard Institute for Space Studies. Available at: http://www.giss.nasa.gov/research/features/201608_extremeheat/ (accessed 18 December 2016).

Wade, J., Mitchell, F. and Baylis, G. (2005) *Unaccompanied asylum seeking children: The response of social work services*, London: British Association for Adoption and Fostering.

Walton, R.G. and Abo El Nasr, M.M. (1988) 'Indigenization and authentization in terms of social work in Egypt', *International Social Work*, 31(2): 135–44.

Wang, S. (2012) 'The new measures and directions for social work development in China', *Social Dialogue*, 2: 14–17.

Wastell, D. and White, S. (2017) *Blinded by science: Social implications of neuroscience and epigenetics*, Bristol: Policy Press.

Watkins, S. (2016) 'Oppositions', *New Left Review*, 98, March/April. Available at: https://newleftreview.org/II/98/susan-watkins-oppositions (accessed 21 December 2016).

Watts, J. (2016) 'Rio's famous beaches take battering as scientists issue climate change warning', *The Guardian*, 1 November. Available at: https://www.theguardian.com/world/2016/nov/01/rio-de-janerio-beaches-climate-change-storms (accessed 18 December 2016).

Webb, S. and Gray, M. (2013) 'The speculative left and new politics of social work', in M. Gray and S. Webb (eds), *The new politics of social work*, Basingstoke: Palgrave Macmillan, p 215.

White, A. (2016) *Shadow state*, London: Oneworld.

White, S., Hall, C. and Peckover, S. (2009) 'The descriptive tyranny of the common assessment framework: technologies of categorization and professional practice in child welfare', *British Journal of Social Work*, 39(7): 1197–217.

Wilkinson, R. and Pickett, K. (2009) *The spirit level: Why more equal societies almost always do better*, London: Allen Lane.

Williams, C. and Graham, M. (2014) 'Migration, mobilities and social work', *British Journal of Social Work*, 44(Suppl1): i1–i17.

Wolf, M. (2013) 'Austerity in the Eurozone and the UK: kill or cure?'. Available at: http://blogs.ft.com/martin-wolf-exchange/2013/05/23/austerity-in-the-eurozone-and-the-uk-kill-or-cure/ (accessed 21 December 2016).

Wolf, M. (2014) *The shifts and the shocks*, London: Allen Lane.

World Bank (2010) 'Country profile: China'. Available at: http://povertydata.worldbank.org/poverty/country/CHN (accessed 18 December 2016).

Wrenn-Lewis, S. (2015) 'The austerity con'. Available at: http://www.lrb.co.uk/v37/n04/simon-wren-lewis/the-austerity-con (accessed 21 December 2016).

Wroe, L. (2016) 'Volunteering in Greece showed me how vital social work is in this refugee crisis', *The Guardian*, 9 March. Available at: https://www.theguardian.com/social-care-network/social-life-blog/2016/mar/09/volunteering-greece-europe-vital-social-work-refugee-crisis (accessed 18 December 2016).

WWF (World Wildlife Fund) (2016) *Living planet report 2016: Risk and resilience in a new era*, Gland, Switzerland: WWF International. Available at: https://www.wnf.nl/custom/LPR_2016_fullreport/ (accessed 18 December 2016).

Yu, A.L. and Ruixe, B. (2010) 'Contemporary labor resistance in China 1989-2009', China Labor Net. Available at: www.worldlabour.org/eng (accessed 18 December 2016).

Yunong, H. and Xiong, Z. (2008) 'A reaction on the indigenization discourse in social work', *International Social Work*, 51(5): 611–22.

Zentner, C. and Friedemann, B. (1991) *The encyclopedia of the Third Reich*, New York, NY: Macmillan.

Index

A

Aboriginal Justice Implementation Commission 62
Aboriginal Protection Act 1869 (Australia) 62
accountability 48–9
Action for Employment (A4E) 47–8
Addams, J. 100–1
advocacy 129–30
agency 149–50
Alayón, N. 78, 156
Alexander, A. 145
Ali, Tariq 20
Alliance for Progress 76, 78
Amnesty International 93, 106
Anderson, P. 138, 151
Andrews, J. 53, 85, 156
Angten, J. 164
Angus, I. 119, 121, 123, 124
Anthropocene 119–22, 124
Arab Spring 22, 141, 145
Araxa Document 80–1
Argentina 71, 72, 73, 80, 156–7
assimilation, colonial 61–3
Asylum Access and Refugee Work Rights Coalition 107–8
Asylum Link Merseyside 94
asylum seekers
  in Australia 93
  children 106–7
  incarceration of 105–6
  and right to work 107–8
  social work with 94, 101, 109–10
  terminology 95–6
  in UK 94, 106, 109–10
  see also refugees and migrants
ATOS 47
Attlee, Clement 24, 39–40
austerity 1, 8–9
  concept of 16
  effect on recovery 13–14
  failure of 16
  in Greece 11–12, 16–18, 27, 34–5, 161–2
  in Hungary 160–1
  impact of 15–20
  and neoliberalism 14
  and relationship between state and citizens 27
  resistance to 11–12
  in Spain 11–12
  in UK 15–16, 18–19
  see also recession
Australia
  child migration to 65–7
  Green Social Work network 175

and immigration 100
indigenous children 62–3
and refugees/asylum seekers 93, 106

B

Badiou, Alain 136, 137
Bailey, R. 31
banks, bailout of 13, 15, 16, 18, 22, 160
Barnet Council, London 48
Barreix, J. 78, 81
Bean, P. 64, 65, 66
Belkin Martinez, D. 170
benefits, and austerity 19
Berry, M. 90, 95
Bevan, A. 49
Boggs, B. 69
Bond, P. 41
Boston Liberation Health Group (US) 170
Bourdieu, Pierre. 23
Brake, M. 31
Braverman, H. 140
Brazil 26, 79, 80–1, 167
  Freire, Paulo 72, 79, 83, 84, 85, 109, 159, 169
Brazilian Association of Teaching and Research in Social Work 167
Breaking the Silence (NBVT) (Sweden) 172
Britain see UK
Buckley, C. 115
Buendía, F.H. 59

C

Cameron, D. 15
Canada 62, 64, 100
Canada Scoops 62
capitalism
  and agency 149–50
  and climate change 122–5
  crises in 12–15
  and inequality 155
  and migrants and refugees 98–100
  and nationalisation 38–40
  and nature 38
  and reconceptualisation movement 81, 84, 85
  see also neoliberalism; post-Marxism
capitalist ecocide 124
carbon dioxide 116–17
Care Quality Commission (CQC) 43
care workers 43
Carney, M. 7
Carr, M. 92, 93, 95, 96, 102, 105
Carr, S. 146–7
Cassiner, E. 78

Castro Villacanas, A. 57
CCTs (conditional cash transfer programmes) 26
Chakrabortty, A. 48
Chalalet, S.A. 97–8
Charity Organisation Society (COS) 67, 158
Chenery, S. 65–6
'child-gathering' (Greece) 59–61
Child Migrants Trust 66–7
children
   'child-gathering' in Greece 59–61
   'children of empire' 64–7
   under Franco 58–9, 89
   indigenous children 61–3
   under the Nazis 56–7, 68
   refugees and migrants 97, 101, 103, 106–7
   and social work histories 55–67
Children Act 1989 (UK) 106
Chile 37, 71, 82
China 25, 29–30, 100, 164–5
China Labour Net 29
Choonara, J. 14
class essentialism 138, 139–41
Cliff, T. 7, 39–40
climate change 111–32
   and advocacy 129–30
   Anthropocene 119–22, 124
   and capitalism 122–5
   and environmental justice 128–32
   extent of the problem 113–15
   and food waste 131
   impact of 118–19
   and pollution 130–1
   science of 116–19
   and social work 118–19, 122, 125–32
   and water supplies 122, 131–2
Coates, J. 125
Cocker, C. 135–6, 142
Collins, P.H. 146, 147, 148
Colombia 72, 85–7, 153–4, 175
colonialism 61–3, 74–6
community development 177
competition 43, 123
conditional cash transfer programmes (CCTs) 26
Connolly, K. 68
conscientisation 78–9, 87, 110, 159
Cook, J. 118
Costa, M. das Dores 84
Crenshaw, K. 146, 147
Critical and Radical Social Work: An International Journal 171, 177, 178
Crouch, C. 2
Curtis, P. 15
Cyprus 175

D

Daily Record (Scotland) 63
Dalianis, M. 60
Davies, J.B. 155
definition of social work *see* social work definition
Denmark 63
developmentalism 76–8
disabled people, ATOS assessments 47

Dominelli, L. 126, 128
Donadiooct, R. 115
Donovan, T. 118–19

E

Eagleton, Terry 136
Ecowatch 113
Edelman, M. 95
Edwards, Thyra 70
Egypt 22, 41–2, 141, 145
Engels, F. 99, 122, 142, 145–6
environmental issues *see* climate change
Esping-Andersen, G. 39
eugenics 56, 65, 67–8, 69
European Union, and refugees 92–3, 95, 104
EZLN (Mexico) 163–4

F

Fareshare 125
Ferenzc, Norbert 160–1, 172–3
Ferguson 31, 165
Feuer, A. 116
financial crash *see* recession
Fine, B. 40
First International Conference of Social Work (1928) 61
floods 113, 118–19
food charity 19, 124–5, 131
Food Cycle 125
food waste 124–5, 131
Forgacs, D. 144
Foucault, M. 135–6, 147–8, 149
France 118
Franco, Francisco 57–9
Freire, Paulo 72, 79, 83, 84, 85, 109, 159, 169
Friedemann, B. 56
Friedrich 121
Früm, L. 72, 73–4

G

Gagneten, M. 83
Galeano, E. 74, 75, 76, 110
GEAR strategy (South Africa) 31, 46
'Generation 65' 80
Geras, N. 142–3, 150
Germany, under the Nazis 55–7
Giles, G. 57
Giovanopoulos, Christos 35
GISS (Goddard Institute for Space Studies) 113, 114–15
Global Social Work Conference (2010) 165
Global Social Work Conference (2016) 171
Global Social Work Congress (2014) 162–3
global warming *see* climate change
Gluckstein, D. 39–40
Gómez, F.G. 59
Gonzales, M. 122
González Duro, E. 58, 59
Gosling, P. 42
Gove, M. 33
Graham, M. 96, 109
Graham-Harrison, E. 92

Gramsci, Antonio 142, 143–4
Gray, M. 125, 135, 136, 139, 149–50, 163
Greece
  austerity 11–12, 16–18, 27, 34–5, 161–2
  'child-gathering' 59–61
  military dictatorship of 54
  refugees 97–8
  social work and the state 33–5
  social work education 61
  solidarity movement 33–5
Greek Association of Social Workers (GASW)
  54, 61, 161–2
Greek Social Work Action Network 161–2
green social work 111
Greenland 63
Greenspan, Alan 11
Growth, Employment and Redistribution
  (GEAR) strategy (South Africa) 31, 46
Guardian, The (UK) 7, 48
Gustavsson, J. 131
Gutierrez, G. 78, 159

H

Hafford-Letchfield, T. 135–6, 142
Hallward, P. 137
Hansen, J. 115
Hardman, C. 132
Harman, C. 13, 14, 23, 24, 25, 39, 40, 41, 140
Harris, J. 24, 27–8, 32, 176
Harvey, D. 38, 39
Haste, C. 56
Hawkins, C. 126
Hayter, T. 109
Health and Social Care Act 2012 (UK) 19, 44
health care, and austerity 16–17, 19, 34–5
heatwaves 113–14, 118
Heede, R. 123
Herbert-Boyd, M. 129
Hering, S. 158
Hinestroza, C. 85–7
histories see social work histories
Hobsbawm, E. 61, 75, 139
Home Care (Greece) 17–18
Hong Kong 30, 165, 173–4
Hull House Settlement, Chicago 100–1
Humphreys, M. 65, 66–7
Hungary 160–1, 172–3
Hurricane Sandy 115–16

I

IASSW (International Association of Schools
  of Social Work) 78–9, 101, 102, 153, 154,
  162–3, 178
IFSW (International Federation of Social
  Workers) 101, 104, 153, 154, 160, 167
IMF 41–2
immigration see refugees and migrants
Immigration and Asylum Act 1999 (UK) 94
India 111–13, 126, 127–8, 130–1
indigenisation 162–4
indigenous children 62–3
individualisation 32–3, 43
individualism 179

Internal Displacement Monitoring Centre
  (IDMC) 90
International Association of Schools of Social
  Work see IASSW
International Federation of Social Workers see
  IFSW
International Geosphere Biosphere Programme
  (IGBP) 119–22
International Organisation for Migration (IOM)
  91, 104
International Red Aid 103, 104, 158
intersectionality 146–9
Ioakimidis, V. 17–18, 54, 85–7, 115
Israel 122

J

Jameson, F. 149
Japan 165–6
Jessop, B. 22, 27
Johnson, B. 148–9
Johnson, S. 56–7
Jones, C. 3, 46–6, 67, 97–8, 169–70
Jonsson, J. 44, 45
Jordan, B. 28

K

Kasimode, India 127–8, 130–1
Kentikelenis, A. 17
Kershaw, R. 64, 65
Kesidou, Olga 34
Keynes, J.M. 10, 12–15
Kidron, M. 24
Klein, N. 128–9
Klinenberg, E. 118
Kolakowski, L 150
Konrad, G. 177
Korea 171–2

L

Laclau, E. 137, 138, 139, 142–3, 150, 151
LaingBuisson 48
Latin America
  conditional cash transfer programmes (CCTs)
    26
  and indigenisation 163–4
  liberation theology 158–9
  see also reconceptualisation movement
Latin American Association for Teaching and
  Research in Social Work 167
Lauri, M. 172
Lavalette, M. 108, 115
Lavinas, L. 26
liberation theology 78, 153, 158–9
Lorde, A. 146–7
Lorenz, W. 55–7, 68
Loverdos, Andreas 16
Löwy, M. 7

M

Manchester University 9–10
Mare Nostrum 104
market failure 48

marketisation
  and market failure 48
  of NHS 41
  quasi-markets 42
  of social care 32, 43–4, 45
  of social work 32, 44, 176
  see also privatisation
Martinez, I. 58
Marx, K. 10, 12–15, 24, 99, 122, 145–6, 150
  see also post-Marxism
Matchar, E. 115
Mayo, M. 31
Mazower, M. 60
McDonald, C. 26
McKinnon, J. 126
Melville, J. 64, 65, 66
methane 116, 117
Mexico 93, 163–4
Midgley, J. 163
migrants *see* refugees and migrants
Milman, O. 117
miners' strike (UK) 145
Molyneux, J. 143
Monbiot, G. 179
Moore, J.W. 122
Moorhead, B. 56–7
Moran, R. 108, 109
Moser, M. 104, 158
Mouffe, C. 137, 138, 139, 142–3, 150, 151

N

Named Person 28
nationalisation 38–40
'natural' disasters 113–16, 118–19, 127–9
Nazi Germany 55–7, 67–8
Neale, J. 117
Needham, A. 92
neoliberalism 21–36
  and austerity 14
  impact on welfare services 26–7
  and individualism 179
  relationship-based social work 176–7
  and retreat of the state 24–5
  and the state 22–3
  and the state and social work 27–35
  theorising 23–7
  see also marketisation; privatisation
New Approach Group (Hungary) 172–3
new politics of social work 135–51
  and agency 149–50
  and class essentialism 139–41
  current thinkers 135–8
  intersectionality 146–9
  post-Marxism 136–49
New Social Work Left 135
new social work radicalism 176–8
New Zealand 65, 175–6
NHS and Community Care Act 1990 (UK) 32

O

Occupy movement 115–16
Occupy Sandy 115–16
O'Connor, J. 40

OECD 44
oil pipelines 129–30
Orange Tide (Spain) 162, 174
Osborne, George 27
Oxfam 8, 155

P

Pai, H-H. 29
Palestine 122
Pathways to Work scheme (UK) 47–8
Patkar, Medha 111–13
Paulsen, P. 164
Pearce, F 117
Person Shaped Support 89
personalisation 32–3, 43
Philip, D. 126
Piketty, T. 31
pipelines 129–30
political economy of social work 7–20
  and examples of austerity 15–19
  impact of political developments 8–9
  inequality 7
  and Marx and Keynes 12–15
  recession 7–12
political polarisation 8
pollution 130–1
'popular' social work 115–16, 129
Post-Crisis Economics Society 9–10
post-Marxism 136–7
  key themes of 138–49
power 147–8
Pride (film) 145
privatisation 37–49
  accountability 48–9
  in China 29
  critique of 47–9
  and efficiency 47–8
  and illusion of automatism 41
  market failure 48
  poor performance 47–8
  and quality 43
  rationale for 38–41
  social care and social work 41–9
  in South Africa 45–7
  in Sweden 44–5
  transparency 48–9
  in UK 39, 41, 42–4, 47–9
Procaccini, M. 92
Progressive Welfare Network (Hong Kong) 173–4

Q

quasi-markets 42

R

racial segregation 68–9, 74–5
radical social work
  developing radical theory 177–8
  as global movement 178–9
  initiatives of 169–76
  key elements of new radicalism 176–8
Rangel, M.C.M. 21

Rathbone, Eleanor 89
Real Junk Food Project (UK) 131
recession
    and crises in capitalism 12–15
    effects of 7–9
    reasons for 9–12
    recovering from 12–15
    and role of the state 22
    and social care market 43
    see also austerity
reconceptualisation movement 71–87, 159
    aim of 73
    and colonialism 74–6
    concrete theory 83
    conscientisation 78–9, 87
    end of 82
    ideologies of 80–1
    legacy of 82–7
    origins of 72–9
    and persecution of social workers 71–4
    and radicalisation process 78–81
    rise and fall of 79–82
    and theology and education 77–8
    and transformation of social work 77
Red Aid 103, 104, 158
Rees, N. 130
Refugee and Asylum Seeker Participatory
    Action Research (RAPAR) 109–10
Refugee Convention (UN) (1951) 91, 96, 106,
    107
refugees and migrants 89–110
    and capitalism 98–100
    children 97, 101, 103, 106–7
    contribution to society 109
    controls on 100, 108–9
    deaths of 91–2, 104
    and employment 109
    European response to 92–3, 95, 104
    and family reunification 107
    incarceration of 105–6
    and Islamophobia 96
    media portrayal of 90, 95–6
    and open borders 109
    practical demands for 104–10
    and right to work 107–8
    safe passage for 104–5
    scale of 'crisis' 90–3
    and self-activity 108
    social work with 94, 97–8, 101–4
    and solidarity 102–4, 110, 179
    terminology 95–6
    traffickers 105
Reisch, M. 53, 85, 126, 170
relationship-based social work 176–7
residential social care 42, 43, 48
Richardson, B. 102
Roberts, M. 1, 11, 13, 14
Robinson, K. 96
Roubini, N. 13
Ruixe, B. 29

S

Sacks, J. 64, 65
Samos Refugees (Greece) 97–8
SAPs (Structural Adjustment Programmes) 41–2
Save Narmada Movement (India) 111–13
Saville, J, 25, 38, 39
Schilde, K. 158
Schilling, S. 104
Schraer, R. 103
Scotland 28, 41, 63
Sedwick, Thomas 65
Sendlerowa, Irena 68
Servio, M. 81, 83
Settlement Movement 104, 158
Sewpaul, V. 30, 46–7
Shanks, E. 44–5
Shenker, J. 22, 41–2, 141
Sigley, G. 30
Skidelsky, R. 15
Slezak, M. 114
Smith, L. 31, 69
Smith, M. 139–40
social care
    and austerity 17–18, 19
    marketisation of 32, 43–4, 45
Social Care Institute for Excellence (SCIE) 101
social Darwinism 67–9
Social Services Today 79
Social Work Action Network (SWAN) 102–3,
    160–1, 161–2, 170–2
social work definition 153–67
    contrasting definitions 166–7
    current debates 153–4, 166
    and indigenisation 162–4
    and oppressive practice 156–7
    and social justice 154, 156, 157–62, 167,
        169–79
    and structural inequality 154–6
social work education
    in Colombia 153–4
    and community development 177
    under Franco 58, 59
    in Greece 61
    and reconceptualisation movement 77,
        79–80, 81–2
    social science base of 33, 153–4, 177
    in South Africa 68–9
    in UK 33, 171
Social Work First 103
social work histories 53–70
    and children of empire 64–7
    and colonialism 61–3
    in Greece 54, 59–61
    importance of 53–5
    and indigenous children 61–3
    and military dictatorships 54, 156
    in Nazi Germany 55–7, 67–8
    and selective amnesia 156–7
    and social Darwinism 67–9
    and social justice 158
    in Spain under Franco 57–9

social work, new politics of *see* new politics of
  social work
Social Work Today 79, 80
Social Work Without Borders 103
solidarity 33–5, 179
solidarity movement (Greece) 33–5
Solnit, R. 129
South Africa
  demonstrations by social workers 174
  privatisation 45–7
  racial segregation in 68–9
  social work and the state 30–2
  social work education 68–9
Southern Rhodesia 65
Spain
  austerity 11–12
  under Franco 57–9
  Orange Tide 162, 174
SSCC (Social Services in the Context of
  Conflict) 175
Starr, Ellen Gates 100–1
state *see* neoliberalism; privatisation
Steffen, W. 120–1
sterilisation projects 69
Structural Adjustment Programmes (SAPs) 41–2
Sweden 44–5, 172

T

Teloni, D. 17–18
Toynbee, P. 43
transparency 48–9
Truell, R. 174
Trump, Donald 15
tsunamis 127–8, 128–9

U

UK
  and asylum seekers 94, 106, 109–10
  and austerity 15–16, 18–19
  and blame discourse 33
  and 'children of empire' 64–7
  and climate change 118–19
  and economic crisis 9–10
  and food charity 19, 124–5, 131
  miners' strike 145
  'Named Person' 28
  and privatisation 39, 41, 42–4, 47–9
  and refugees and migrants 100, 102–3, 105,
    106–7, 109–10
  Scotland's lost children 63
  Social Work Action Network (SWAN)
    102–3, 170–2
  social work and the state and neoliberalism
    32–3
  social work education reforms 33, 171
  working class of 139–40
UNESCO, definition of social work 153–4
UNICEF 130
United Nations
  definition of refugee 96
  and refugee rights 91, 96

United Nations High Commissioner for
  Refugees (UNHCR) 90, 91–2, 93, 105–6,
  107
USA
  Boston Liberation Health Group 170
  and climate change 114, 115–17
  and environmental justice 129–30, 131–2
  and eugenics 69
  and Keynesianism 15
  and Latin America 76, 82
  and migrants 93, 100–1, 106

V

Varoufakis, Y. 27
Vázquez, J.M. 59
Vervenioti, T. 60–1
Voiland, A. 111

W

Wade, J. 106–7
Wang, S. 165
water supplies 122, 131–2
Watts, J. 114
Webb, S. 135, 136, 139, 149–50
White, A. 47, 48–9
Williams, C. 96, 109
Wolf, M. 10–11, 12, 16
women
  under Franco 57
  in Greece 60–1
  under the Nazis 56
  refugees and migrants 103
Work Capability Assessments (WCA) 47
working classes 139–46
World Social Work Day 2016 101
Wrenn-Lewis, S. 13
Wroe, L. 103
WWF 118

Y

Yanes, M. 122
Yu, A.L. 29

Z

Zentner, C. 56
Zetkin, Clara 158
Zimbabwe 136